THE NEWS FROM POEMS

The News from Poems

ESSAYS ON THE 21ST-CENTURY AMERICAN POETRY OF ENGAGEMENT

Edited by Jeffrey Gray and Ann Keniston

University of Michigan Press
ANN ARBOR

Published in the United States of America by the
University of Michigan Press
Manufactured in the United States of America
⊗ Printed on acid-free paper

2019   2018   2017   2016   4   3   2   1

A CIP catalog record for this book is available from the British Library.

Library of Congress Cataloging-in-Publication Data

Names: Gray, Jeffrey, 1944– editor. | Keniston, Ann, 1961– editor.
Title: The news from poems : essays on the 21st-century American poetry of engagement /
    edited by Jeffrey Gray and Ann Keniston.
Description: Ann Arbor : University of Michigan Press, [2016] | Includes bibliographical
    references and index.
Identifiers: LCCN 2016030391| ISBN 9780472073184 (hardback : acid-free paper) | ISBN
    9780472053186 (paperback : acid-free paper) | ISBN 9780472122196 (e-book)
Subjects: LCSH: American poetry—21st century—History and criticism. | Politics and
    literature—United States—History—21st century. | Literature and society—United States—
    History—21st century. | Poetics—United States. | BISAC: LITERARY CRITICISM / Poetry.
Classification: LCC PS326 .N49 2016 | DDC 811/.609—dc23
LC record available at https://lccn.loc.gov/2016030391

For our children
Pablo and Maira Duarte Quiroga
and
Jeremy and Paul Novak

Acknowledgments

We wish to thank the manuscript's two anonymous readers, whose thoughtful and detailed comments helped us improve this book, and our research assistants Katlin Kocher and Rebecca Livi of Seton Hall University, and Aaron Schneeberger and Craig Charboneau of University of Nevada, Reno, who patiently and tirelessly helped us compile and systematize it. Thanks to the Seton Hall University English Department; to the University of Nevada, Reno; to the University of Nevada English Department and its Summer Research Assistantships Program; and to UNR's College of Liberal Arts for support of this project. We are also grateful to Aaron McCullough at the University of Michigan Press for his enthusiasm about the project and to his colleagues Elizabeth Frazier and Scott Ham for shepherding it through production.

We also wish to acknowledge the *American Poetry Review*, in which Tony Hoagland's chapter (in different form and under a different title), Eleanor Wilner's chapter, and excerpts from Steven Gould Axelrod's appeared. An earlier and different version of Tony Hoagland's "Getting the World into the Poem" also appeared in *Twenty Poems That Could Save America and Other Essays*, from Graywolf Press, 2014.

Contents

Part Four: Redefining Poetics

It is difficult
to get the news from poems
                yet men die miserably every day
                        for lack
of what is found there.

—William Carlos Williams, "Asphodel, That Greeny Flower"

Introduction

Contemporary Poetry and the Public Sphere

Jeffrey Gray and Ann Keniston

This collection follows our *The New American Poetry of Engagement: A 21ˢᵗ Century Anthology* (2012), which was constructed around the premise that the United States is witnessing a resurgence of public poetry, with poets of all types writing about concerns beyond the personal, epiphanic, or aesthetic. In that book we noted not only the fact of this resurgence but some of its features. We noticed, for example, that the engaged poetry we were reading did not directly correspond to the "poetry of witness," a term associated with much Latin American poetry from the postwar period as well as with Carolyn Forché's well-known anthology *Against Forgetting* (1993). Rather, in recent U.S. poetry, there seemed to be more distance between event and speaking subject, and in fact the notions of both subjectivity and representation were complicated. We also noticed that, like the "hybrid" poetry anthologized in Cole Swensen and David St. John's *American Hybrid* (2009), the new public poetry was coming from many different sources, poetic schools, and perspectives.

A number of poets and critics have made similar observations about the trend toward social engagement in American poetry. In a 2008 essay focusing on mainstream poetry, Robert von Hallberg argues that "in recent years, the most distinguished political poems have all engaged precisely the issue of what holds citizens together in a community." In the same year, David Orr speaks of American poets finding "ways to reach outside themselves," assuring them and us that "the path to a richer political poetry is still open." Charles Altieri notes a similar shift in more innovative poetry by younger poets—including Juliana Spahr, Ben Lerner, and others—who "make a space for a more overt poetry of social responsibility than they felt their immediate [i.e., modernist and midcentury poetic] heritage afforded" ("What Theory" 66) and who "engage the world" in new and more direct ways (71). Altieri associates this engagement with "local versions of history" (71), while Juliana Spahr identifies a very different trend in the Bush administration's cooption of certain poets in the service of a nationalist agenda (685). Although her reading is quite different from those of von Hallberg and Altieri, it too places poetry squarely in the public sphere.

Of course, American poetry has often been concerned with public, even political issues, whether in Whitman's verses on the Civil War or in the work of numerous twentieth-century poets. While space precludes our taking up the argument that all literature is by nature political, the public impulse is evident in Ezra Pound's evocations of World War I in "Hugh Selwyn Mauberley" and in his comments on Jefferson, John Adams, and Mussolini in the *Cantos*. World War I and its aftermath are central to T. S. Eliot's *The Waste Land*, and commentary on economic, gender, and racial inequality is explicit in the work of the poets of the Harlem Renaissance. With respect to the mid- to late twentieth century, as we pointed out in our earlier anthology, a number of important poets—including Kenneth Rexroth, Adrienne Rich, Muriel Rukeyser, Robert Duncan, Robert Bly, Amiri Baraka, June Jordan, and many of those published by City Lights Press, including Allen Ginsberg—wrote political poetry. But the engaged poems of many of these postwar poets—perhaps especially those of women and poets of color—arguably remained marginal until the final decades of the last century, when their work began to find space in mainstream anthologies.

Despite these public voices, most critics agree that the dominant ethos of U.S. poetry throughout the twentieth century was antididactic. No single poem articulated this ethos more than Archibald MacLeish's widely quoted "Ars Poetica": "A poem should not mean / but be," the poem asserts. Poems are meant to be "motionless in time" (the phrase occurs twice), "mute / as a globed fruit," "dumb," "silent," and "wordless." In the 1960s, the poet William Everson, writing about critical disapproval of Robinson Jeffers, asserted, "Our [contemporary U.S.] aesthetic reveres the pure essence; it is anti-polemical, anti-programmatic, basically anti-subject matter." What Everson called an "anti-polemical, anti-programmatic" climate was partly if not largely an effect of the dominance of the New Criticism from the early 1940s (though the phenomenon predates the term by a decade) through at least the early 1970s. The New Critics sought not to explain a poem's cultural milieu but to understand its form and the play of its ambiguities. This was not a hospitable environment for the likes of Allen Ginsberg, Amiri Baraka, or Adrienne Rich and would not be for most poets today.

According to some scholars, the New Critical aesthetic persisted in American poetry even while politically activist poetry was being written. In 1984, well after the heyday of the New Critics, Charles Altieri effectively dismissed much of the poetry of the 1970s for its apoliticism, including works by Robert Hass, James Wright, William Stafford, and Stanley Plumly, which he described as "scenic," characterized, that is, by "highly crafted moments of scenic empathy," culminating in a sense of "numinous awe" (*Self* 452). Jerome McGann, also in the 1980s, used similar terms, including "suburban and personal" to describe the work of John Ashbery, a poet whose work many readers had in fact seen as groundbreaking (146). Walter Kalaidjian echoed these views when he wrote in 1989 that "the course of contemporary American poetry has actually reproduced, rather than contested, formalism's swerve from social change" (4).

What then explains the emergence and particular features of twenty-first-century public poetry? It may still be too early to adequately account for them, but some factors suggest themselves: the collapse of earlier distinctions between mainstream and experimental poetry, with the ensuing sense that the parameters of poetry are by now wide open; the sense that writing about the world is no longer different from writing about the self; and, perhaps most of all, largely as a result of battles fought and slowly won during the latter years of the twentieth century, a greater acceptance of what was once derided as didactic or agenda-driven poetry.

★

Today there remains no shortage of contemporary poets writing "suburban," personal, "scenic" poems, to use the terms of the critics cited above, and no shortage of poems that defy category. But many poets, even those formerly associated with these modes (Robert Hass comes to mind), are writing public and engaged poems in mainstream publications. These poems are as likely to come from Language (or Language-inflected) poets as they are from what Charles Bernstein has for decades called "official verse culture" or from the aesthetically hybrid poetry that some argue now characterizes the contemporary scene.

It is risky or premature to make generalizations about a mode of poetry that is still emerging, but the present volume might be read as a series of preliminary gestures toward such generalizations. Certainly it is motivated, like our earlier anthology, by two observations. First, as we have just implied, a wide range of poets of different aesthetics and backgrounds have been writing engaged poetry in the first years of the twenty-first century, responding to events ranging from the 9/11 attacks to the effects of Hurricane Katrina to climate change. Second, the idea of public or political engagement may have different implications in the contemporary moment than it has had formerly. We began this introduction by noting that today's poetry seems quite different from the poetry of witness predominant in the 1990s. That this is the case is indicated by Carolyn Forché, who in 2011 reframed the concept of witness, calling it "a mode of reading rather than of writing, of readerly encounter with the literature of that-which-happened" and noting that "its mode is evidentiary rather than representational" (163). Cathy Park Hong, in a 2015 essay titled "Against Witness," goes further, asking, "What kind of proximity do I need to write as witness? Do I have to experience the event myself? If I watched the video, can I write about it? Do I have to be related to the victim? And what do you mean by relation?" (161).

The essays collected here elaborate on the implications of these statements. They suggest that twenty-first-century engaged poetry tends to be characterized by suspicion and doubt about positions of witness, authority, and omniscience. They don't necessarily contradict this sense of suspicion and often acknowledge the poet's complicity in these positions. In fact, nearly all the poems discussed in this volume consider the ways public events are represented by the government, politics, and/or the media. This heightened awareness of mediation is particularly evident in the use of cited or appropriated discourse, whether from presidential speeches, newspapers, scientific texts, official or corporate directives, or popular culture; it is apparent in the work of poets ranging from the purportedly confessional Frank Bidart to the supposedly antisubjective Kenneth Goldsmith, to say nothing of the more directly political Claudia Rankine.

Several contemporary critics have noticed this documentary or appropriative trend in recent poems, notably Marjorie Perloff in her book *Unoriginal Genius: Poetry by Other Means in the New Century*, which discusses both recent poetry's departures from and its continuities with early twentieth-century practices of objet trouvé. Rachel Blau DuPlessis notes the recurrence of "citation strategies" in recent poems, which enable "the author . . . to account for, perhaps absorb, perhaps confront, provocative alterity" (993) through practices ranging from juxtaposed passages to "torque[d]" texts (994) to what she calls "neo-reportage" (996). The chapters below extend these observations, placing these formal practices in a twenty-first-century context in which official or public discourse is both ubiquitous and highly suspect.

*

We have organized this volume to foreground the ways that twenty-first-century poets challenge long-standing assumptions about politics, authorship, identity, and poetics. These four categories are broad, and they necessarily overlap. Indeed, chapters from different sections can be usefully juxtaposed: Lynn Keller's discussion of poets considering environmental degradation and climate change in Part One anticipates James McCorkle's reading of the ways a number of female African-American poets depict Hurricane Katrina in Part Two; Kevin Prufer's discussion of the ambivalence of recent engaged poems in Part Four recalls Vernon Shetley's use of the same term in Part One. In the remainder of this introduction, we set out some of the recurrent terms and continuities within each of the book's four parts in order to identify the ways the chapters characterize, modify, and expand each of the four categories.

The three chapters in Part One, "Redefining the Political," argue that both recent engaged poetry and its reception differ in crucial ways from those of earlier periods. Eleanor Wilner's "Homeland Insecurity and the Poetry of Engagement" takes on this issue directly, challenging the "more or less received notion that what was called 'political poetry' was . . . bad poetry in which a polemical purpose must necessarily overwhelm the poetic." The term *engagement* (with its international analogues and, as Wilner notes, its etymological link with *pledge*) offers a more neutral and capacious way of understanding the turn in recent poetry. The term also marks the recent breakdown of dated distinctions between the private and the public or political. Vernon Shetley's chapter, "The Poetry of Engagement and the Politics of Reading," considers the effects of engaged poems on the reader, arguing that poems must be understood in relation to their authors' intentions, a concept whose nuances he elaborates throughout the chapter. Lynn Keller addresses the topic of politics less directly. Her "Twenty-First-Century Ecopoetry and the Scalar Challenges of the Anthropocene" examines the ways several recent poets depict climate change and species loss in terms of incommensurability, evident in a concern with both the microscopic and the enormous.

All three of these initial chapters take up issues of the extrapoetic. Keller points to recent poems that chronicle not only the effects of global events on individuals but also, as the epochal term *anthropocene* reveals, the human effect on the physical world. Wilner makes a related point, arguing that due partly to the "foundational cracks and sinkholes" that "have opened in the American illusion of invulnerability and exceptionalism," recent poetry emphasizes "how much outer world the inner self contains." Shetley, citing the legacy of the New Critical idea of "intentional fallacy," argues that extrapoetic factors play a large role in our making sense of poems, especially poems about real-world events. Considering such factors, he claims, often complicates the way poems first appear, creating "an ambivalence that is redoubled in the reader's response."

Part Two, "Redefining Authorship," directly considers the implications of poetry's reliance on appropriated or found language, a practice that ranges from small-scale or intermittent sampling, often from multiple texts, to the wholesale appropriation of a single source text. These modes are the topic of Joseph Harrington's chapter, "The Politics of Docupoetry," which distinguishes between documentary poets who "make *use* of sources" (emphasis added) and those poets who reproduce extant texts. Harrington sees "docupo" as a critique on behalf of marginalized or voiceless people, one formally distinct from the didactic modes of twentieth-century documentary films and prose. Because contemporary docupoets have inherited the postmodern distrust of referentiality, they often exhibit a "reflexive" turn, in which the focus moves from historical reference to the properties and problems of the text itself. These poets, in other words, are at least as involved in questioning the strategies and materials of representation as they are in representing—as in the case of Kaia Sand, whom Harrington discusses—the fates of Japanese prisoners interred in Vanport, Oregon. Harrington interviews several documentary poets whose responses illuminate the place of the documentary poem in its sense-making function, the link it offers between self and others, and the type of activism it is capable of.

Jeffrey Gray's chapter, "'Hands Off': Official Language in Contemporary Poetry," surveys the contested ground between an appropriative poetry of engagement, one that, in Jasper Johns's phrase, "does things" to found materials, and one that, as Kenneth Goldsmith says, "leaves them alone." Gray's chapter suggests that the contemporary poetics of appropriation may be linked to a larger movement in Western thinking away from interpretation and toward information, and ultimately toward a view of data as implicitly incomprehensible. The irony of a poetry of engagement existing alongside the postmodern legacy of the repudiation of the self is at least partly resolved, says Gray, by the tendency of engaged poems to comment on or subvert neutral or inert languages (guides, catalogs, corporate directives, and the like) by writing *through* them.

Bob Perelman's chapter, "Delivering Difficult News," offers a witty annotation of a 2013 appearance by the most celebrated contemporary appropriator, Kenneth Goldsmith, on *The Colbert Report*. In a brief discussion of Goldsmith's *Seven Deaths and Disasters*, Colbert manages to maneuver Goldsmith, "the conceptual poet who skewers authenticity," into revealing himself as both Romantically retrograde, and even, contrary to his usual persona, a poet of witness. Perelman's play-by-play commentary assesses the situation of the contemporary avant-garde vis-à-vis popular media, indicating "how art can best face the glare of the present."

Like "political," the term "identity" has undergone revision in relation to American poetry. Often associated with the discourse of ethnicity as well as with the personal revelations of the confessional poets and their heirs, it also evokes an older discourse with essentialist tendencies. The chapters in Part Three offer an important counterclaim, reimagining identity in ways that reveal its relevance for twenty-first-century poets, even (or perhaps especially) those who disavow the "personal" or "autobiographical." Steven Gould Axelrod, in "Frank Bidart's Poetics of Engagement," considers that poet's turn away from the intensely personal toward a stance of observation and witness. Yet, as Axelrod notes in his reading of three Bidart poems, this apparent turn is not altogether unforeseen. Through considerations of Bidart's allusions to a range of precursors, notably his mentor Robert Lowell, Axelrod argues that Bidart's poems are "shaped by the intersection of public event with introspection and intertextuality."

Similarly, the work of Claudia Rankine, according to Elisabeth Frost's "Claudia Rankine and the Body Politic," departs from personal experience, engaging the experiences of those who live precariously. In *Don't Let Me Be Lonely* and in her collaborative video essays, Rankine reveals the inextricability of abject, invisible, or injured bodies from the social conditions that ensured their vulnerability to harm. This interrelation between individual and collective is also evident in the work of the three African-American women poets writing about Hurricane Katrina that James McCorkle considers in "Beyond Katrina: Ecopoetics, Memory, and Race." In these poems, acts of mediated witness raise questions about what constitutes value in human life.

All three chapters in this part challenge or complicate the process of bearing witness, and all three react both to traumatic events and to the political and cultural mechanisms that separate spectators from what they see. Frost directly considers how various works by Rankine "move beyond the positivist assumptions of identity politics." McCorkle's reading of the Katrina poems shows how personal narratives expose "the shortcomings of the neoliberal state and its implicit racist underpinnings" as well as the racist underpinnings of classic environmentalism. And, as Axelrod reveals, Bidart's recent poems assert a mode of witness that is both allusive and depersonalized.

Part Four, "Redefining Poetics," turns directly to a question implicit in earlier chapters: how do twenty-first-century engaged poets imagine poetry itself? Does this poetry have distinctive features and traits and, if so, what are they? The part's three chapters approach these questions in quite different ways: Ann Keniston focuses on the twenty-first-century implications of formal choices; Kevin Prufer considers the emotional and philosophical stance of recent poetry; and Tony Hoagland considers the ways that poetry incorporates a range of tones and a variety of information. Read together, these chapters imply that recent poets are reimagining traditional forms, orientations, and poetic structures to express the contradictory and mediated nature of contemporary American existence.

Keniston's chapter, "Echo Revisions: Repetition, Politics, and the Problem of Value in Contemporary Engaged Poetry," focuses on varieties of repetition in contemporary poems, including both iterative patterns within poems and the repetition of preexisting language. Several recent poems in forms, including the pantoum and the villanelle, she argues, simultaneously adopt and mock hegemonic discourse, revealing that repetition is implicated in contemporary patterns of domination and subjugation.

While Keniston's chapter joins the formal with the thematic, the section's subsequent chapters by practicing poets consider these issues separately. Kevin Prufer's "Ambivalence and Despair" and Tony Hoagland's "Getting the World into the Poem" both attempt to define the distinctive features of recent poems, offering rubrics that, while different, respond to the information overload of contemporary life. Prufer transforms a contemporary sense of paralysis into something more positive, beginning by chronicling his own sense of being overcome by the rhetoric of news reports during the U.S.-led wars of the early 2000s. Through a discussion of early twentieth-century attitudes toward sentimentality and didacticism, Prufer argues in favor of an explicit acknowledgment of the "simultaneity of conflicting meanings," meanings that originate at least partly in a distinctively twenty-first-century information overload. This acknowledgment leads to what Prufer calls a "muscular ambivalence" evident in recent poems' concern with "the motions of thought."

While Prufer's partly autobiographical chapter focuses on subjectivity, Hoagland, in the final chapter, considers a similar topic to a different end: poetry, in privileging the inner life, has tended to excise current events and history. For this reason, Hoagland identifies and favors an alternate mode in contemporary poetry, which he calls the "composite" or "layered" poem, whose structure enables the juxtaposition not only of the conflicting subject positions to which Prufer refers but of different registers of experience. Thus, the composite poem can include what Hoagland calls "samples of worldly information" (including data about the sparrow populations of Florida, a portrait of the local prostitute, and discussion of weather patterns—to use examples from a Spencer Reece poem) *alongside* "passionate testimonies to subjective life."

*

In defining an emerging trend in American poetry, the chapters that follow offer a response to long-standing complaints that contemporary poetry is irrelevant to its readers. They demonstrate instead that poetry is deeply concerned with political, environmental, and sociological events as well as with the ways those events are conveyed. Whatever their poetic orientation, twenty-first-century poets have found ways, often very different from those of the twentieth century, to evoke, examine, and engage the material situations of our time, demonstrating that it is still (or again) possible to make of poetry what Pound called "news that stays news."

Works Cited

Altieri, Charles. *Self and Sensibility in Contemporary American Poetry*. New York: Cambridge UP, 1984. Print.

Altieri, Charles. "What Theory Can Learn from New Directions in Contemporary American Poetry." *New Literary History* 43.1 (2012): 65–87. Web. 30 July 2014.

DuPlessis, Rachel Blau. "Agency, Social Authorship, and the Political Aura of Contemporary Poetry." *Textual Practice* 23.6 (2009): 987–99. Web. 30 July 2014.

Everson, William. Correspondence and papers: 75/5 c, Carton 10: Robinson Jeffers material. Bancroft Library. University of California, Berkeley, CA.

Forché, Carolyn. *Against Forgetting: Twentieth Century Poetry of Witness*. New York: Norton, 1993. Print.

Forché, Carolyn. "Reading the Living Archives: The Witness of Literary Art." *Poetry* 198.2 (May 2011): 159–74. Print.

Hong, Cathy Park. "Against Witness." *Poetry* 204.2 (May 2015): 151–61. Print.

Kalaidjan, Walter. *Languages of Liberation: The Social Text in Contemporary American Poetry*. New York: Columbia UP, 1989. Print.

MacLeish, Archibald. "Ars Poetica." *Collected Poems 1917 to 1982*. Boston: Mariner, 1985. Print.

McGann, Jerome. "Contemporary Poetry, Alternate Routes." *Politics and Poetic Value*. Ed. Robert von Hallberg. London: U Chicago P, 1987. 253–76. Print.

Orr, David. "The Politics of Poetry." Poetry Foundation, 1 July 2008. Web. 30 July 2014.

Spahr, Juliana. "Contemporary U. S. Poetry and Its Nationalisms." *Contemporary Literature* 52.4 (2011): 684–715. Print.

Swensen, Cole, and David St. John, eds. *American Hybrid: A Norton Anthology of New Poetry*. New York: Norton, 2009. Print.

von Hallberg, Robert. "Poets and the People: Reflections on Solidarity during Wartime." *Boston Review*, 1 September 2008. Web. 30 July 2014.

PART ONE

REDEFINING THE POLITICAL

ONE

Homeland Insecurity and the Poetry of Engagement

Eleanor Wilner

Words are a poet's medium and material—symbolic carriers of meaning and instruments of perception, so when the common coinage of words changes, the poet becomes hyperalert. Inevitably, when a new usage arises, something has changed to account for it, something that undermines old assumptions—the way, over time, in a porous underground, a top layer will thin, a subterranean hollow become a sinkhole, and your home, once the safest place on earth, suddenly will disappear into it. From this situation is bred a radical kind of insecurity, a widespread loss of trust in what had been assured. In such circumstances, language, and what it signifies, changes.

When, for example, did prisoners of war become "detainees?" When did torture become "enhanced interrogation?" When did bombing raids become "airstrikes?" When did our nation become the Homeland,[1] its police powers, vastly expanded, designated as Homeland Security? Each of these euphemistic new terms registers a change for the worse in our culture, and with it, an increasing distance between public language and actuality.

So it is not surprising that poets should be impelled, by the very nature of their enterprise, to confront the growing public gulf between words and actions, and to engage language critically and expressively with respect to new realities. Along with this has come a change in the reception of poetry concerned with current history, as the once negatively loaded term in America, "political poetry," has lately been designated as "the poetry of engagement," borrowing respected European usage, an English version of *poésie engagée*, associated in the twentieth century with French resistance poetry during the Nazi occupation, and very much an honorific. At the very least, poetry engaging the larger world has lately been granted neutrality, becoming "public poetry," the usage in a recent *Poetry* magazine—a respectable civic term that sheds the old pejorative so often attached to "political poetry."[2]

Along with changed attitudes reflected in the gift of a good name comes the recent proliferation of poems fitting that name—poems engaging intimately with public events and the large movements of history; not, this time, voices that can be identified (often dismissively) with a protest movement or ghettoized as a counterculture by a complacent mainstream, but coming from everywhere in the society, across separatisms and generations. The individual consciousness (is it necessary to say?) is the nexus of a private and a public world, of the singular and the choral, a unique instance in a collective and cultural continuum—and increasingly our poets are conscious of working at that intersection—not so much by choice as by circumstance. As people and poets, "we are set contextual" (Randall 159); we do not choose our subjects, but our subjects are given by the moment in which we live, and which lives in us.

This shift in both our poetry and the attitude toward it has been brought about largely by a change in the world. As foundational cracks and sinkholes have opened in the American illusion of invulnerability and exceptionalism, history has moved inside. New and intrusive realities have begun to undermine the smug or impervious attitudes that made the larger history seem peripheral, that permitted or encouraged a willed and/or manipulated ignorance of the less savory facts of privilege and our own nation's actions in the world. Those sinkholes, along with rising oceans and shrinking opportunities, have begun to change the perception of publically engaged poetry into something existential rather than "political": history lived, suffered within, as internally driven as any first-person lyric; our public life become a private woe—our dreams uneasy, our sleep disturbed.

In addition, and importantly, our poetry has become far more representative of the diversity of our mixed-origin nation, and that, too, has had a profound effect on the attitudes about a poetry with social, historical concerns, as has the growing body of poetry by former soldiers bearing internal wounds from our wars abroad. This change of attitude is reflected in students and apprentice poets who no longer ask *why* we write poetry that engages history and public events, but *how* it is done.

There is a new urgency about and acceptance of what earlier was exiled to silence or suspicion in our poetry (what Vietnam vet and poet Bruce Weigl called "the stories that no one wants to hear" [Wilner 38]). As a nation, the wars we waged were distant, and if they produced an unacknowledged ethical anxiety, the need to keep it unacknowledged may have fed the resistance to poetry that expressed what was stirring the curtains

Meanwhile, the revealing of private woes was authorized by a culture focused on the first-person singular, our poetry reflecting the mainstream society's tendency to assign personal responsibility for problems, even those arising from intractable material circumstances, institutionalized inequality, and the failure of public systems. As to those failures, and our actions abroad, we had, as a nation, the luxury of ignorance and could afford our illusions. After all, though armed with flaming swords and other antipersonnel weapons, ours were the better angels, weren't they?

But the Garden has been breached. On the cover of the poetry anthology, *The New American Poetry of Engagement*, that spawned the present essay collection is, not surprisingly, the well-known photo of the ruined World Trade towers, uncannily like Max Ernst's painting of the unfinished tower of Babel. In place of those ghostly towers, beside their monolithic, soaring replacement, is the huge open wound that changed our lives as Americans, and changed "political" to "engaged" poetry.

It is a commonplace that poetry often flows from hidden sources, finding expression and image for things erased, effaced, denied, or insulted—a wound will sometimes open these hidden places, vulnerability enabling disclosure. It is my sense that vulnerability is, for poetry, necessary, and, paradoxically, a source of its power; the forms and figures of poetry create the protective distance required for its revelations, what Seamus Heaney has called its "redress," poetry offering knowledge in a way that helps us endure it.

"What will always be to poetry's credit," Heaney once wrote, himself a poet of humane conscience faced with articulating a response to a bloody history, is "the power to persuade that vulnerable part of our consciousness of its rightness in spite of the evidence of wrongness all around it." "Rightness" for Heaney is not to be confused with "righteousness"; what he describes as a "condition of illuminated rightness" occurs when, through poetry, "consciousness is given access to a dimension . . . where an overbrimming, totally resourceful expressiveness becomes suddenly available" (Heaney xvii).

When applied to the expressive vision of our newly experienced vulnerability as a nation, we can discover, or poetry can discover for us, an identity with the unprotected of the world, a straying of sympathy; from an open wound, a suffering with, and with it, an increase in the frequency and amplitude of awareness. In sum, a less blinkered vision, one of greater complexity, exposing conflicting loyalties, mixed emotions, revealing the questions under the given answers.

For, as to that "wrongness all around it," it is the "given answers," the other human response to vulnerability, that is more easily tapped—a hardening: popular fear accepting a government's heightened security, a refusal to tolerate dissent, cries for revenge, a justification of violence, a resurgence of the illusion of invulnerable power, based on a gross simplification of reality ("with us or against us"). A prescient friend working at the Library of Congress looked out the window that September 11, saw the smoke rising from the direction of the Pentagon, and said to herself: "There go our civil liberties."

I remember, too, the vituperation that was visited on Susan Sontag for her suggestion in her *New Yorker* essay that there was some causality here, an assertion that was immediately and falsely confused with exculpation by her many detractors. She hoped that this atrocity might at least open a much needed public discussion of America's actions abroad, a hope many of us shared. But in the wake of that shattering event, after the initial shock and horror, the first response, predictably, was not soul searching, but its opposite: a paroxysm of patriotism, fanned by opportunistic leaders, who appropriated the occasion for their own ends, and falsified language to justify their actions.

As the storm gathers over our own heads as Americans, and as dread moves within, it seems to me that poets no longer need feel defensive about their public concerns, subjects that, for so long, were treated with suspicion, and sometimes with a sneer, a symptomatic disdain. How unfashionable, how uncool, conviction had become.

I was taken aback when reading, in a recent *New York Times* (February 2014) obituary for Maxine Kumin, a fine and laudatory review of her life and work, to find this paragraph, which typifies, I think, the kind of past resistance to poems, especially poems by women, that stray too far from the personal hearth, as if that were the boundary of the self and its most heartfelt concerns:

> Most critics agreed that Ms. Kumin's finest poems were those that trained their focus close to home. Those on large political subjects like mankind's dubious stewardship of the land, reviewers said, sometimes read better as prose than as poetry.

What struck me about the language here (beside the fact that the Kumins have built and worked together a small farm, and have long been quite personally concerned with stewardship of the land) was the attribution of opinion to some kind of large but unidentifiable majority: "Most critics agreed . . ." and "reviewers said . . ." This vague and settled plurality creates a kind of spurious authority that arouses the very skepticism it fails to document, and seems one example of what had been a prevailing attitude.

In spite of this undertow of the past, a new nomenclature for poetry now exists, a poetry recognized as engaged with the larger world, the very root of engagement in Latin being "pledge," an intimacy and bond between self and subject, which reveals a growing acceptance of a poetry about large events, driven by the most grievous personal necessity, as in Galway Kinnell's "When the Towers Fell" (Kinnell 37):

> As each tower goes down, it concentrates
> into itself, transforms itself
> infinitely slowly into a black hole

infinitesimally small: mass
without space, where each light,
each life, put out, lies down within us.

In this way, public wound becomes private injury, experienced within one-self to emerge as an expression of a painful awareness. And it also leads, as we saw, oppositely, to desire for revenge, permission to wound others, to a heightened nationalism, a carelessness about rights, and a political pretext to pursue self-serving goals without mercy or judgment, as in the all-too-revealing description of the bombing of Baghdad as producing "shock and awe,"[3] a mirror image of 9/11's death and destruction, but misdirected and amplified.

I fear that gazing into that open wound—perpetuated in the new memorial and tourist attraction in New York, described by Adam Gopnik in a recent *New Yorker*[4] as "a pair of chasms that correspond to the vacant footprints of the old Twin Towers" (Gopnik 39)—is dangerously seductive in the indulgence of a self-justifying national victim image. In more reflective circumstances, however, it might produce a heightened awareness of the suffering that war, so distant to most Americans—in spite of our role in foreign wars—really entails for those who must endure it; and awareness, too, of the "blowback," what the CIA calls unintended consequences—some of them, inevitably, to ourselves.

Kinnell's words above come at the end of his harrowing poem, whose work is to imagine the horror of those who were in the towers, or were waiting for someone who was—scenes to which most Americans had been exposed—but it is what Kinnell did with them that is the poet's work: to bring home to us, through sympathy with our own, all those others; to put it in perspective with the record of violence to our own human kind in the last century, to strip away all the sanctimonious language that is used to veil merciless mass slaughter:

They come before us now not as a likeness,
but as a corollary, a small instance in the immense
lineage of the twentieth century's history of violent death—
black men in the South castrated and strung up from trees,
soldiers advancing through mud at ninety thousand dead per mile,
train upon train of boxcars heading eastward shoved full to the
    corners with Jews and Roma to be enslaved or gassed,
state murder of twenty, thirty, forty million of its own,
state starvation of a hundred million farmers,
atomic blasts erasing cities off the earth, firebombings the same,
death marches, assassinations, disappearances,
entire countries become rubble, minefields, mass graves. (Kinnell 40)

Kinnell's lines comprise a traditional form of lamentation: they are mega-litanies of the human dead caused by other humans, reminding us that the greater the power, the larger the terror—first and foremost, from the state. And within his poem, in their own languages, are the words of poets François Villon, Paul Celan, Hart Crane, Aleksander Wat, and Walt Whitman: a single community of outcry that knows no national or temporal boundaries, and no cause except a measureless grief.

For many of our poets, of course, violence had already, long since come home, and its wound carried within. Our soldier and veteran poets were al-tering the very nature of war poetry, even as the nature of war had radically changed. This change, as well as in civilian attitudes, is tracked in Lorrie Goldensohn's essential anthology, a record of American poetry's response to war from the colonial wars of 1746–63 to the recent wars in Afghanistan and Iraq: *American War Poetry: An Anthology*, and its companion critical volume, *Dismantling Glory*, an exploration of the changing poetry of war by soldiers of the twentieth century.

In the anthology, each group of poems begins with a discussion of the historical setting from which the poems arise. As the years pass, and warfare changes, and slaughter grows general, the weapons more lethal, and, in the wars from Vietnam on, civilians become most of the casualties, what you see is how the poems, written by witnesses, victims and combatants, move from the sense of victory to that of utter waste: from the anonymous "The Song of Braddock's Men," 1755: "'Tis nobly done,—the day's our own—huzzah, huz-zah!" (Goldensohn 4) to the book's final lines, from the Iraq War, by veteran poet Brian Turner: "here, Bullet / here is where the world ends, every time" (Goldensohn 366).

Nor is historical violence and social injustice, felt passionately and per-sonally, new to our civilian poetry. Obviously, African American poets, from the Harlem Renaissance to the Black Arts movement of the 1960s, and since, have necessarily been engaged with the larger social and historical issues be-cause—it brooks no argument—they have been in a different political situa-tion from that of white Americans: that is, vulnerable from the first; groups oppressed and misprized within a culture do not have the psychological lux-ury of ignoring the larger society and history in which they have their personal existence.

Not surprisingly, the established literary world traditionally viewed the so-cial concerns of writers of color with the same attitude as that directed at all "political" poetry, all too frequently branding it partial, narrow, and didactic. In addition, white readers too often failed to see the injustices and suffering expressed by writers of color as specific instances of universal human experience, though poetry, by its very nature, expresses universals through the local and particular, something that mainstream prejudice managed to overlook.[5]

Additionally, writers of color, including Hispanic and Asian American writers, have, especially in the past, complained of the opposite expectation: that is, of being expected by the larger world and sometimes by their own community to write in a politically and ethnically engaged manner, attitudes that, when mandated, can be seen as limiting artistic freedom, that is, the choice to write out of one's own aesthetic necessities, whatever they may be.

While acknowledging awareness of these significant internal differences among us, let us look now at the mainstream mythology that fed the more or less received notion that what was called "political poetry" was, almost by definition, no matter one's ethnicity, bad poetry in which the polemical purpose must necessarily overwhelm the poetic. Since there is bad poetry of every kind, to single out socially engaged poetry in this way speaks, I believe, of our shrunken, isolating definition of the individual, one that damages our commonality, and hides our common plight. Writing in 2002 in *The American Poetry Review* about W. H. Auden's eerily apposite poem "September 1, 1939," which went viral in response to 9/11, Lucia Perillo spoke of a lost tradition of "nobility of expression" in poetry and its relation to the general suspicion of poetry in the civil tradition. "I remember, as a student," she wrote, "being advised not to use 'we' as my mode of address, not to try to speak on behalf of anyone but myself" (28). This is the ultimate separatism; islanded in autobiography, we have been drawn away, even in speech, from the company of others. Of course I say "we," for such isolation is a shared condition, and its recognition a powerful source of change.

Our popular psychology, which swallowed Freud whole, and was underwritten by commercial and political forces, had for so long reduced our perception of problems to the immediate personal: you and your little family were offered as sufficient cause for so many effects—a perspective that not only robbed us of history, depth, and connection, but kept us from seeing how we were manipulated to an unthinking conformity, encouraged in self-absorption and envy; how we and our world are shaped and defined by "invisible hands," to borrow Adam Smith's image, and our vaunted autonomy a commercially engineered mirage: "The Marlboro man thinks for himself."

This illusory, mythic, self-created individual, free of history and the evils of the Old World, is itself an inherited product of America's immigrant history, and draws on the well-known foundational myths of the "American Adam," an innocent inventing himself in a new and Edenic world, a myth understandably risen from the immigrant need to shed the pain of remembrance of a lost language and world, while embracing optimism and new beginnings.[6] Over time, however, our relative safety and well-being as an increasingly rich and imperial nation encouraged ignorance of the larger world, and of America's action in it, an ignorance necessary to the maintenance of the myth that our exercise of power was, unlike that of other nations, well intentioned and benign. We as a nation, had become, over time, self-hypnotized and confident of our virtue and our invulnerability.

And this measured our distance from other nations, for whom one category of respected poetry had always been poems in response to public and historical events, reflections political and philosophical: in France, as mentioned before, *poésie engagée*; in Spain and Latin America, *poesía de compromiso* (commitment); in Russia, *grazdanskaya poesiya* (citizen's poetry). For other nations, war, tyranny, and the vulnerability that large-scale violence ensures could not be experienced apart from the self; the personal was necessarily integral with the larger, public world, and history a deadly presence.

But since revision of myth in the light of the actual is one of the imagination's tasks, in spite of prevailing attitudes about the boundaries of the personal being more or less at one's front door, some of our poets have all along been challenging both the American ("you can be anything you want") myth of the autonomous and self-created individual, and the myth that our foreign interventions were virtuous, our recent wars furthering "freedom" and "democracy." There is not room enough or time to discuss or even enumerate the American poets of the twentieth century who engaged with public events, with the forces ranged against the individual, and, in particular, with the wars and violent interventions—some open, some covert—by the United States in the affairs of other nations.

It is not that current history is a new subject for our poets; what is new is its more widespread internalization, resulting in the proliferation of engaged poetry, and its broad acceptance in what are history's changing circumstances, an acknowledged enlargement of how much outer world the inner self contains. In a bewilderment of violations and violence, the sense of a common condition animates the poetry of engagement—this time consciously crossing bloody borders marked "enemy."

Walt Whitman's ancestral voice comes to mind—"my enemy is dead, a man as beautiful as myself is dead" (271)—as, out of the carnage of the Civil War, he made an identification of self and other on which all poetry depends—as Homer has Achilles seeing in the tears of his enemy Priam those of his own father—and which empathy, if it were general, would forever tarnish glory and disable war, its slaughter being dependent on successful dehumanization of the "enemy." Forever postponed, it seems, that empathy, for, in all my years, only the name of the enemy has changed.

For here I must speak from my own place in time. For those of us of a certain age, who, like C. K. Williams, have been there before, and all along, personally and therefore poetically engaged with history; who were children when the images of both Shoah and atomic holocaust shattered all we'd been taught; who were given our subject by virtue of circumstance and not virtue; who were, in his words, "of the generation of the bomb, Hiroshima, the broiling bubble at Bikini, ICBMs" (Williams 190)—who had, post-Hiroshima/Nagasaki, crouched under our desks at school, taught as children thereby to be afraid that others would do unto us as we had done unto them (though no one said this). To our otherwise fortunate generation none of this was really new, only more grievous, more implacable: "these fearful burdens to be borne, complicity, contrition, grief" (Williams 189). Reading Williams's poems of 2001 and the years after, I find my own conflicted consciousness given voice, as in his poem "Fear" (190):

> I still want to believe we'll cure the human heart, heal it
> Of its anxieties, and the mistrust and barbarousness they spawn,
> But hasn't that metaphorical heart been slashed, dissected,
> Cauterized and slashed again, and has the carnage relented, ever?

As history, and its terrible and escalating repetitions, invades our twenty-first-century waking world, and moves within, we are torn—afraid to look, afraid to look away; for such contradictions, poetry becomes more than ever an expressive necessity. And even if the way we know sanctity now, as C. K. Williams suggests, is through its desecration, then desecration must become our subject.

That the desecration of the other, designated as "enemy" and therefore disqualified as human, enters and poisons our most intimate and private moments is made powerfully evident in the poem "Gift" by Nell Altizer, which measures the personal effect of those pornographic images of the treatment of Iraqi prisoners by our soldiers:

Gift

> Had I known the last love of my life
> would be a girl whose early holler
> in my arms awakened the short ditch,
> alarms of loss, the rose thorn under
> the lavender fingernail, who after
> pulling out the Groovy Girl that was
> the present, thrust the bag over
> her crow black bangs down to hair
> feathering her narrow shoulders
> and twirled her wrists in the dark thrill

> of being lost and not found turning
> outward the quick flair of trapped wings
> beating the air, I would not have thought
> of Abu Ghraib or caught her close
> or torn the hood from her head—
> the only one I could. (Altizer 178)

A woman is speaking of how the love of her granddaughter has reopened the pain of the past and her fear of loss through the child's vulnerability—love and mortality at their usual odds, when a gift-giving scene is interrupted by the girl's childish thrill at putting the bag over her head, both playfully hiding and tempting the dark in a situation she feels is safe. To her grandmother, the image brings horror with it, and her sudden action, the last line of the poem registering her felt helplessness at atrocity that we can protest but not prevent. In the condensed force of this poem—driven by its wrenched syntax and periodic sentence, as if holding off this inevitable awareness and her response—we feel a larger truth in its central trope: that innocence itself has been injured by the internally felt, no longer distant events.

Similarly, W. S. Merwin registers the public world's inner damage to the most peaceful and precious personal moments in his poem of 2004, "Ogres" (26), which, in his characteristic unpunctuated lines that dramatize their syntax, comprise one 17-line periodic sentence, a cascading structure of linked units, one prepositional phrase cupped within another, miming a tranquil world of connectedness: "all night waking to the sound / of light rain falling softly / through the leaves in the quiet / valley below the window / and to Paula lying there," and as his appreciation deepens into amazement "at the fortune / of this moment . . . this breathing peace," it is that sweet word "peace" that awakens awareness of its opposite:

> this breathing peace and then I
> think of the frauds in office
> at this instant devising
> their massacres in my name
> what part of me could they have
> come from were they made of my
> loathing itself and dredged from
> the bitter depths of my shame. (Merwin 26)

As the long rhapsodic sentence turns to anguished questions, its self-accusation is what catches us off guard, as it questions what identity he might have with these degraded actions done in his name, throwing away the moral ease of simply saying "Not in our name," which was a catchphrase of the movement against the preemptive invasion of Iraq. This suggests, too, how political writing per se (and necessarily so) differs from poetry faced with the same issues.

Speaking of the inner imperative that drives her late-life poems of engagement, Maxine Kumin says: "My political poems were wrung from me. Thematically [they] are linked by my despair at the monstrous contempt American officialdom has displayed for justice and morality in the years since the 9/11 attacks" (Kumin, "Metamorphosis" 734). Even as, in Merwin's poem, the most private peace is invaded by knowledge of these violations, so, too, is the perception of nature distorted by it, as in the poem from her recent book, *Still to Mow* (2007), "Extraordinary Rendition" (33), which takes on that newly invented euphemism for the U.S. act of exporting prisoners to other countries to be tortured. Nature is shown bearing the marks of human acts: the oak leaves in autumn are "bruised the color of those / [beaten] insurgent boys"; the beech leaves, too, "curl undefended." And in the next lines Kumin offers an understated challenge to the aesthetics of lyric disinterestedness: "Art redeems us from time, it has been written." She then measures the falsifying new verbiage against actual practice, actions that tear from her the old human root meanings: "Meanwhile we've exported stress positions, shackles, / dog attacks, sleep deprivation, waterboarding. / To rend: *to tear (one's garments or hair) / in anguish or rage.* To render: *to give what is due / or owed.*" The poem's tercets close with a return to the falsifying legalese in the title, ironically twisting the tarnished language back toward meaning:

Extraordinary how the sun comes up
with its rendition of daybreak
staining the sky with indifference. (Kumin 33)

"Rendition" is returned here to its original meaning as performance, interpretation, version—and, in her rendition of the sun, along with its habitual indifference, there is, in that word "staining," our own culpable indifference that comes to light at the poem's end.

Now, closing this essay, I turn to a poem, "The Innocent," by Jean Nordhaus, as it exemplifies powerfully both the new sense of vulnerability and the way poetry can expressively destabilize the dangerous simplifications of common usage and political parlance, and can complicate, deepen, and humanize a subject at the same time. In this case, the language the poem explores is the well-worn phrase "innocent victims," an attribution that has historically too often been used as a carte blanche for more violence. The first-person speaker in this poem, reflecting the enlargement of the personal to include the public domain, has become the collective pronoun; the first of its two stanzas describes "us": "a mob of strangers awaiting a train. There may be / among us a wifebeater, surely a thief . . . none of us blameless / not one of us pure. Greedy, covetous, / selfish, vain, we have trafficked in lies; we / have practiced small cruelties. Even the baby, / asleep in a sling on his mother's breast / has been willful, has shaken with rage" (50). Then comes the second stanza, the shattering moment—the poem, while radically questioning what "innocence" means, ends by shocking us back to our human, utterly contingent, and ultimately unprotected commonality when faced with the violence of our own kind:

> Yet, if fate arrives, as a wind, in a bullet,
> a bomb, at the instant of shock, in the silent
> heart of conflagration, we will all
> be transformed into innocents, cleansed
> in the fires of violence, punished not for any sins
> committed—but for standing where we stand,
> together in the soft, the vulnerable flesh.

Notes

1. There is something obtuse about arrogant power that makes it deaf to connotations. The modern association of "homeland" is with the English name for the Bantustan, the restrictive areas to which the apartheid government of South Africa banished the black South African majority.

2. Perhaps no better or more impassioned example of this once-prevalent and pejorative attitude could be cited than the extended rant by Harold Bloom introducing *The Best of the Best American Poetry* (Scribner's, 1998), epitomized here: "If you urge political responsibilities upon a poet, then you are asking her to prefer to poetry what can destroy her poem" (24).

3. I have read the prologue and first two chapters (more than enough to get the point) of the document from which this method of using massive force with the goal to destroy the enemy's will to resist gets its name and objectives: "Shock and Awe, Achieving Rapid Dominance," by Harlan K. Ullman and James P. Wade, prepared by Defense Group Inc. for the National Defense University, 1996. A sobering experience of rationally advanced and discussed mass horror to be visited on a population.

I quote one statement that struck me: "With declining numbers of worthy and sufficiently equipped adversaries against whom to apply this doctrine, justifying it to a questioning Congress and public will prove more difficult."

4. The rest of the quote is telling: "Although officially described as 'reflecting pools,' they are not pools, and they leave no room for reflection. Wildly out of scale with the rest of the site in their immensity, they are subterranean waterfalls. . . . Their constant roar interrupts any elegiac feeling that the list of engraved names of the dead which enclose them might engender."

5. I recall a lecture by Carl Phillips in which he described a class response to a poem as one about loss and grief, but when he then identified the poet as Langston Hughes, the students narrowed the interpretive lens and saw it instead as about the African American condition.

6. These social and historical circumstances that narrowed the personal in last century's American poetry exaggerated the influence of certain European literary movements on our mainstream poetics. Citing the literary influences on what he characterizes as "the relative non-engagement of the bulk of 20th century U.S. poetry," Jeffrey Gray (in an essay in progress) describes "the poetic zeitgeist in broad strokes, from its roots in 19th century l'art pour l'art, the English Aesthetic Movement (and Edgar Allan Poe in this country), and from the French Symbolists who shaped T. S. Eliot's poetry, through the decidedly anti-didactic ethos of the New Critics, crystallized in the idea of the poem as autotelic, and Archibald MacLeish's dictum 'A poem should not mean but be.' In this atmosphere, there was little space in the . . . mainstream for explicitly engaged poetry."

Works Cited

Altizer, Nell. "Gift." *Hawai'i Review* 67/68, 29.2 (2009):15 Print.

Goldensohn, Lorrie, ed. *American War Poetry: An Anthology.* New York: Columbia UP, 2006. Print.

Gopnik, Adam. "Stones and Bones: Visiting the 9/11 Memorial and Museum." *New Yorker,* 7 and 14 July 2014: 38–41. Print.

Heaney, Seamus. "Preface." *The Redress of Poetry.* London: Faber and Faber, 1996. Print.

Kinnell, Galway. "When the Towers Fell." *Strong Is Your Hold: Poems.* Boston: Houghton Mifflin Harcourt, 2006. 37–43. Print.

Kumin, Maxine. "Extraordinary Rendition." *Still to Mow.* New York: Norton, 2007: 33. Print.

Kumin, Maxine. "Metamorphosis: From Light Verse to the Poetry of Witness." *Georgia Review,* Winter (2012): 724–34. Print.

Merwin, W. S. "Ogres." *American Poetry Review,* May–June, 33.3 (2004): 26. Print.

Nordhaus, Jean. "The Innocent." *West Branch,* Fall–Winter, 59 (2006); reprinted in *Pushcart Prize XXXI Best of the Small Presses,* ed. Bill Henderson et al. Wainscott, NY: Pushcart P, 2007. Print.

Perillo, Lucia. "W.H. Auden: '9/1/39'." *American Poetry Review,* September–October 2002: 28–29. Print.

Randall, Julia. "Moving in Memory." *The Path to Fairview: New and Selected Poems.* Baton Rouge: LSU P, 1992. Print.

Sontag, Susan. In "Talk of the Town: Tuesday and After." *New Yorker,* 24 September 2001. Web. Archive.

Whitman, Walt. "Reconciliation." *Leaves of Grass.* New York: Signet Classics, 2005. Print.

Williams, C. K. "War; September–October 2001." "Fear; September 2001–August 2002." *Collected Poems.* New York: Farrar, Straus and Giroux, 2006. Reprinted in *The New American Poetry of Engagement: A 21st Century Anthology,* ed. Ann Keniston and Jeffrey Gray. Jefferson, NC: McFarland, 2012. Print.

Wilner, Eleanor. "Poetry and the Pentagon: Unholy Alliance?" *Poetry,* October 2004: 37–42. Print.

TWO

The Poetry of Engagement and the Politics of Reading

Vernon Shetley

My argument depends on an assertion and an observation. The assertion has to do with the nature of interpretation: when dealing with politically engaged poetry, our readings of poems depend crucially on the ideas we hold about their authors' intentions. No poem, at least no politically engaged poem, can sufficiently internalize its context to render externally derived understandings unnecessary. This assertion might seem pointless, given that the intentional fallacy, according to conventional wisdom, was long ago exiled from respectable theoretical company, along with the New Critical horse it rode in on. In fact, though, current ideas about intention exist in a curious superposition of incompatible states. In principle most of us remain committed to what Toril Moi refers to as "the . . . skepticism and suspicion that pervades . . . contemporary theory" (193), a skepticism particularly hostile to ideas of subjectivity, intention, and expression. Even if one possessed a self capable of forming an intention, this view holds, language would be incapable of communicating that intention. In practice, interpretation frequently mobilizes accounts of intention, particularly when praising ideologically congenial authors, though, as I note in my discussion of Amiri Baraka below, a supposedly superseded anti-intentionalism stands ready, under the right circumstances, to rescue authors from themselves. As readers, most of us, I suspect, remain unable fully to commit either to the theoretical clarity of poststructuralist skepticism, or to what now seems like a naive faith in the ability of language to embody the lyric subject. As critics and readers, we continually revert to ideas of intention that as theorists we reject.

The observation is that American poetry has fractured into niches structured by different, often radically different, ideas about poetry: about what constitutes a poem, about what ends poetry should serve, about the social role poetry performs, about the politics of the poet and the reader. The microclimate in which mainstream crowd-pleasers like Billy Collins and Mary Oliver flourish is a world away from that inhabited by post-Ashberyans like Tim Donnelly and Marcella Durand, which is in turn a different country from the "high cultural pluralism," to adapt a term from Mark McGurl's analysis of contemporary American fiction (56–63), of Vijay Sheshadri or Rita Dove, which inhabits a separate universe from the conceptualism of Kenneth Goldsmith and Vanessa Place, which is in turn stationed at an unbridgeable divide from the traditionalism of A. E. Stallings and R. S. Gwynn—and I could go on. The interaction between the niche-ification of American poetry and the salience of authorial intention has important implications for how we read poetry, implications that are particularly powerful for our understanding of the contemporary poetry of engagement.

Those implications gain urgency if we accept the premise that intention can never be adequately communicated by language alone. Language can be the bearer of intention only when placed within a dense network of social relations, preexisting knowledge, and conventions of discourse and action. Here I follow the thinking of the philosopher Nancy Bauer in her powerful reinterpretation of J. L. Austin's work. Bauer discusses a hypothetical common in philosophy, the woman who "walks into a coffee shop desiring exactly one dry-measure cup of coffee beans and tells the waiter, 'Bring me a cup of coffee'" (99). Bauer rejects the usual idea that the waiter, when he brings her a cup of brewed coffee, has failed to understand her intention; rather, Bauer insists, given what she said and the context in which she said it, "It doesn't matter . . . that she intended to order a cup of beans" (99). Since there exists no social context in which one orders a dry-measure cup of coffee in a coffee shop—such a context might exist, but doesn't—the woman's words could not possibly have communicated the request she wished to make, and were the woman to make clear, by further explanation, what she wanted, the waiter would surely not feel that he was at fault for failing to understand her initially. The contexts within which poetry is read are in many ways more amorphous and more complex than the simple example of an order in a coffee shop, even in cultural situations where more shared assumptions about poetry prevail than in the contemporary United States. The dependence of intention on context suggests that the fracturing of American poetry into mutually exclusive niches multiplies the opportunities for misunderstanding when the borders of those groupings are crossed.

Space does not permit a rehearsal of the series of battles over the issue of intention in interpretation that have repeatedly broken out through the history of literary criticism and theory, but a few observations are in order. Bakhtin is surely correct that "in world literature there are probably many works whose parodic nature has not even been suspected" (374). A corollary of Bakhtin's hypothesis is that our judgments of literary excellence or interest must to some extent be detachable from our understanding of how the work was intended to be read or experienced. The afterlife of the Ern Malley hoax supports Bakhtin's idea; for a substantial number of readers the poems have overcome their origins as an antimodernist stunt to constitute a significant poetic achievement, demonstrating, as David Lehman puts it, that "intentions may be irrelevant to results." And yet all of us, in our experience of artworks, have surely had moments when the question of intention has arisen with urgency, when it feels as if we cannot decide how to respond to a work, or achieve any kind of understanding of it, without knowing how the maker intended it to be read or seen. W. H. Auden refers to the pleasure of "baiting the critic with the problem of the comically bad poem"; he quotes a poem by Ebenezer Elliott, one that Aldous Huxley had singled out for the "peculiar repulsiveness" of its "complacent . . . genteel feelings" (207–8), in order to offer the thought-experiment of reading it as if it were a satirical "comic dramatic monologue" by John Betjeman (45). Auden presents this kind of duck/rabbit problem as an outlier, an occasion for laddish amusement, but the issues raised by Auden's thought-experiment may not be so easily contained.

I'll begin with a few examples outside of poetry, to illustrate the generality of the problem. Surely many listeners, perhaps most, have enjoyed the Beatles' "Yer Blues" without hearing in it the "parody of British blues" that John Lennon apparently intended (Everett 170), and even knowing that Lennon's impulse was parodic might not change significantly our response to the song. But cases in which our sense of the orientation of the author to his or her work feels like a crucial element of our response are probably more numerous than those in which the presence of a parodic intention is indifferent. Critics go round and round arguing whether John Currin's and Lisa Yuskavage's kitsch nudes are meant to challenge the male gaze (good) or pander to it (bad). Many viewers of the film Black Swan found its tone an urgent question; was it intentionally risible, or was it an example of unconscious camp?[1] The issue isn't confined to what we traditionally think of as artworks. Media scholar Heather Lamarre and her fellow researchers demonstrated in a 2009 paper that many conservative viewers of the Colbert Report took Colbert to be advocating seriously the right-wing perspectives he was in fact satirizing. Interestingly, these conservative viewers found the show no less funny than did viewers who understood Colbert's satire as it was intended. Surely, though, viewers who misidentify the targets of Colbert's satire are in effect watching a different show from those who grasp Colbert's intentions. The political effect Colbert means his show to have depends on the viewer's prior knowledge of Colbert's political orientation.

To explore the way that the interpretive demands of reading the poetry of engagement interact with the fractioning of American poetry into niches, I'll discuss poems by three poets, chosen to maximize the range of styles and political orientations represented. Paul Lake is perhaps the rarest kind of poet in America today: a political conservative. Conservative viewpoints were once well represented among American poets, from Ezra Pound, propagandist for fascism, and T. S. Eliot, purveyor of a gracefully abstracted monarchist nostalgia (though with a decidedly graceless anti-Semitic note), to Ike-likers Robert Frost and Wallace Stevens. But conservative political views have almost entirely disappeared from American poetry—a consequence, perhaps, of poetry's incorporation into the academy, where professors' political orientations, at least in humanities departments, fall almost entirely on a spectrum from centrist liberal to radical Left.[2] The outlier status of Lake's conservatism within the field of American poetry (despite his having published in mainstream venues such as *Iowa Review, Poetry*, and *Threepenny Review*) raises some distinctive questions of response. Amiri Baraka's radical leftism, on the other hand, is something of an outlier on the opposite end of the political spectrum, even if, as Joseph Lease notes, from the perspective of Language writers like Bruce Andrews and Charles Bernstein, Baraka's work remains wedded to the "reactionary" strategies of the lyric "I" and self-expression (390). I will try to bring into focus the specific reading strategies demanded by a poem like Baraka's "Somebody Blew Up America." Finally, I will discuss a poem by Robert Hass, who might be placed on the mainstream left in terms of both politics and poetic style. Hass's "Some of David's Story" offers a self-reflexive probing of the ways in which understanding is enabled or derailed by differences in political orientation, and of the effects created by the forms of political exhortation and representation mobilized by the poetry of engagement. Hass's poem cultivates ambivalence of response, at the same time that it depends, perhaps no less than Lake's or Baraka's work, on an address to a quite specific segment of the poetry-reading audience, and on our sense of the poet's own placement within the landscape of American poetry.

Before I focus on individual poems, it may be useful to explore briefly the concept of "intention" I deploy here, given that I use the term to refer to several different elements of our orientation to an encounter with poetry. The most basic sense refers to the question of whether the poet intends the poem as parody or not, whether we are meant to read literally or ironically. Another sense has to do with the alignment between the poetic speaker and the poet him- or herself; even if we assume, in New Critical fashion, that poet and speaker are not equivalent, poems still depend on, and assert, a sense of the poet's identity. The choice of a dramatic speaker tells us something about the kind of poet and person who has made that choice. Even if we value the Ern

Malley poems more highly than their authors did, knowing their origins in a hoax informs our reading of the works, and turns admiring them into a different kind of act from what it would be had Ern Malley actually existed. This is the case even in the kind of conceptual work that claims to have done away with intention altogether, such as Kenneth Goldsmith's "uncreative writing." Transcribing a year's worth of weather reports may seem like a radical abandonment of intentionality (The Weather), but the project communicates to us a good deal about Goldsmith himself: for starters, it tells us that he is the kind of writer who would transcribe a year's worth of weather reports and present the results as poetry. Finally, there is the form of intention that might be called verifiability; certain kinds of poetry make assertions about the world, and about the poet's relation to the world he or she represents. It is central to the effect of such poetry that we take what the poet asserts to be true, or at least credible; the poem makes a claim, not simply on imagination, but on belief. Different forms of poetry mobilize different understandings of intention, but our readings of poems are always crucially inflected by the alignment, or lack of it, between the reader's idea of the poet and poet's idea of the reader.

The speaker of Paul Lake's "Concord" is Henry David Thoreau, its subject the night Thoreau spent in jail for his refusal to pay taxes because of the government's support for the Mexican-American War and slavery (Walking Backward 35–36). Thoreau's action, and the essay that it inspired, "Civil Disobedience," have been key inspirations for many on the left in the twentieth century, from Martin Luther King to Gandhi. Much of Lake's poem versifies the account presented in "Civil Disobedience": the inmates chatting until lockup time, the courtesy of Thoreau's cellmate, the breakfast of bread and hot chocolate served before Thoreau was released. Lake's Thoreau begins his story, though, in a self-aggrandizing vein rather unlike the persona projected in "Civil Disobedience":

> To stop the wheels of state, I made
> My life a kind of counter friction
> And went to jail, my tax unpaid.

And the ending of the poem raises acutely the question of the tone we are meant to register in the lines

> Let out myself, I then proceeded
> Across the street to fetch the shoe
> I'd left to mend, then unimpeded
> Strolled slowly down an avenue

And past the square and when last seen
On top a hill two miles from town,
Was lost in huckleberrying,
My conscience clear, my duty done.

Nothing in the language itself prevents one from reading these lines as a celebration of Thoreau, an endorsement of his righteous action. Read this way, the disproportion between huckleberrying and "stop[ping] the wheels of state" is an irony that turns back on the political sphere; enjoying the simple pleasures of nature constitutes a form of resistance to the state's coercive claims on the individual. The only problem with reading the poem this way is that it becomes an uninteresting poem, the ending of which simply tells us what to think about the questions raised within it. I take it that Lake means us, instead, to hear these lines as mocking, to hear the voice that speaks in them as touched with smugness and an unpleasant self-dramatizing quality. Lake implicitly contrasts Thoreau to his cellmate, "who spent mornings haying / In neighboring fields," and who, upon parting with Thoreau, says he "doubted we'd be meeting soon." The cellmate's hard, productive labor shows up Thoreau's self-indulgent huckleberrying, while his parting remark demonstrates that he has taken Thoreau's measure: having spent a night in jail for show, the privileged Thoreau will not be returning. What makes me think that we should hear Lake as taking an ironic distance on Thoreau's self-satisfaction, rather than celebrating his principled stand? Partly my sense that the poem is simply a more interesting poem if read this way, partly Lake's own self-presentation, in essays and interviews, as a political conservative, partly other poems in *Walking Backward*, the title poem and "Epitaph for a Draft Dodger," which depict as selfish or morally culpable Vietnam-era draft resisters, whose refusal to participate in the war "machine" parallels Thoreau's refusal to pay taxes for war. Nothing in the language of "Concord" itself can tell us definitively how to read it, what attitude toward its speaker the poet intends us to take. And yet our sense of that attitude is crucial in our response to the poem. Even if we bracket the idea that there is a correct way to read the poem, even if we abandon the idea that we should read the poem in accord with its author's intentions, we find ourselves compelled to make a choice in our reading, as the poem is a fundamentally different work of art read one way versus the other.

"Revised Standard Version," from Lake's most recent volume, *The Republic of Virtue*, offers an even more acute example of this kind of ambiguity (30–31). The poem is a dramatic monologue spoken by the Samarian woman Jesus meets in chapter 4 of the Gospel of John. In John, the woman accepts the justice of Jesus's rebuke for having sex outside marriage. In Lake's poem, she reject's Jesus's authority to judge her:

> My sex life, sir, is none of your damn business.
> I don't know where you got your information,
> But if you try this sort of thing again,
> I'll haul you into court, you stalker, you.
> Who do you think you are, harassing me?

A crowd of women surrounds the two, joining with the Samarian in mocking Jesus for his arrogance: "I'll take charge of my sexuality, / With no advice from you," one states. Given my sense of Lake's position, I assume he endorses Jesus's authority to deliver judgment and police women's sexuality. But again, how are Lake's intentions made legible to the reader? One might imagine a poem pretty much identical to this one written by a feminist poet, a poem whose aim was precisely to critique the patriarchal assumptions of the biblical episode, to reject the idea that women's sexuality should be regulated by male religious authority. The only verbal quality that might in isolation push one toward viewing Lake's poem as antifeminist is the flat, clichéd language that the poet gives to the women's critique of Jesus: "keep your phony doctrines off my body," "Mr. Misogynist." But is it impossible to imagine a poet of antipatriarchal views expressing his or her position this unimaginatively? The ending of "Revised Standard Version" is exactly what we might expect from this hypothetical revisionist feminist poem: the Samarian women return to their homes "singing / Words not set down in your official Greek." I take it that Lake means that these songs embody a vulgar, obscene sexuality; the Samarian women revel in their own impurity. But this line might easily be taken to express, and celebrate, the feminist idea that women's words embody meanings inexpressible in the "official" language of patriarchy. Only a reader already familiar with Lake's ideological commitments could parse the attitude the lines are meant to convey; nothing in the language itself can confirm that the point of the satire is antifeminist rather than feminist. Even if we suppose that, in the absence of context, Lake's occasional uses of anachronistic language would communicate satiric intent, how are we to know that the poem is not intended as a parody, rather than an instance, of conservative satire? We know this, if we know it, not because of anything in the poem's language, but rather through context, because we know that satire with a conservative orientation does not occupy a sufficiently prominent place in the contemporary poetic landscape to motivate anyone to bother parodying it.

Lake's poetry, then, is ambiguous, but only in a contingent sense; the ambiguity is not the poet's aim, and it dissipates once we understand his intentions. If we might at first mistake those intentions, it is only because Lake's particular political orientation is so unusual among contemporary American poets, not because the poet's irony is meant to veil those intentions. The problem, poetically, with Lake's approach, in my view, is its implicit construction of irony as the polar opposite of sincerity, which is perhaps simply another way of saying that the absence of sympathy for opposing points of view that characterizes Lake's work connects it to some of the less attractive currents of contemporary American conservatism. Lake's irony resembles the stable ironies of eighteenth-century satire, which are frequently read as reinforcing, rather than undermining, authority and hierarchical norms. Rose Zimbardo's description of the function of Restoration and eighteenth-century satire might easily be applied to Lake's work:

> The new ordered and ordering language of satire establishes a bond of trust between the discursively central I-narrator . . . and the "obedient" Model Reader and carefully discriminates the narrator + reader "us" from "them," the foolish or vicious "others" at whom the "reader" and the "author" gaze through the telescope of mediating discourse. (141)

The "bond" Zimbardo posits here depends on a fundamental identity of perspective between writer and reader, or at least on the reader's willingness to adopt the writer's frame of reference; Zimbardo connects this form of satire to Paul de Man's account of irony as embodying a "will to power" that is also a will "to educate and improve" (140). In aiming to educate and improve, Lake shares the goals of many of the "engaged" poets collected in *The New American Poetry of Engagement*. But the 18th-century satirists were speaking on behalf of values widely shared among the literate classes of their time; when a poet's work is substantially out of alignment with the values of its time, we are more likely to call it prophecy than satire. Perhaps Lake will, by writing as if a shared body of values were available to ground his satire, call into being the Model Readers his work demands. But he has his work cut out for him.

Much lyric poetry we might take to be a report on experience: "This is what it feels like to be in the situation I inhabit." What the poem asks for is less assent than empathy; by experiencing the poem we are trying on, inhabiting, a particular mode of experience (which is quite different from sharing the experience that the poem takes as its subject, though that can be part of what it means to read certain poems). The poetry of engagement often goes further, asking us to share the sentiment the poem expresses, or aiming to produce a specific feeling, even to catalyze action, in the reader. I. A. Richards proposed the concept of "pseudo-statements" as a means of preserving the value of past poetry written within a framework of beliefs, especially religious beliefs, that no longer held the assent of most readers (66–79). Richards's strategy reaches back to that proto–New Critic Sir Philip Sidney's insistence, against philosophical and religious views accusing poetry of spreading falsehoods, that "for the poet, he nothing affirmeth, and therefore never lieth" (136). The whole point of the "poetry of witness," conversely, is affirmation, that this particular event happened, that the poet has either experienced the event or encountered its traces. The outraged response in some quarters to the Araki Yasusada hoax, in which an American professor of literature fabricated poems that he passed off as those of a survivor of the Hiroshima bombing, attests to the importance of beliefs about "truth" or "authenticity" in "witness" poetry. Margaret Soltan, expressing a widely held feeling of outrage in unusually heated language, writes that the hoaxer, Kent Johnson, "has distorted a complex, sensitive, and important historical record by pretending to have experienced personally that which he did not experience; he has furthered the degradation of modern poetry into victim pathography; he has, through his success, and through the subsequent attention he has received, encouraged other pranksters to contrive their own pseudo-victims; he has permanently destroyed his credibility as a writer and the reputation of a number of editorial boards; and he has volitionally placed his work among a rapidly proliferating body of similarly destructive fraudulent work in the world at large" (222). Conversely, Ron Silliman and others have suggested bracketing the moral dimension of the hoax; for Silliman, the value of the Yasusada oeuvre is that it "makes the argument for anti-essentialism," that it supports, in other words, the poststructuralist ideas about the "death of the author" to which Silliman and like-minded writers subscribe. Reading poems in this way, though, emphasizes their literary-theoretical functioning over any other possible motive for reading. Perhaps that's all that's left after the revelation of the hoax has destroyed their sense of historical weight and rendered it impossible for them to mobilize the depths of pathos with which they had first seemed to be endowed. The literary-theoretical is hardly without interest, but it seems pretty thin compared to the intensities of physical suffering and horror, pain and struggle, into which the poetry of witness attempts to immerse us.

Engaged poetry frequently demands, then, that we accept the affirmations of historical fact upon which it builds, and demands as well that we share a specific political orientation toward them. If were to discover that, let us say, a massacre depicted in the work of a "poet of witness" did not in fact take place, it seems inevitable that the impact of the poem for us would be diminished, unless we were already poststructuralist readers for whom no text could ever have the power to put us in touch with the real. It seems equally unlikely that a supporter of the Contra war would respond to, for instance, Carolyn Forché's poetry about Central America in the way she intends. For Forché's generation of American poets of engagement, the poetry depends both on a kind of literalism of content and on an implicit alignment between the reader's perspective and the poet's, based on the assumption that poet and reader share a generally left/liberal political orientation. While Forché and her peers at times express skepticism about language, that skepticism turns on fears that language is inadequate to communicate the extraordinary experiences of trauma the poets wish to render, rather than on more encompassing poststructuralist doubts about the capacity of language to afford any contact with reality whatsoever.

Ann Keniston and Jeffrey Gray, in their introduction to *The New American Poetry of Engagement*, distinguish the kind of "engagement" they observe in recent poetry from the French concept of *littérature engagée* and the South American and Eastern European political poetry that provided models for this earlier generation of American poets, arguing that recent "engaged" poetry, while resisting "postmodernism's decontextualization," nevertheless incorporates "postmodern destabilizations of identity and reality" (7). Within the context of those destabilizations, though, the reality-effects that once were the *raison-d'être* of engaged writing come to perform a very different role. Keniston and Gray cite Timothy Donnelly as typifying the shift from hermetic postmodernism to, in Donnelly's words, "admitting reality." When Donnelly describes that shift himself, though, "reality" has a purely poetic function: "Admitting reality into my work . . . allowed for the kind of tonal complexity and amped-up artfulness I couldn't forsake" (215). "Reality" enters the poetry to increase its palette of tones, to enhance, not its political traction or its ability to effect change in the world, but its "artfulness." Poets who still aim to move hearts and minds are likely to remain wedded to a different view of the role of "reality" in poetry, one that sees reality not as a source of poetic effects but as a ground of political utterance and action. The distinctive reading strategies appropriate for poetry that aims for some form of political or social efficacy always threaten to displace reader response from the work itself to the underlying political, social, and historical situations and events that inspire the poetry. Arguments about engaged poetry, at least that segment of it aligned with activism, always risk becoming arguments not about poetry but about politics or history.

So it is in the case of Amiri Baraka's "Somebody Blew Up America." Disproving Auden's famous dictum "Poetry makes nothing happen," Baraka's poem made the position of poet laureate of New Jersey disappear, though the question remains whether it was the poetry in the poem, or something else, that had that effect. The poem has received a spirited defense by Piotr Gwiazda, who insists that "Somebody Blew Up America" should be read "as a poem," and whose chief accusation against the poem's critics is that they fail to do so. As Gwiazda himself recognizes, this raises the question, "What does it mean to call 'Somebody Blew Up America' a poem" (471)? Within the New Critical protocols that for many decades governed the reading of poetry, the answer to this question is clear: to read a text as a poem is to read it as the utterance of a dramatic speaker, who is not to be identified with the poet. This way of reading rejects the idea that the poem asserts propositional content, and thus brackets any truth-claims the poem appears to be making. To use a trivial example, it doesn't matter, if we are reading Keats's poem as a poem, that he mistakes Cortés for Balboa in "On First Looking into Chapman's Homer"; whatever truth the poem contains is not to be found in the details of history it alludes to but in the experience it communicates to the reader.[3] Poststructuralism dissolved the dramatic speaker, while warring even more militantly against the idea that poems should be read as making truth-claims. Without precisely dismissing the New Critical approach, Gwiazda offers a different emphasis: to read a poem as a poem "means to pay attention not only to what it says but also to how it says what it says" (471). So Gwiazda launches on an extended examination of the rhetorical strategies and stylistic characteristics in Baraka's poem. Throughout these pages, Gwiazda proceeds as if demonstrating that the poem displays highly patterned and technically skillful uses of language were a defense against charges that it purveys falsehoods. But the mere presence of rhetorical devices in a text does not bracket its truth-claims; one could find in a mendacious speech by Sarah Palin many of the same strategies Gwiazda points out in Baraka's poem. Gwiazda's analysis depends on an unstated, maybe not even consciously held, New Critical assumption: that a text's being a poem absolves it of a responsibility to documentary truth. Only in the New Critical universe is the accusation "This text contains defamatory falsehoods" properly disarmed by the response "This text is a poem, and thus makes no truth-claims."

Ultimately Gwiazda is forced to acknowledge the incompatibility between his defense of the poem as poem and the demands of the engaged artwork: "What is problematic about reading 'Somebody Blew Up America' exclusively as a poem is the fact that Baraka unequivocally stands by his words" (478). Precisely. If a poem intends, to use a formulation encountered constantly on the left, to "speak truth to power," it follows that the poem must speak truth, and that the truth it speaks cannot be merely a poetic truth. In his reply to the Anti-Defamation League, Baraka says nothing about any failure to read his poem "as a poem"; instead he asserts the documentary truth of the poem's assertions. In response to criticism of the lines "Who told 4000 Israeli workers at the Twin Towers / to stay home that day / Why did Sharon stay away?," for instance, Baraka says nothing about their status as poetry but rather appeals to his version of historical fact: "I do believe . . . that the Israeli government, certainly it's [sic] security force, SHABAK knew about the attack in advance," and goes on to give a list of news sources he claims support his version of events. It is possible to imagine reading the poem as a dramatic monologue, as a poet's representation of the ranting, paranoid consciousness of a speaker driven to endorse conspiracy theories in his or her outrage at the long history of criminality and oppression perpetrated by the powerful against the weak. But reading the poem that way would violate Baraka's aims and transform it into a fundamentally different poem.

Exploring more fully the "Israeli workers" passage may help bring into focus the incompatibility between Baraka's intentions and Gwiazda's interpretive method:

Who set the Reichstag Fire

Who knew the World Trade Center was gonna get bombed
Who told 4000 Israeli workers at the Twin Towers
To stay home that day

Gwiazda notes first that the line about the Reichstag fire refers to the way that the Nazis used the event to inflame anti-Semitic sentiment and consolidate their power; he uses Baraka's own defense of the poem to certify his account of what Baraka is trying to communicate.[4] When discussing the assertion that follows, however, he ignores Baraka's own remarks and writes instead that it "refers to a rumor, this time the one spread in the Arab world insinuating Israel's foreknowledge of the events of September 11" (469). Even if we did not have Baraka's own statement, the interpretation Gwiazda proposes here would make these lines decidedly out of character with the rest of the poem. Gwiazda deploys a typical New Critical reading strategy, taking the lines to be an expression not of the author's own views, but of those of a dramatic speaker, someone whose perspective is to be, if not entirely rejected, understood as potentially mistaken or distorted, the expression not of truth but of the kind of partial understanding humans inevitably inhabit. Nowhere else, however, does the poem adopt this kind of distanced speaker, and it seems unlikely that Baraka would be critiquing the Arab world for its credulity in swallowing an anti-Semitic myth when Baraka elsewhere professes his belief in the "rumor" Gwiazda takes him to be criticizing. Baraka complains, not that hostile readers have failed to understand that the poem is a dramatic utterance, but that they have misread his intended meaning. The ADL takes Baraka to be purveying the anti-Semitic conspiracy theory that Jews were responsible for the Reichstag fire, while Baraka in fact endorses the left-wing conspiracy theory that asserts that the Nazis set the fire themselves.[5] Baraka understands that the kind of political poetry he is writing depends on a fusion of poet and speaker; only a reader on board with Baraka's worldview is in a position to read the poem the way the poet intends. Though their politics are radically different, and Baraka embraces the prophetic role that Lake seems to shy away from, the rhetorical strategies Baraka deploys closely resemble Lake's; we could describe both poets as being ironic without being ambiguous. The misreadings to which "Somebody Blew Up America" has been subject spring not from any deliberate polysemy in the poem's language, but from certain readers' lack of familiarity with Baraka's views, a situation that arose when the poem traveled outside the microclimate of readers knowledgeable about Baraka to a wider public.

Gwiazda credits Baraka, at least in the passage about Israeli workers, with a view of human understanding as partial—necessarily both fragmentary and prone to bias—that I take to be foreign to Baraka's poetic voice, which depends on supremely confident assertions of authority. Later I will take a brief look at some of Baraka's earlier work, which inhabited an anxious space of partial knowledge and manifested an acute and painful awareness of the difficulty of determining both one's own thoughts and those of others. I'll turn now to a poem, Robert Hass's "Some of David's Story," that thematizes the ways in which our presuppositions shape our responses, the ways in which our grasp of our own intentions and those of others is necessarily baffled and uncertain, and the ways that the political commitments of others challenge our own understanding—in the sense both of comprehension and of sympathy. The poem, clearly the utterance of a dramatic speaker, unfolds entirely within quotes. Given that the convention of the dramatic monologue has been well established for over a century, a poet hardly needs to signal the dramatic mode by quotation marks. Their presence insists with particular force on the distinction between poet and speaker, introducing an additional layer between speaker and reader, as if Hass means to tip the balance of sympathy and distance that constitutes the dynamic of the dramatic monologue toward the latter. The poem is presented as "David's" account of a failed love affair, one that begins in a recognizably Petrarchan key. The first meeting with "her" seems to hold out to the speaker the possibility of self-transformation; the love-object appears endowed with a freedom and completeness the speaker himself lacks: "I thought . . . she had made herself up entirely." The second section of the poem is a Petrarchan blazon:

> Her neck was the thing, and that tangle of copper hair.
> And, in those days, her laugh, the way
> she moved through a room. Like Landor's line—
> she was meandering gold, pellucid gold.

How are we meant to take this? No attitude is explicitly signaled, yet Hass surely expects that his audience is familiar with the withering feminist critiques of objectification, critiques that render the blazon, with its focus on physical attributes, its fragmentation of a woman's wholeness into separate parts, deeply suspect. The reference to Landor raises further suspicions, in some measure simply because feminism has alerted us to the troubling aspects of seeing a woman as if she were an artwork. The trouble deepens when we seek out the source of the quotation, Walter Savage Landor's poem "On Seeing a Hair of Lucretia Borgia." Though Landor takes a curiously reverential tone toward her in the poem, Lucrezia Borgia has long been a byword for shocking notoriety, with a reputation blackened by accusations of incest and murder. The speaker's impercipience in likening his beloved to Lucrezia Borgia suggests that we should be skeptical about his attitudes toward the woman he describes.

"David" moves from describing his infatuation with the (never-named) woman to recounting the tensions that ultimately ended their relationship. The woman becomes "obsessed" with her work at "Amnesty" (the poem assumes we are the kind of readers who know that "Amnesty" is short for Amnesty International), an obsession that estranges her from the speaker: "Political torture, mostly. / Abu Ghraib, the photographs. She had every one of them . . . / And Africa, / of course, Darfur, starvation, genital mutilation. / The whole starter kit of anguished causes." Again, the tone here seems complex, and also dependent on the reader's being positioned in a particular way with regard to the speaker, the woman, and the atrocities that come to preoccupy her. On one hand we sympathize with the exasperation "David" expresses here, his sense that there is something unhealthy about the woman's single-minded fixation on suffering and oppression. Perhaps we are meant to understand this partly as the speaker's retrospective bitterness, a feeling that has developed only after he has found himself in competition for his beloved's attention with torture and atrocity. At the same time, the speaker's dismissiveness seems intended to grate. "She had every one of them" belittles the woman, making her impulse to know the extent of the Abu Ghraib horrors into something that resembles collecting baseball cards, an impression amplified in the phrase "starter kit," which likens the woman's human-rights activism to a childhood hobby or a packaged consumer product. Hass intends, I think, that the sympathy we feel for "David" in his view that the woman's obsession with suffering is in some way excessive or self-damaging will be leavened with a guilty sense that there is something admirable about her commitment, something we might envy, in moral terms, without being willing to emulate. The speaker's irony hints at a defensiveness in his tone, an ambivalence that is redoubled in the reader's response to that tone; we are meant to find it patronizing, and yet can easily imagine ourselves adopting a similar attitude were we to find ourselves in the speaker's situation.

The incident that the speaker identifies as "the beginning of the end" seems calculated to put us on his side. The woman introduces him to one of her colleagues, a "girl" with "absolutely white skin," whom the speaker describes as a "wan English beauty." "Not really. She has lymphoma," the woman replies. "I wasn't being callow. I just didn't know," the speaker protests. Surely the woman is wrong to hold this remark against the speaker, if that is indeed what she does, and yet the poem's persistent questioning of the speaker's perspective may make us wonder whether we might not be meant to doubt the speaker's view here. Though he insists that he "wasn't being callow," he comes off as callow more than once in the poem; readers who suspect that "David" is an unreliable narrator might wonder whether the woman would agree with the man that this incident was "the beginning of the end," or whether she might date it to some other incident in which the speaker was more genuinely culpable.

The closing section of the poem further layers misunderstandings and obliviousness in a way that seems designed to impress upon the reader both the difficulty of any kind of human understanding and the speaker's own failures of perception. He recounts a concert that he and the woman attend near the end of their relationship: "we went to hear a friend / perform some music of Benjamin Britten." The choice of Britten, famously a pacifist, connects with the speaker's account of reading back issues of T. S. Eliot's journal *Criterion* and "noticing / again that neither Eliot nor any of the others / seemed to have had a clue to the coming horror," that horror being World War II. Eliot and his contributors exhibit a perfectly understandable failure to grasp the pattern in which they are enmeshed, however obvious that pattern may seem in retrospect. The speaker remarks on the woman's "beautiful hands," an image that recalls the earlier mention of "the hands of some Iranian feminist journalist / that the police had taken pliers to," though whether we are meant to criticize the speaker's aestheticized perception, or reflect on the luck of those whose lives have been unmarked by the "horror" so prevalent in other parts of the world, or see the speaker's attention to the woman's hands as precisely the kind of distraction that causes one to miss the "horror" all around, remains ambiguous.

The speaker imagines the woman as "carrying the whole of the world's violence / and cruelty in her body, or trying to, because / she thought the rest of us couldn't or wouldn't." The formulation reworks a common metaphor, "carrying the weight of the world on her shoulders," in the direction of greater internalization, a more vivid and immediate taking in, beyond taking on, of the world's pain. The ending of the sentence poses an alternative, "couldn't or wouldn't," without making clear who is posing that choice. Is it the woman who remains poised between a more sympathetic view of "the rest of us," one that sees us as incapable of a long, hard look at the worst, and a view that sees "us" as culpably unfeeling, choosing to ignore the pain we know exists? Or is it the speaker who, despite his intimacy with the woman, remains unable to decipher the view she holds? The poem ends with a literary allusion that balances the reference to Landor in the poem's opening: "that line of Eliot's / from *The Wasteland* came into my head: / 'This music crept by me upon the waters.'" Eliot's vision of a blighted world is presumably meant to resonate with the woman's vision of a world of "violence" and "cruelty." This raises a potentially troubling possibility, however: that we should see the woman's response to a world of "violence" and "cruelty," a world she knows through "photographs" and "report[s]," images and narratives, as analogous to aesthetic responses, the kinds of responses we have to fictional narratives and images that move us. The atrocities that weigh so heavily on the woman are real, rather than imagined, certainly, and yet the question remains of how her responses to real events differ from those of a reader or viewer to fictional happenings. And what of our response to the poem itself? Its title suspends any truth-claim; ascribing the "story" to "David" suggests its origin in a real person's experience, while the term "story" applies equally to fictional and factual narratives. The imponderables extend even to the poem's final line, which the speaker identifies as a quotation from T. S. Eliot. The line certainly occurs in *The Waste Land*, but within quotes, because it is one of Eliot's many quotations, in this case from Shakespeare's *The Tempest*, where Prince Ferdinand describes the music he hears as "allaying" both the "fury" of nature and his own "passion." The speaker's ascribing this line to Eliot rather than Shakespeare relocates the consolations of Shakespearean pastoral romance into the darker realm of Eliot's blighted cityscape, and emphasizes the different effects of the music in Shakespeare's play and Hass's poem, where the music, rather than calming turmoil, seems somehow connected to the end of the relationship. And what of David's error about the title of Eliot's poem, which he makes into one word with an article, "*The Wasteland*," rather than two? Most readers of Hass's poem will notice the mistake, but outside of seasoned Eliot scholars, how many of us could fail to experience a tiny flicker of self-doubt, a moment of suspicion that it might be we, as opposed to David, or rather the faceless narrator who reports David's words to us, whose memory is mistaken?

That the questions the poem raises about the poet's attitude toward "David," and the attitude we are meant to have toward him, could never be answered on the basis of the poem's language does not make them feel less necessary. If we are to read the poem at all, we are compelled to grapple with them, just as, if we are to live in a world with others, we must grapple with, try to decipher, their meanings and intentions, despite the strong possibility that those meanings and intentions are unknown or unfathomable to the people themselves, or that they are too shifting, unstable, and mixed ever to grasp. What we can say with some certainty is that the poem positions the reader in specific ways, and that the effects the poem achieves depend crucially on the attitudes the reader brings to it. We are encouraged to identify with "David," even as we recognize the "callow" edge to his way of describing the woman and his relation to her. The energy of the poem emerges from the play of sympathy and distance typical of the dramatic monologue, to which has been added a complicated play of attitudes toward the woman the speaker describes. The poem both mobilizes the kind of delicately nuanced sensitivity to complex attitudes that characterized the New Critical way of reading, and offers a critique of that way of reading. The poem seems to deny that resolution, harmony, or clarification of experience has been achieved; the relationship it describes has ended, it is not at all clear that anything was learned from it, and the poem ends with the puzzle of the blindness or obliviousness of the *Criterion* writers, people whose education and intellect should have enabled them to achieve some measure of foresight. Rather than placing us at an ironic distance, the poem seems to want to force us continually to experience the impossibility of the impossible choices it represents. But only a specific kind of reader will experience the poem the way Hass intends.

If the poem offers any kind of answer to the questions it raises, it lies in the activity of the poem itself, its open-ended investigation of uncertainties, continually circling them without imagining that it could settle them. In its multilayered distance from the terrible political facts it invokes—the poet's report of David's account of the woman's experience of representations of oppression—the poem implicates itself in the failure to confront and protest the world's suffering that so upsets the woman. Hass means, I take it, to provoke ambivalence about our own response to the poem; to what extent does it put us in the morally uncomfortable position of acknowledging our own failures to work toward justice as fully as we might, and to what extent is the poem itself, writing it and reading it, an example of just such failure? The poem hints at the possibility that there exists a fundamental incompatibility between poetry and political action, one that has tension and power only for readers who can be made uncomfortable by being reminded that we are not doing all we can to alleviate suffering, by our awareness that those who have dedicated themselves to fighting oppression are doing work that we in some way feel we ought to be doing but aren't. Against the explicit moralizing of much engaged poetry, Hass offers an uneasy experience focused precisely on the difficulties of reading. In our interactions with others in the world, and in our interactions with poems on the page, we are constantly reading intentions, always with the risk that we will misread, that the frameworks we use to enable understanding will overlay or distort it. "David" may strike us as impercipient, but can any of us be sure our understanding is superior to his? Hass suggests that our responsibilities, and our struggles, as readers of poetry are a version of our responsibilities and struggles in any human situation in which we are engaged in reading the intentions of others. There is a profound ethical responsibility involved in reading, even if, Hass implies, we will never know if we have gotten it right.

As a brief coda, let me return to Amiri Baraka—return, in fact, to a time when he was LeRoi Jones. *The Dead Lecturer*, from 1964, makes powerful poetry out of conflicts and ambivalences that Baraka resolved in later transformations of his poetic style and political orientation. Throughout the volume, the "I" of the poems seems at once riven with internal tensions and caught in an explosive dissonance with the world it confronts; this situation compels and at the same time threatens to stifle expression, with the effect that the poems frequently become, either implicitly or explicitly, strings of questions. "Somebody Blew Up America" is constructed largely of questions as well, but the questions are rhetorical; Baraka knows the answers, and expects his reader to know them as well. The questions that suffuse *The Dead Lecturer* are, in contrast, open-ended, uncertain, prompts for what often seems a desperate seeking:

> It cannot come
> except you make it
> from materials
> it is not
> caught from. (The philosophers
> of need, of which
> I am lately
> one,
> will tell you. "The People,"
> (and not think themselves
> liable
> to the same
> trembling flesh). I say now, "The People,"
> as some lesson repeated, now,
> the lights are off, to myself,
> as a lover, or at the cold wind. (10)

These lines, the opening of "Balboa, The Entertainer," seem suspended between entirely private and expansively public utterance. Beginning with a pronoun that lacks an antecedent suggests that we have caught the speaker in the middle of a dialogue with himself, but this utterance is reframed as the presumably public pronouncement of "The philosophers of need," though no antecedent for "it" is ever provided. The poem invokes the vast abstraction "The People," and yet "The People" seems to occupy the same scale as "a lover." Parentheses repeatedly break the lines, suggesting that the speaker is digressing, or reformulating, or reframing his thoughts; all but one of these parentheses remains unclosed. The shape of the poem emerges from the speaker's inability to settle on what he is trying to communicate, as if seeing what he has just said reroutes what he is about to say. Or consider the poem that closes the book, "The Liar" (79). The homophony between the title of the poem and the instrument that gives lyric poetry its name suggests the impossibility of embodying truth in poetry, given that the poet finds both that he misrecognizes his own feelings ("What I thought was love / in me, I find a thousand instances / as fear") and that any expression transforms the self he is trying to express ("their chanting weight, / erased familiarity / from my face"). The poem's final lines seem almost like a riddle: "When they say, 'It is Roi / who is dead?' I wonder / who will they mean?" Grammatically, the quoted words form a statement, but they are shifted into the interrogative by the question mark at the end, modeling the continual sliding of assertion into perplexity that characterizes the volume. The poet wonders how others see him, how they perceive what he refers to as "I," but he also is uncertain about his own identity, about who he is, in part because his self is constituted out of the perceptions of others, so that he cannot know fully how others see him and, lacking that knowledge, cannot know what he is himself. It is not surprising that Jones/Baraka was unable to sustain the tension and ambivalence that inform *The Dead Lecturer*; the volume is shot through with an intensity of pain and struggle that must have seemed almost intolerable to the poet who experienced it. But I cannot help but prefer the poet of *The Dead Lecturer*, who had nothing but questions, to the later Baraka, who has all the answers.

Notes

1. Dennis Lim offers a useful account of the stakes of the debate.

2. Neil Gross's *Why Are Professors Liberal and Why Do Conservatives Care?* offers a level-headed discussion of the two questions raised by its title.

3. Recent scholarship has proposed that Keats's apparent mistake was in fact deliberate; see Rzepka.

4. Baraka's response to his critics refers to "Hitler's destruction of the Reichstag," assuming that the Nazis were responsible for the arson; sober historians have generally been skeptical of that theory, though, of course, responsible commentators join in deploring the uses to which the Nazis put the ensuing panic.

5. Most responsible historians hold that the fire was set by the Dutch Communist Marinus van der Lubbe; Evans presents an account of the back-and-forth among historians.

Works Cited

Auden, W. H. *The Dyer's Hand*. New York: Random House, 1962. Print.

Bakhtin, Mikhail. *The Dialogic Imagination: Four Essays*. Ed. Michael Holquist. Trans. Caryl Emerson and Michael Holquist. Austin: U of Texas P, 1982. Print.

Baraka, Amiri. "The ADL Smear Campaign against Me." *Counterpunch*, 7 October 2002. Web. 12 May 2014.

Baraka, Amiri. "Somebody Blew Up America." *African-American Review* 37.2–3 (Summer–Autumn 2003): 198–203. JSTOR. Web. 14 July 2014.

Bauer, Nancy. *How to Do Things with Pornography*. Cambridge, MA: Harvard UP, 2015. Print.

Donnelly, Timothy. "Statement." Keniston and Gray. 213–15. Print.

Evans, Richard. "The Conspiracists." *London Review of Books* 36.9 (May 8, 2014): 3, 6, 8–9. Print.

Everett, Walter. *The Beatles as Musicians: "Revolver" through the Anthology*. New York: Oxford UP, 1999. Print.

Goldsmith, Kenneth. *The Weather*. Los Angeles: Make Now Press, 2005. Print.

Gross, Neil. *Why Are Professors Liberal and Why Do Conservatives Care?* Cambridge, MA: Harvard UP, 2013. Print.

Gwiazda, Piotr. "The Aesthetics of Politics / The Politics of Aesthetics: Amiri Baraka's 'Somebody Blew Up America.'" *Contemporary Literature* 45.3 (Fall 2004): 460–85. JSTOR. Web. 14 July 2014.

Hass, Robert. "Some of David's Story." Keniston and Gray. 89–93. Print.

Huxley, Aldous. *Text and Pretexts*. New York: Harpers, 1933. Print.

Jones, LeRoi. *The Dead Lecturer*. New York: Grove Press, 1964. Print.

Keniston, Ann, and Jeffrey Gray. *The New American Poetry of Engagement: A 21st Century Anthology*. Jefferson, NC: McFarland, 2012. Print.

Lake, Paul. *The Republic of Virtue*. Evansville, IL: Evansville UP, 2013. Print.

Lake, Paul. *Walking Backward*. Ashland, OR: Story Line Press, 1999. Print.

LaMarre, Heather L., Kristen D. Landreville, and Michael A. Beam. "The Irony of Satire: Political Ideology and the Motivation to See What You Want to See in *The Colbert Report*." *International Journal of Press/Politics* 14.2 (April 2009): 212–31. Sage. Web. 14 July 2014.

Lease, Joseph. "'Progressive Lit.': Amiri Baraka, Bruce Andrews, and the Politics of the Lyric 'I.'" *African-American Review* 37.2–3 (Summer–Autumn 2003): 389–98. JSTOR. Web. 14 July 2014.

Lehman, David. "The Ern Malley Poetry Hoax." *Jacket Magazine* 17, originally published in *Jacket* 2 (1998). Web. 18 July 2014.

Lim, Dennis. "Dirty Dancing." *Slate*, 29 December 2010. Web. 14 July 2014.

McGurl, Mark. *The Program Era: Postwar Fiction and the Rise of Creative Writing*. Cambridge, MA: Harvard UP, 2009. Print.

Moi, Toril. "Thinking through Examples: What Ordinary Language Philosophy Can

Do for Feminist Theory." *New Literary History* 46.2 (Spring 2015): 191–216. *Project Muse*. Web. 26 January 2016.

Richards, I. A. *Science and Poetry*. New York: Norton, 1926. Print.

Rzepka, Charles. "'Cortez, or Balboa, or Somebody Like That': Form, Fact, and Forgetting in Keats's 'Chapman's Homer' Sonnet." *Keats-Shelley Journal* 51 (2002): 35–75. JSTOR. Web. 14 July 2014.

Sidney, Sir Philip. *Selected Prose and Poetry*. Ed. Robert Kimbrough. Madison: U of Wisconsin P, 1983. Print.

Silliman, Ron. Cover copy, *Doubled Flowering: From the Notebooks of Araki Yasusada*. New York: Roof Books, 1997. Print.

Soltan, Margaret. "Bicameral Mind." *Angelaki: Journal of the Theoretical Humanities* 6.3 (2001): 221–24. Web. 14 July 2014.

Zimbardo, Rose. *At Zero Point: Discourse, Culture, and Satire in Restoration England*. Lexington: U of Kentucky P, 1998. Print.

THREE

Twenty-First-Century Ecopoetry and the Scalar Challenges of the Anthropocene

Lynn Keller

The purview of environmentally engaged poetry and poetry criticism, like that of environmentalism itself, has been expanding dramatically in recent years. No longer limited to nature poetry, twenty-first-century ecopoetry treats a diversity of places, including urban and degraded landscapes, while it attends increasingly to issues of environmental justice and of broadly conceived environmental health affecting human and nonhuman beings.[1] In addition, poets now are grappling with the often frightening challenges posed by rapid climate change, by accelerating rates of extinction, and by the recalcitrance of governments and multinational corporations in responding to dire anthropogenic planetary alterations. Given that environmental scientists have not been successful in generating appropriate behavioral and policy changes, artists and scholars in the environmental humanities are challenged to more effectively advance environmentally sound agendas. As poets invite us to imagine more fully the environmental conditions in which we live and toward which we seem to be moving, they participate in a profoundly important realm of public discourse. Examining works by three poets who are committed to doing just that, this essay will highlight the distinctive imaginative, rhetorical, and formal strategies each uses to help readers confront a crucial intellectual challenge of our immediate environmental situation: the scalar disparities of this period of human-generated planetary transformation now labeled the Anthropocene. The poets' different strategies imply differing visions of poetry's role in enabling change in the world, although the poetry of all three reveals an instability—not a vacillation or an inconsistency so much as a refusal of certainty—a dance between a desire to locate in poetry effective resources for changing perception and understanding and a counterrecognition of language's limited powers, particularly in the face of extreme—and for humans, quite possibly catastrophic—environmental disruption.

Among the challenges encountered in trying to address current environmental crises are those of imagining at unfamiliar scales, both minute and vast. The concept of the Anthropocene brings these challenges into focus. The term was introduced in 2002 by Nobel Prize–winning chemist Paul Crutzen, who proposed that the earth is no longer in the Holocene epoch of geological history because human activity since the beginning of the Industrial Revolution has changed the oceans, the atmosphere, and the earth's surfaces on a scale comparable to the cataclysmic geological events that determined prior periods or epochs. The idea that we have entered the Anthropocene epoch has caught on among both scientists and the broader public partly because it provides a way of bringing together a great variety of anthropogenic changes in order to consider their cumulative and interactive impacts.[2]

The shifts in thinking prompted by the concept of the Anthropocene are profound. Some people claim that "there is no more *nature* that is independent of human beings" (Purdy).[3] Such statements exaggerate to the extent that they overlook the inherent instability of the planet or the unchanging laws governing its processes; as geographer Nigel Clark notes, "With or without the destabilizing surcharge of human activities, the conditions most of us take for granted could be taken away, quite suddenly, and with very little warning" (xi). But certainly, as Clark also acknowledges, "The awareness that humankind has grown into a preeminent force in planetary nature—and all the associated questions about how to deal with this situation—is undoubtedly one of the most momentous events our species has ever had to cope with" (xiii).

Thinking about the human in terms of the Anthropocene produces a down-the-rabbit-hole experience, as humankind can seem at one moment dominant, huge, and the next minuscule and utterly unimportant. Seen in geological time frames, the few hundred years since the Industrial Revolution massively expanded human use of fossil fuels constitute an infinitesimal unit. Holding in view the small scale of human habitation on Earth highlights nature's indifference to the survival of *Homo sapiens* or to the maintenance of the atmospheric or oceanic conditions on which the survival of many Holocene species depends. Such a perspective could encourage humility about our importance as well as concern about a long-term future. Yet even as thinking in terms of geological time renders the human tiny and ultimately insignificant, the name "Anthropocene" itself points to how very big humans have come to be on the planet, both because of huge population growth and because of the vast chemical and biological effects of human activity. Perceiving humans as significant geological actors whose behavior during a few hundred years will impact the biosphere for hundreds of thousands of years could prompt a desire to put humankind in more proportional relation to the planetary change.[4] Alternatively, it might only compound the anthropocentric hubris evident in industrialized humanity's behavior to date, perhaps encouraging faith in geo-engineering as the solution to whatever environmental problems arise. However one sees its implications for public policy, a fundamental aspect of the concept of the Anthropocene is its bringing together—even into collision—vastly discrepant scales of time and space.

That the Anthropocene implicitly lumps all humans into a monolithic collectivity might be considered another of its troubling scalar implications. As historian Dipesh Chakrabarty points out, while humans have always been biological agents, both collectively and as individuals, "We can become geological agents only historically and collectively, that is, when we have reached numbers and invented technologies that are on a scale large enough to have an impact on the planet itself" (206–7). The collective emphasis of the concept draws attention away from the inequities across the globe in responsibility for anthropogenic planetary changes, in access to the benefits of those developments, and in distribution of their environmental costs. Chakrabarty goes so far as to ask, "Does not the talk of species or mankind simply serve to hide the reality of capitalist production and the logic of imperial . . . domination that it fosters?" (216).

Even leaving aside the myriad issues of environmental justice that the generalizing term "Anthropocene" risks eliding, the species-oriented nature of the term—like the scale of the accumulated kinds of environmental disturbance it encompasses—obscures the role or nature of individual agency, the possibilities for future individual freedoms, and the potential impact of economic and social changes within particular social, regional, or national groups. The question of how to think about the possibility of piecemeal and nonglobal responses to what Chakrabarty calls the "shared catastrophe" of the Anthropocene (218), and of how to position oneself in relation to it all, proves a daunting one.

From this emerges a dimension of Anthropocene scalar challenges that I think of as "scalar dissonance"—my coinage for the cognitive and affective dissonance between what feels like minute individual agency and a context of enormous collective impact. As we collectively lurch toward one biological tipping point after another, each of which has cascading consequences of scales and complexities one can barely comprehend, the individual feels tiny and helpless. One's conscientious choices—not to travel by airplane, say—lack meaningful impact. Ruling political, corporate, and economic systems responsible for environmental degradation are evidently beyond the individual's control, even as few individuals in industrialized nations can avoid participating in them.

Juliana Spahr's "Unnamed Dragonfly Species" effectively exposes this scalar dissonance and the structures of feeling that accompany it because of the way in which the poem's rhetoric and construction draw the reader into that experience. This poem in prose from Spahr's 2011 collection *Well Then There Now* presents information about global warming and species extinction and may thereby educate its readers, but its focus is less on the data than on the difficulties nonscientists experience in trying to process the reality particularly of global warming and in trying to locate appropriate responses.[5] One of its two interwoven strands is a narrative concerning an unspecified but socially cohesive "they" who, in a year when hot summer temperatures came so early in April that the daffodils died almost as soon as they bloomed, became preoccupied with the melting of glaciers, which they learned about and observed on the Internet. Inserted between each of the sentences in that narrative is the boldfaced name of a plant or animal species. These approximately 150 names, which constitute the second strand, are alphabetically organized entries from a list of "endangered, threatened and special concern plant, fish, and wildlife species of New York State" found on a state government website (6–7).

Spahr's presentation of the experience of the people learning about glacial melting positions the reader not just as audience to their story but also as participant in the analogous experience provided not by the Internet but by the poem. Thus, while some sections report the struggles "they" went through as they grew increasingly preoccupied with and informed about the geological evidence of global warming, others provide enough of the factual information "they" were trying to process that the reader has to struggle as "they" did to confront the astonishing scale of this global transformation. On the one hand, the reader is being invited to process information, the scale of which is difficult to absorb; on the other, she or he is prompted to examine the conceptual and psychological drama this information produces, not only by reading about others who confronted this information but also by examining his or her own responses.

Although a map that precedes the poem shows that it was written in Manhattan, the place where "they" are experiencing the Anthropocene is the indeterminate space of the information-overloaded World Wide Web, which can be difficult to connect to one's non-Internet reality in some specific locale. However, in the section beginning "On the internet they realized," Spahr does not announce how difficult it is to grasp the actual scale, let alone the significance of the facts about glacial melting that follow. She simply lists facts "they" were learning, such as "the Bering Glacier in Alaska recently lost as much as seven and a half miles in a sixty day period" (78), saying nothing about how "they" reacted to this information. By suspending the narrative of "they" while providing factual data, Spahr allows her readers to have, and reflect on, their independent experience of this information.

By moving in the following section to how oblivious the younger "they" were to the climate change going on in 1988, a key year in the history of global warming, Spahr uses the narrative of "they" to help readers acknowledge how little people tend to think of anything outside their own immediate context and very personal needs. The scale of human attention tends to be small and self-centered, not attuned to what Rob Nixon has called "slow violence." Even changes that geologists easily recognize as alarmingly rapid can, because of their geographical distance and their suprahuman scale, remain abstracted from ordinary lives. Readers may well recognize themselves in the younger "they" who spent their time thinking about getting jobs or hitting baseballs or ridding themselves of drunk boyfriends rather than pondering locally imperceptible changes in global climate.

In the present time of "Unnamed Dragonfly Species," however, "they" have been drawn into an obsessive quest for more information, drawing the reader, too, into more engagement. The next section begins, "After the piece of the Antarctic Pine Island glacier broke off, they could not stop thinking about glaciers and the way they thought about glaciers the most was by reading about them on the internet late at night, their eyes blurring and their shoulders tight" (82). Now Spahr recounts not just the facts but the shifting responses "they" have to the accumulating data and the scale of change they cumulatively suggest—thereby encouraging readers to attend to their own perhaps volatile responses. At one point, "they" try to take comfort in a statistic "liked by oil drillers" that the melting away of the entire Antarctic Pine Island Glacier wouldn't matter much "because it would only raise sea levels by a quarter of an inch" (82). But because further questions "would surface through this blurry comfort of small amounts of rising ocean," they can't avoid seeing that the oil drillers haven't grasped how scale works in this scenario. With so many glaciers melting at once, the statistics for one need to be added to the others. Moreover, a quarter inch of water in the ocean is not like a quarter inch in a can with vertical sides; a rise of one foot of ocean level, they learn, "typically means that shorelines end up one hundred feet or more inland" (83). So much for attempts to minimize the scale of the ongoing changes. The section ends with data on island nations that are already being overtaken by rising seas, while the next begins with "they" recognizing themselves as island dwellers for whom what's happening to Pine Island Glacier has a "scary relevance." The collapse of spatial and temporal distances taking place in Anthropocene conditions calls into question categorizations of environmental changes as insignificantly small or as "far away."

The remaining sections offer a compelling portrayal of the psychology of "they," with which the mental states of Spahr's readers have come to be aligned. By matter-of-factly recording "their" thoughts and behaviors, Spahr effectively registers the difficulties most Americans are likely to face in trying to maintain an awareness of alterations that are overwhelmingly vast, complexly interrelated, but as yet largely "far away from them"—or so they tell themselves (76). Hypocrisy, inconsistency, and self-deluding fantasy are all part of the picture. Often seeking comfort, they try out positive ways of thinking about these incipient transformations: trying "to see climate change as just one more tendency of life towards change"; attempting to look forward to having more fjords to visit or new plants evolving; or latching onto theories about anthropogenic warming counteracting the earth's movement into a new ice age. Most of all, "They tried to balance out all their anxiety with loud attempts at celebrations of life" (92). The work's longest sentence lists some of those ineffectual attempts, all of which are efforts to convince themselves that their lives are good enough that the melting doesn't matter. In this final section, their—and the readers'—dissonant fix emerges starkly: it seems impossible to sustain such self-delusion and equally impossible to face reality in the full scale of its terrifying transformation—the rapidity of the changes taking place, their vastness in themselves, their cascading and inconceivably varied, frightening consequences, and "their" complicity in it all. After the fifteen-line sentence about the various ways in which they try loudly to savor the social and sensual pleasures in their lives, Spahr concludes the poem with the following scale-conscious passage:

> **Unnamed Dragonfly Species** They were anxious and they were paralyzed by the largeness and the connectedness of systems, a largeness of relation that they liked to think about and often celebrated but now seemed unbearably tragic. **Upland Sandpiper** The connected relationship between water and land seemed deeply damaged, perhaps beyond repair in numerous places. **Vesper Sparrow** The systems of relation between living things of all sorts seemed to have become in recent centuries so hierarchically human that things not human were dying at an unprecedented rate. **Wavy-rayed Lampmussel** And the systems of human governments and corporations felt so large and unchangeable and so distant from them yet the effects of their actions felt so connected and so immediate to what was happening. **Whip-poor-will** They knew this but didn't know what else to do. **Wood Turtle** And so they just went on living while talking loudly. **Worm Snake** Living and watching on a screen things far away from them melting. **Yellow-breasted Chat** (92–93)

The work ends there, with Spahr having exposed and re-created the dynamics of scalar dissonance but offering no program or inspiring model for "what else to do." On the contrary, she has presented the reader with a further challenge, explicitly identified only here at the end of the work with the line "things not human were dying at an unprecedented rate": the challenge not just of facing rising sea levels and global warming but also of thinking about mass extinction, a key aspect of the early Anthropocene (and of the beginning of any new geological epoch). The title phrase, "Unnamed Dragonfly Species," highlights the limits of scientific knowledge about anthropogenic change. The other species on the New York State government list have names, often carefully descriptive ones like "Brook Floater Buffalo Pebble Snail." However, this one species that is disappearing or has disappeared before it has even been named signals that we in the industrialized nations are losing life-forms in our immediate environments before we even recognize them or can add them to official taxonomies. Scientists have barely scratched the surface when it comes to identifying the beetles on this planet, for instance, let alone the microfauna and microflora so crucial to soil and plant life.[6] It is no wonder people find it difficult to know "what else to do"; as we are unintentionally destroying habitats and blindly eliminating species, it seems we do not even know in the most literal ways what we are already doing. We may imagine our collective knowledge to be large, but it proves small and extremely partial.

Spahr's work's primary aim seems to be to expose and explore the stymying dilemmas of Anthropocene scalar dissonance. Yet I detect a countercurrent, generated by the species list, that may point readers in a particular direction of political engagement as an alternative. The species whose names relentlessly interrupt the narrative are endangered (or extinct) in a specific place that is not distant and not in the cloud, the place where she and "they" live their embodied lives. The list brings to a local level a worldwide problem that is often connected to global warming and that is certainly part of the Anthropocene.[7] Spahr's not putting punctuation between each species name and the sentence that follows invites readers to think of the two strands of the work as part of one thing. If a reader in the United States can barely imagine what it means that "Kilimanjaro in East Africa has lost eighty-two percent of its area in eighty-eight years" (78) and has no idea what she might do about it, she may be able to imagine what her life would be without whip-poor-wills, and perhaps there is something she could do locally to help prevent that loss. It is true, of course, that many of the species listed would be unfamiliar to most American readers, but at least some, like the cougar or the nation's emblem, the bald eagle, are guaranteed to be recognizable. Moreover, the poem's unrelenting naming of animals that are immediately endangered casts a shadow of self-indulgence on the emotional struggles of "they." In the underlying dance of this poem, even as Spahr encourages readers to examine their own near-paralyzing dilemmas in the presence of dramatically discrepant scales, by interweaving the two threads of this work she directs her reader to the possibilities of local action as a response to "what else to do" when globally effective action seems beyond conception.

We have seen that Spahr in "Unnamed Dragonfly Species" approaches Anthropocene awareness as in large part an emotional challenge, one that produces what we might call affective confounding. The works I will consider by Forrest Gander and Ed Roberson, in contrast, treat the challenges as more perceptual than affective. Perhaps because their training in the natural sciences makes imagination at extreme scales come more easily, they find scalar dissonance less problematic and model possible strategies for apprehending processes and phenomena at suprahuman scales. Both suggest that poetry's ability to help us grasp the colliding scales of the Anthropocene is a crucial resource for humans now, although, even with that resource in place, hopes for meaningful change remain at best tentative.

Gander's poetic prose in the first part of "The Carboniferous and Ecopoetics" (from *Redstart: An Ecological Poetics* [2012])[8] deploys the observational skills and knowledge that he cultivated partly through undergraduate training in geology along with the expressive resources of a highly sensuous lyricism to draw his readers imaginatively into a non-anthropocentrically scaled understanding of planetary history. One notable achievement of this work is to make deep evolutionary time imaginable to the nonscientist without trivializing or in effect shrinking it, without making it fit accustomed scales. Inviting readers into the distant past in ways that draw upon familiar references and literary conventions without rendering the scene itself familiar, he translates scientific understandings so that his readers will grasp the brevity of human habitation as well as the limits of the planet's carbon resources.[9] Only after that is accomplished does he introduce more straightforward data to convey a collision of scales as human habitation, which occupies a minuscule part of geological time, suddenly overwhelms planetary space, consuming resources whose effectively imagined history makes their irreplaceableness evident.

The piece begins by echoing the inviting opening of countless origin stories—not "in the beginning," but "in one of the beginnings." The story Gander tells is in present tense, with each paragraph making a colossal leap forward in time, so that the reader is immersed in an always changing now that traverses hundreds of millions of years. The first two paragraphs are representative:

In one of the beginnings, below the fluff- and leaf-encrusted surface of a wide, shallow body of water, microscopic spores swirl with bat-winged algae. A cloudy soup of exertions and excretions, the sea drizzles its grit into rich mud.

Trilobites are dying off. (Miles Davis could have been quoting nature when he said, "I listen to what I can leave out.") Brachiopods, mollusks, and corals cluster in wide, shallow seas riven by sharks. Thick fish with lungs and lobes are giving way to a new species, the lung reconfigured as a swim bladder. Like surreal, underwater candelabra, crinoids effloresce; on long branching stems they stretch up toward the waves, each arm filtering small animals and plants through the calyx where a mouth is hidden. (*Redstart* 5)

The alien richness of this temporally distant world is conveyed as much by an aural density ("drizzles its grit into rich mud") and by a striking, sometimes scientific vocabulary ("riven," "effloresce," "calix") as by the visual phenomena depicted (surreally waving underwater candelabra). Yet at the same time that the geological past is made sensorily vivid, Gander's interjection of references to works of art or to modern artists, as with the quote from Miles Davis above, reminds the reader that one's understanding of nature, even one's best effort to imagine accurately, is inescapably mediated by and entwined with culture. Additionally, these parenthetic interjections, in linking the distant past to recent art, suggest art's transtemporal relevance, its adequacy to even prehuman worlds.

Vividly immersed in earth's evolutionary drama, readers witness the transformations of organic material during a radically distant era in which layers of plant life are laid down so thickly and rapidly that "they don't have time to decay" and instead are pressed into coal, the planet's legacy from the Carboniferous period. By the time Gander identifies coal as a form of sunlight, readers are prepared to accept that startling vision as nonmetaphoric: "When we pick up a piece of coal, it is the fossil residue of photosynthesis, a condensation of Paleozoic sunlight that we hold in our hands" (7).

With the arrival of the human, Gander's narrative accelerates and he begins to introduce statistics, but still as part of a story, which readers now understand to have been all along the story of coal: "and then, about three decades ago, mountaintop removal mining. In West Virginia alone, more than 350,000 acres of forested mountains are lopped off, and 1,200 miles of streams are buried. The overburden or leftover rock fills adjacent valleys" (8). The narrative of section I concludes as follows:

In China, where more than 6,000 men died in mines in 2004, where coal seams in the north hiss in unstoppable fires started by small-scale mining operators, and where the deserts are yawning wider at an alarming rate, coal is powering unprecedented industrialization. Some scientists estimate that coal will provide half the world's energy by the year 2100. And a hundred years after that, all the exploitable reserves of coal in the earth will be exhausted. (9)

What took nearly a hundred million years to form more than three hundred million years ago will have been consumed by a single species in less than three hundred years; "the relation between those two sets of numbers," Gander notes, "represents six orders of magnitude." A reader who has taken the journey of this story of coal from its enchanting beginnings to its sudden end can't avoid registering the significance of this shocking scalar disproportion. While no specific alternatives are proposed, the error of continued consumption of fossil fuels is driven home.

Yet the section is in fact not quite done. Or perhaps what follows after a dividing line at the end of section I should be thought of as the "and" linking "The Carboniferous" and "Ecopoetics." This passage reads: "A poem, even excavated from its context and the time of its writing, is a curiously renewable form of energy. It is hard to be sure whether it is from the future or the past that the poet Henry Vaughan writes, 'They are all gone into the world of light! / And I alone sit ling'ring here'" (10). At this point, as past and future blur, questions of scale fade to the background. Rather than dwelling further on the horror of coal's planet-poisoning consumption, or on the straits in which that leaves us, Gander shifts to considering the powers of art, inviting readers to light their lives with the energy to be discovered in poems. What I find startling here is the use made of metaphor. "The Carboniferous" contains a number of similes—for example, "Beneath hundreds of thousands of meters of overlying rot, the peat beds contract like a frog's iris into thin, horizontal lines"—and an occasional metaphor—for example, "At full throttle, technologies advance"—that help the reader envision the planetary changes depicted. Here, however, there's a striking disjunction between the very literal problems of the combustion of nonrenewable coal that Gander has just been emphasizing and the claim that poems are a form of "renewable energy"; for, however much poems may warm our hearts or illuminate our souls, poems cannot warm our homes or power our industries unless through the burning of the paper they are printed on; they cannot in any direct way solve our energy problems or slow climate change.

I suspect Gander intends this abrupt shift to highlight a widespread problem in ecopoetics: the disjunction between the perhaps quixotic hope many poets, including himself, place in poetry's explorations and the limited agency of any writing that relies on shifts in consciousness and awareness to generate social or political change. Part II, "Ecopoetics," wrestles with the claims made for ecopoetics and what should be expected from it, still mulling over whether, as Auden announced, "Poetry makes nothing happen" (14). Although much of this section takes the form of questions, cautions, and qualifications, Gander ultimately gives weight to several recent anthropological studies of indigenous languages and cultures markedly different from the West's as "register[ing] support for the argument that language, perception, and conception are irrevocably interconnected" (15), with changed conception opening the way to changed behavior. Yet Gander carefully qualifies his claims:

> If language does affect the way we think about being in the world, poetry *can* make something happen. I would suggest that it does. Certainly, I feel it has profoundly influenced the way I experience the world. But it probably doesn't affect perception nearly as directly as poets might wish. Getting rid of the capital I, eliminating pronouns altogether, deconstructing normative syntax, making the word "wordy"—these techniques, all more than a century old, impact the reader. But the effects are complex and subtle and may not correspond to a writer's intentions at all. (16–17)

Gander goes on to offer the possibility that "poems might be seen to take responsibility for certain ways of thinking and writing, as Charles Altieri notes, 'precisely by inviting audiences to see what powers they take on as they adapt themselves to how the texts ask to be read'" (17). Part I of "The Carboniferous and Ecopoetics" constitutes such an invitation. It employs several of the techniques he lists, such as eliminating the "I" and stressing the materiality of language—strategies that, he notes, "look a lot like innovative poetic strategies championed for the last hundred years" (11)—to provide the audience with powers of vision less focused on the human subject and human scale. By enabling readers to imagine unaccustomed realms and time scales in richly sensuous ways, "The Carboniferous" conveys a physically based understanding of anthropogenic environmental damage and of the planetary limits humans are up against. Yet in "Ecopoetics" the question of whether taking on those perceptual powers will translate into "ways of *being* in the world that might lead to less exploitative and destructive histories" (15) remains. In putting the two parts (with the unsettling "and") together into one work, Gander has demonstrated his own impassioned investment in and hopes for the powers of language, while also exposing his uncertainties around claims that have been made by multiple avant-gardes throughout the twentieth and into the twenty-first century—claims he himself wants to make—linking linguistic to social or political transformation.

If Gander in "The Carboniferous" works to cultivate in his readers a sensorily perceptive imagination that will enable them to grasp Anthropocene scales, Ed Roberson highlights people's already functioning perceptive and perspectival range and flexibility. His writing in *To See the Earth before the End of the World* (2010) conveys an awareness that humans have adapted before to changing perceptual scales—for instance, in the changes brought through aerial views made available by plane flight and more recently by photos of Earth from space—and even suggests that humans move through the world perceiving in a kind of constantly shifting scalar kaleidoscope. Roberson—who has studied both painting and limnology—implies that apprehending Anthropocene scales is only an extension of an adjustment that, however astonishing, has long been part of the human tool kit. Despite this hopeful vision of human perceptual power, his title poem, as I will demonstrate, seems to reject any hope that this ability, or a poet's calling attention to it, will prove helpful in averting environmental disaster. Yet he seems the least anxious of the three poets treated here, advocating an attention to one's immediate sensory world that refuses absorption in guilt, fear, or concerns about language's power.

Roberson ponders the adaptability of human scalar perception in "Topoi," whose speaker describes the geography observed from a plane descending into Newark and then wonders,

> . . . at
> what point did we become so familiar with
>
> such long perspective we could look down
> and recognize the pile of Denver by the drop off
> and crumble of the plate up   into the Rockies,
> or say   That's Detroit!   by the link of lakes by
>
> Lake St. Clair some thirty-thousand feet
> above Lake Erie . . . ? (11)

He goes on to note that earlier humans who survived by hunting had similar maps in their heads, though those were limited to terrain traversed on foot. He notes, too, that we have lost the hunter's vision and that we are now in a situation of extreme precarity, figured with a cartoon-like image of humankind as a dancing bear suddenly realizing it is hanging unsupported over the abyss: "Like trained bear / dancing on a circus ball, we look down, our feet in a step / from which there is no step off" (11). The scale of perception has shifted: the earth itself is tiny, and it is all we've got.

Repeatedly in the volume Roberson places human experience within a larger context of space and time that challenges anthropocentrism in its dwarfing of the human. "The oceans of the time men don't exist," he notes, "include only a drop that we do / and see / above them another ocean's spray of stars" (21). He frequently incorporates mention that the sun's light travels for ninety-three million miles to reach us or that the stars whose light we see may well have burned out eons ago. But rather than making such perception daunting, he suggests, often quite subtly, how many shifting scales we accommodate all the time. "Deep Time," for instance, puts the return of the cicadas after their song died seventeen years earlier into play with the generation of stars—what he calls "heard but unseen / insect star births / [that] have yet to reach us." The poem ends noting "that one / day our own / insect sun" will explode, hissing "in deep time into deepsong" (7). That vision of our puny sun disappearing into deep time is, however, no more of a scalar wonder than the depiction of trees and cicadas' whirring songs with which the poem opens:

> Where trees are a sky
> whose spider web
> radio antennas'
> search receives
> the rhythmic static
> of cicadas. (7)

There, the tree canopy assumes the scale of the entire sky, before an abrupt shift in which the trees' branches shrink to being delicate spiderwebs. Then those strands—through the rapid shifts of what he calls "polyphonic syntax" ("Interview" 412)—become figurative radio antennas receiving signals from the cicadas. Such language invites readers to embrace the challenge of planetary scalar transformation as an operation particularly familiar to poets and poetry readers via the action of metaphor. Readers of poetry are accustomed to phrases such as "insect sun"—and Roberson seems convinced that that kind of imaginative practice prepares people to see the human in its Anthropocene smallness.

His poems reveal continuities between past, present, and possible future adaptations in ways that make clear what is calamitously at stake now while also suggesting that the conceptual shifts we need to make are within our grasp because grounded in earlier human perceptual skills. He acknowledges losses, but also suggests the possibility of nondeclensionist narratives rooted in a turning toward what our senses have taught and can teach us. While calling attention to humankind's ultimate insignificance, shrinking us in our own eyes, Roberson asks his readers also to see through enlarging lenses—to "widen . . . the tube of that measure // of sight we are given" (127)—so as "to see ourselves / in the brief moment / that we are / of the earth" (22).

Thus, his title poem, which concerns global warming, challenges us to be fully present to our current crisis, not in an anxious way, but in an attentive one, and to live in that present space. The opening of "To See the Earth before the End of the World" emphasizes the scalar discrepancies of the Anthropocene: the world is dying piece by piece, and each of those pieces is "longer than we"—not just longer than a human lifetime but longer than the existence of humankind.

> People are grabbing at the chance to see
> the earth before the end of the world,
> the world's death piece by piece each longer than we.
>
> Some endings of the world overlap our lived
> time, skidding for generations
> to the crash scene of species extinction
> the five minutes it takes for the plane to fall,
> the mile ago it takes to stop the train,
> the small bay   to coast the liner into the ground,
>
> the line of title to a nation   until the land dies,
> the continent uninhabitable. (3)

Because some of those endings of monumental phenomena overlap with our little lifetimes, we are able to witness the final moments of some of these pieces—comparable, on another scale, to someone's witnessing the last five minutes in the flight of a crashing plane or to being present at the small bay where a sinking ocean liner comes to rest. Human constructs like nations (often invoked in ocean liners' names) last only as long as the land is habitable, as today's climate refugees from small island nations are discovering. In the first half of the poem, Roberson works to give his readers a feeling for that almost unimaginable coming together of the discrepant large and small scales, what he calls here "[t]hat very subtlety of time between // large and small" which finds us witnessing, in a revision of that formulation, "a subtle collapse of time between large // and our small human extinction."

After that important line, the poet meditates first on his individual situation and then on how humankind got to this point. "If I have a table / at this event, mine bears an ice sculpture." So, while others may be "grabbing" at last chances and "chasing" after glaciers, he imagines himself sitting still before a segment of one of the pieces "longer than we" that is small enough for him to contemplate. It is, additionally, a sculpture, a work of art (bringing to mind Gander's turning to poetry at the close of "The Carboniferous"). "Of whatever loss it is," Roberson observes, "it lasts as long as ice / does until it disappears." There is no obvious anxiety here; rather than focusing on mourning loss, he focuses on present duration. There is an attitude of acceptance; the time he has is the time he has, what he has to observe is what he has to observe, and, seen as ice sculpture, his bit of the earth is not only fascinating in its constant change but also implicitly beautiful.

In saying the artwork made of ice that adorns the speaker's table will melt into air, Roberson alludes to Marx's critique of capitalism,[10] perhaps thereby pointing to capitalism's responsibility for the climate change described in the poem. The close of the poem, however, indicates that Roberson sees the disappearance and loss we are witnessing as consequences of irreversible choices made much earlier:

> . . . All that once chased us and we
> chased to a balance chasing back, tooth for spear,
> knife for claw,
>> locks us in this grip
> we just now see
>>> our own lives taken by
> taking them out.   Hunting the bear,
> we hunt the glacier with the changes come
>> of that choice. (3)

Again thinking in terms of human continuities across eras, Roberson locates the origins of our climate crisis with the earliest human hunters, who devised spears and knives to gain advantage over other species. By assuming such dominion over nature we humans initiated the process of killing the glaciers as well; our lives are being taken by our "taking out" the lives of other species. This is something "we just now see"—that is, we only now see clearly what we have done, and we see it for only a moment before we too, mortal beings on a rapidly warming planet, melt into vapor and air. Demonstrating the unfixed assessment of the power of poetic perception and language already observed in Spahr and Gander, Roberson in the deterministic vision that closes this poem denies the usefulness, in averting or delaying ecocatastrophe, of the human ability to flexibly perceive in shifting scales that other poems in the volume more hopefully highlight.

I began this essay by noting that poets like these three are engaging in crucial conversations of great political urgency. Yet even as Spahr, Gander, and Roberson resourcefully deploy a variety of formal and linguistic strategies in this effort, the implicit and explicit claims they make for poetry's public interventions remain qualified and modest. Let us put it this way: none seems willing to relinquish all hope that poetry has a contribution to make to positive ecopolitical change—whether by highlighting for its readers particular perceptual abilities with ecoethical implications, cultivating particular ways of conceptualizing the relations of nature and culture or human interrelations with natural processes, or suggesting avenues for activism.

Notes

1. There is not yet consensus about the meaning of "ecopoetry." Some use it to identify all environmentally engaged poetry of any period, including nature poetry. In a chronologically restricted version of that position, Ann Fisher-Wirth and Laura-Gray Street use "ecopoetry" as an umbrella term for poetry since 1960 that responds to environmental crisis; within that they locate the subcategories of nature poetry, environmental poetry, and ecological poetry (xxviii–xxix). Some reserve "ecopoetry" for recent work that diverges from traditional nature poetry in being formally and linguistically experimental (what Fisher-Wirth and Street call "ecological poetry"). Using the term in distinction from traditional nature poetry, I join those who apply it to poetry that approaches environmental writing with an interest in the intertwining of nature and culture.

2. This claim is made in Zalasiewicz et al. 2230–31.

3. Here Purdy seems to echo Bill McKibben's *The End of Nature*, which can be seen as reflecting an Anthropocene awareness *avant la lettre*. As Zalasiewicz, Crutzen, and their coauthors acknowledge, people considerably earlier had proposed terms "to denote the idea of humans as a new global forcing agent" (Zalasiewicz et al. 2228).

4. This was Crutzen's hope in introducing the term: "Rather than representing yet another sign of human hubris, this name change would stress the enormity of humanity's responsibility as stewards of the Earth" (Crutzen and Schwägerl).

5. Spahr refers to this work as a poem; both she and Gander often move between lineated and nonlineated writing and, like many contemporary poets, often refer to their creative work that doesn't easily fit into established categories of prose as poetry.

6. According to the Wikipedia entry "Microfauna," "Out of the estimated 10–20 million animal species in the world, only 1.8 million have been given scientific names, and many of the remaining millions are likely microfauna, much of it from the tropics."

7. Extinction rates are so high now that biologists say we have entered the planet's Sixth Great Extinction event. The dinosaurs were killed off in the preceding mass extinction, the Cretaceous-Paleogene extinction event, 66 million years ago.

8. The book is coauthored with John Kinsella, but this piece is identified as Gander's.

9. Gander is a very active translator from several foreign languages; I use the term to extend critical understanding of his role as translator.

10. In the *Manifesto of the Communist Party*, Marx and Engels say that capitalism, with its "constant revolutionizing of production" and "uninterrupted disturbance of all social conditions," results in everything solid melting into air, leaving man to "face with sober sense his real conditions of life, and his relations with his kind." For discussion of capitalism's relation to climate change, see Naomi Klein.

Works Cited

Chakrabarty, Dipesh. "The Climate of History: Four Theses." *Critical Inquiry* 35 (Winter 2009): 197–222. Print.

Clark, Nigel. *Inhuman Nature: Sociable Life on a Dynamic Planet*. London: Sage, 2011. Print.

Crutzen, Paul J., and Christian Schwägerl. "Living in the Anthropocene: Toward a New Global Ethos." *Yale Environment 360*. 24 January 2011. Web. 9 September 2013.

Fisher-Wirth, Ann, and Laura-Gray Street. *The Ecopoetry Anthology*. San Antonio: Trinity UP, 2013. Print.

Gander, Forrest, and John Kinsella, *Redstart: An Ecological Poetics*. Iowa City: U of Iowa P, 2012. Print.

Klein, Naomi. *This Changes Everything: Capitalism vs. the Climate*. New York: Simon & Schuster, 2014. Print.

Marx, Karl. *Yale Law School: The Avalon Project. Manifesto of the Communist Party*, "I. Bourgeois and Proletarians," 2008. Web. 1 August 2014.

McKibben, Bill. *The End of Nature*. New York: Anchor, 1989. Print.

"Microfauna." *Wikipedia*. Web. 14 February 2014.

Nixon, Rob. *Slow Violence and the Environmentalism of the Poor*. Cambridge, MA: Harvard UP, 2011. Print.

Purdy, Jed. "Losing Nature: Living in the Anthropocene." *Fieldwork*, April 8, 2013. Web. August 1, 2014.

Roberson, Ed. "An Interview with Ed Roberson." Conducted by Lynn Keller and Steel Wagstaff. *Contemporary Literature* 52 (2011): 397–429. Print.

Roberson, Ed. *To See the Earth before the End of the World*. Middletown, CT: Wesleyan UP, 2010. Print.

Spahr, Juliana. *Well Then There Now*. Boston: David R. Godine, 2011. Print.

Zalasiewicz, Ian, Mark Williams, Will Steffe, and Paul Crutzen. "The New World of the Anthropocene." *Environmental Science and Technology* 44 (2010): 2228–31. Print.

PART TWO

REDEFINING AUTHORSHIP

FOUR

The Politics of Docupoetry

Joseph Harrington

Twenty-first-century documentary poetry (or "docupoetry") implicitly questions the status of both poetry and documents. North American poets who incorporate historical narratives derived from research do so by combining forms, genres, and media in a manner that calls attention to the materiality and mediation of the text. However, documentary depends upon mimesis: to document is to refer to a reality beyond the document. I see this creative friction within current docupoetry as being directly related to its creators' circumscribed political goals: whatever political efficacy they lay claim to is limited and resides within the individual writer and reader or within the communities of which those writers and readers are part. The modesty of the poets' political aspirations for their work stems from their simultaneous belief in and mistrust of referentiality—a conflict that makes for a poetics at odds with itself. Epistemological doubt collides with ethical imperatives. Documentary as fact is appealing—we hunger for it. But documentary is always a form of mediation and so always problematized by language. The new docupoetry embodies this contradiction: it narrates history at the same time that the form of the narrative makes us aware of how we construct, perceive, and interpret history.[1]

The term "documentary" was coined to describe a type of film rather than a type of poem.[2] Documentary films from the 1930s in the mold of Pare Lorentz's *The Plow That Broke the Plains* (1936) and *The River* (1938) represent what critic Bill Nichols, in his landmark work *Representing Reality* (1991), terms the "expository" mode, mounting arguments and evidence for a partisan position. U.S. documentary literature followed suit, combining writing and photography in works such as Erskine Caldwell and Margaret Bourke-White's *You Have Seen Their Faces* (1937) or Archibald MacLeish's *Land of the Free* (1938). These works, in Susan Briante's words, exemplify "the documentary book genre common in the 1930s which used text and image to describe a social condition to invoke sympathy if not political action in middle-class readers."

In short, they used realism to produce a political effect. Likewise, much of the poetry in the *Daily Worker* and other left publications depicted workers' victimization or resistance.

The first poem in English to call itself "documentary" is probably Canadian Dorothy Livesay's "Call My People Home," originally subtitled "A Documentary Poem for Radio" (1949; the poem was performed on CBC radio that same year).[3] The poem, based on transcripts of interviews with Japanese Canadians who were interned and dispossessed during World War II, uses the realism of voice to articulate a scathing indictment of the government's treatment of its citizens. Documentary poetry, Livesay would write in 1969, entails "employment of the actual data itself"—the *ding an sich* of empirical reality ("Documentary Poem" 267). Seven years later, Ed Sanders, in his influential work *Investigative Poetry*, echoes Livesay's language ("Lines of lyric beauty descend from the data clusters" [9]) and declares that "poetry should again assume responsibility for the description of history" (3).

For all of these twentieth-century poets, documentary poetry contains fact, those facts are hard, and poets should use them to fight oppression and neglect. By the twenty-first century, however, both documentary film and poetry had changed substantially. Cinema verité and oral histories, examples of what Nichols terms "observational" and "interactive" modes, respectively, became more common from the 1960s onward. Moreover, the late twentieth century saw the growth of the "reflexive" documentary, in which "the focus of the text slides from the realm of historical reference to the properties of the text itself" (57).[4] That is, the film defamiliarizes the process of representation even as it represents history.

This reflexive tendency in documentary film in the late twentieth century can be seen in documentary poetry in the twenty-first. It is not surprising that the 1930s documentary poem that has received the lion's share of critical attention in the last fifteen years, Muriel Rukeyser's "Book of the Dead," is also one of the most reflexive.[5] Rukeyser's refusal to set forth a linear, unambiguous argument, and her critique of the documentary gaze have become hallmarks of twenty-first-century North American documentary poetics. At the same time, however, the principal function of documentary has not disappeared—that is, to document, to "bear an indexical relation to the historical world" (Nichols 27). Although many of these poets have political and ethical commitments, they also live in an era of intensive manipulation of images and information by the politically and economically powerful. Documentary poets' ability to reconcile—or at least to acknowledge—these competing forces makes for some of the most interesting work in recent years. Although, given the current boom in documentary poetry, there are many examples one could cite, Craig Santos Perez, Kaia Sand, and Kristin Prevallet present especially clear instances of politically committed poets who, in their different ways, draw upon research sources even as they interrogate the status of the results.

Chamorro poet Craig Santos Perez tells several different stories at once in his series of book-length docupoems about the history of his native island. The first, *From Unincorporated Territory [hacha]* (2008), relates the colonization of Guåhån (or Guam) by the Spanish to his grandparents' account of the Japanese occupation of the Pacific island, as well as to his memories of collecting achiote pods as a child, and to U.S. militarization of the island. He makes these connections using long-lined, loose-limbed passages that interweave the various narratives using both documentary sources and his own words. Critic Paul Lai writes of Perez's work that it "challenges a linear unfolding of these interwoven excerpts, emphasizing a recursive and multi-layered knowledge that refuses a straightforward argument. . . . [T]he poet disperses them in a way that creates new meanings in the juxtaposition of different sections or the interruption of an excerpt by another poem" (7). In *"from* Flowering Plumeria," for example, the parallel narratives of Perez's emigrant cousin's traffic death in the mainland United States and the arrival of the exotic invasive brown tree snake in Guam juxtapose the personal ache of economic exile and loss in the present day with the ongoing ecological tragedy wrought by parasites and stowaways of various empires that have marked the land. The correlation between these two bodies of knowledge is not spelled out; it exists at least in part on a nonnarrative, perhaps nonverbal, level, signified by white space between the two texts at the bottom and top of the page.

Likewise, within the section titled "Achiote," the book relates the slaying of the Jesuit priest Diego Luis de San Vitores in 1672 at the hands of Chief Mata'pang (for baptizing the Chief's newborn daughter without his consent) and the subsequent twenty-five years of Spanish-Chamorro wars:

> —the frail blind body of father sanvitores [1672]
> is led around by a rope tied to his waist he refused glasses because "if
>   the poor were too poor for glasses"
> etc *evangelizare pauperibus misi te*
> a small satchel: a breviary, a new testament, lumps of sugar for
>   children who could recite their prayers and catechism lessons. (19)

But the poet's knowledge of San Vitores's legacy is not derived from research sources alone. Farther down the page we find a refrain from childhood: "he's always i fi'on-mu [near you]: a sunday school warning: if you don't say your prayers you wake / with bruises" (19). Finally, at the very bottom of the page, we learn that "[*achiote can be used to treat skin problems, burns, venereal disease, and hypertension*]." The plant, with its blood-red pods, was brought to Guam from the Spanish Caribbean—and, coincidentally, is a "home remedy" for many of the ills that were also introduced by the Spanish.

Indeed, Perez relates, "[*after the death of sanvitores, the native population dropped from 200,000 to 5,000 in two generations as a result of spanish military conquest*]" (21). We also learn that the "red tide" algae blooms offshore are said to be the blood of the martyr; that "the shrine of father sanvitores [is located] between *Guam Reef Hotel* and *Sails Restaurant*" (22); and that the eponym "mata'pang" "used to mean 'alert eyes'" but "now it means 'silly' or 'rude' or 'misbehaved' or 'uncivil'" (23). The relationship between these various facts and etymologies is not spelled out, nor are we told what to make of them. The interplay of (auto)biography and history, Chamorro and English, drives the poem, which, taken as a whole, attempts to make a case for Guamanian sovereignty. Yet it does so by both utilizing and problematizing "the status, conventions, effects, and values" historically associated with documentary (Nichols 63). Perez is acutely aware of the thinness of the line between documentary and propaganda, given that the latter has been used very effectively by each of the several colonizers of his native land.

One cause of the formal and epistemological tension in the book is that narrative passages are interspersed with lyric poems, some of which reduce the documentary sources to one- or two-word phonemes or microquotations recontextualized in a largely associative manner. In other words, the lyrics self-consciously draw on the very tradition of poetry that is often conceived of as the "other" of narrative (and of documentation). The lyric poems, however, suggest a politics by virtue of their form. In the "Tidelands" series, Perez repurposes the preeminently Japanese form of syllabic verse: the number of syllables in each line (1-8-9-8) in the first stanza reveals the date of Guam's official colonization by the United States; in the second (2-0-0-6—the middle two lines of the first stanza are missing in the second), the date the poems were composed:

> taut
> "shadows almost" visible be–
>   low the dispersal of "forms—swathe" this
> small touch "no maps sown" to hallow
>
> [tano]
>
> hold "alms that shell" this pulse (25)

"Tano" is glossed as "land, soil, earth, ground." But this definition does not give the reader much of a toehold—the poem works via elliptical, laconic utterances. At the outset, Perez introduces the word *reducción*, which "the Spanish used to name their efforts of subduing, converting, and gathering natives" (11). Later in the book, a "reduced" form of the above poem appears:

taut
"shadows" visible
  the dispersal of "forms" this
"no maps sown" to hollow

[ ]

hold "alms that shell" (88; brackets in original)

The shadows become fully visible; "form(s)" becomes an operative word; "hallow" becomes "hollow"; the Chamorros' "tano" disappears; and "shell" takes on a double meaning. Each of these features resonates with the narrative sections but adds neither information nor any unambiguous interpretations.

Beyond mixing several strains of lyric and narrative, Perez embeds graphics, as do many other docupoets today. Thus the book includes a map showing the massive presence of the U.S. military on the island (85). The inclusion of website addresses, under the heading "8,000?" (the number of troops the U.S. military was proposing to redeploy from Okinawa to Guam at the time of publication), opens up this archive to others with different, though overlapping, boundaries (83).[6] In one series, for instance, a schematic diagram of the routes of Spanish galleons in the seventeenth century faces a diagram of the movements of navies in the Pacific in World War II. The next page reveals another, not dissimilar, graphic rendering of the same territory, this time in terms of present-day transpacific airports and flight routes (28–30). All of these graphics serve as off-rhymes with the textual accounts of the United States' use of Guam as a glorified aircraft carrier; causal connections may be inferred, but they are not spelled out.

This multimedia, multinarrative invocation of / resistance to the fiction of documentary transparency is evident in many other contemporary documentary poets as well. Kaia Sand renders the verse and prose of her book *Remember to Wave* (2010) on a typewriter, and she also includes photographs, primary documents, and hand-stitching. The book, like Livesay's, recounts the internment of Japanese citizens, but in a different context, namely, that of the history of the Vanport section of Portland, Oregon. Sand charts the various other phases of the local history as well—from the building of housing for workers

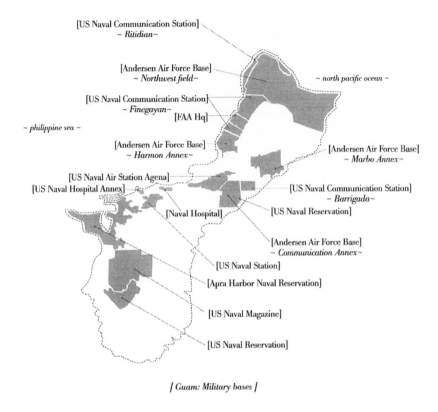

[US Naval Communication Station]
~ Ritidian~

[Andersen Air Force Base]
~ Northwest field~

~ north pacific ocean ~

[US Naval Communication Station]
~ Finegayan~
[FAA Hq]

~ philippine sea ~

[Andersen Air Force Base]
~ Harmon Annex~

[Andersen Air Force Base]
~ Marbo Annex~

[US Naval Air Station Agena]
[US Naval Hospital Annex]

[US Naval Communication Station]
~ Barrigada~

[Naval Hospital]

[US Naval Reservation]

[Andersen Air Force Base]
~ Communication Annex~

[US Naval Station]

[Apra Harbor Naval Reservation]

[US Naval Magazine]

[US Naval Reservation]

[Guam: Military bases]

Fig. 1. Graphic in *from unincorporated territory [hacha]*, by Craig Santos Perez, showing geographical extent of the U.S. military's control over Guåhån (Guam)

in the defense industry in the 1930s, to the internment center in the war, to the flood that washed the whole place away in 1948, to the area's present-day condition as industrial wasteland cum nature preserve. The book's combination of layered images and writing conveys the difficulty of imagining and representing Vanport in all its various historical incarnations. As Briante writes, "These collages, faithfully reprinted, give the book the feel of a scrapbook, a work of individual labor, in opposition to the regular typography and design of traditional history books, suggesting another way to challenge the manner in which conventional histories have been written"—and, one might add, to compile histories where none exist. But one is always aware of the mediating physical presence of this history-poetry book and of the complexity of interpreting material historical traces.

This complexity and difficulty weigh heavily upon the author. At the center of the map-collage that is the frontispiece of the book, amid all the typing and clipped photos, one reads: "I feel like a spectator / of the present. History, help" (n.p.).[7] Sand's layout does not "lay out" an argument, but questions both the form and motivation of documentary argument itself. Does looking at the past make one *not* feel like a spectator of the present? How can one represent that past without doing further violence to it? Sand continues this direct address on subsequent pages, but to humans: "To those who were held prisoner in the Portland Assembly Center, and to those whose lives were ended or rent by the Vanport flood—to you I acknowledge a responsibility," she writes. "Here is one small attempt at addressing that responsibility through committed inquiry, through pedestrian investigation." It is significant that Sand chooses the word "addressing," not "redressing." This is an inquiry—even an indictment, perhaps—but not an incitement. She doesn't propose that her work will change anything in the world she investigates. Nonetheless, hers is an ethically *committed* inquiry.

So, while *Remember to Wave* is undeniably imaginative and reflexive, it is at the same time decidedly documentary, that is, representational. Sand implicitly compares the temporary housing for wartime shipbuilders with the "Assembly Center" for Japanese Americans and with the PODS company's marketing of eight-foot by eight-foot by sixteen-foot "hurricane housing" units for climate refugees. This oblique reminder of Katrina also echoes the 1948 Vanport flood, which literally washed the houses and people away. The Dalles Dam, built in response to that flood, has, unlike the levees in New Orleans, held very well—but at the cost of wiping out centuries-old indigenous lifeways. Sand declares herself "inexpert" at the outset, yet, as she remarks, a poet has something to bring to the cityscape: "A poetic imagination can be an insistent one, comfortable enough in uncertainties to demand meaning," to find parallels, without imposing a map that subsumes the territory.

Sand uses this negative capability in her extensive research, inexpert or otherwise. For materials, she delved into issues of the *Evacuazette*, the newspaper of the internment center at Vanport. She treats the topic of the relocation of people of Japanese descent differently than does Livesay, resisting the temptation to speak for or through the "evacuees" or to dilate upon their suffering in a realist or expository mode. Instead, she addresses them, in a Whitmanesque/Ginsbergesque catalog, using material gleaned from the paper and interviews:

hello, Midora Baker, separated from your parents, carceral childhood, sixty years later and I worry about you.

hello, Akira Shimura 6 years old & dead on July 10, 1942

hello Midora Baker, separated from your parents, carceral childhood,
sixty years later and I worry about you

hello Akira Shimura 6 years old & dead on July 10, 1942

hello to the cook on break in the sun 'too near' the fence, suddenly shot
by guards, the blood on your white coat another man remembers, wondering
what happened, so do I

hello to the journalist watching the Jantzen Beach ferris wheel lights
from the Evacuazette balcony, 'knowing that is outside,' hello Sunday
visitors speaking at the barbed fence

hello Michi Yasunaga & James Wakagawa betrothed June 29, 1942

hello Madame Fifi Suzette, talent show impresario, hello Chiseo Shoji,
cartooning the flyswatters, the toe-stompers, the clog-clompers

bound for Minidoka, Heart Mountain

hello Rose Katagiri, Evacuazette typist bound for Tule Lake June 10 1942,
the Katagiri family & Akagis & Moriokas & Yamaguchis & Watanabes bound
for Tule Lake, bound, carceral

there are so many of us on this planet

Fig. 2. From *Remember to Wave*, by Kaia Sand. The drawing is from the *Evacuzette*, the
internees' newspaper; Sand renders her poem below with manual typewriter.

hello to the cook on break in the sun "too near" the fence, suddenly shot by guards, the blood on your white coat another man remembers, wondering what happened, so do I

The reader is here reading over the poet's shoulder. At times the poet seems stunned into speechlessness, as when she simply retypes words of the "Instructions to All Persons of Japanese Ancestry" poster issued by the Wartime Civil Control Administration. "Civil control" is retyped several times on the poster itself, as if in disbelief (or recognition). But like Perez's "Tidelands" series, the second part of *Remember to Wave*, "Uptick," is an elliptical meditation upon the partial narratives that have preceded it:

> in the use of the, in the many of the, in the use of the
> in the many of the
>
> that circle is showing the behavior of a sun
>
> sun inked out
> is night

"Uptick" also extrapolates into the present, often in a rather pointed manner: "a centigrade uptick— / crops, deserted in desert dust / mountains melting, run-off rising." This series serves both as meditation and coda, a chance for the reader to absorb the implications of what she or he has read by seeing it through a very different form.

Some docupoets' work is even more reflexive, self-conscious, and less directly referential than the work of Perez and Sand. Kristen Prevallet's work, for example, is just as likely to travesty or *détourner* the documentary form as to utilize it. In her 2002 book *Scratch Sides: Poetry, Documentation, and Image-Text Projects*, the sequence called "The Catalogue of Lost Glimpses" consists of random video stills, taken by a camera slung over her shoulder, accompanied by "faux-ethnographic text" (72). "False but Elegant Supreme" is a "lyric infiltration" of a news story about the recount of Florida votes in the 2000 U.S. presidential election. Through a complex procedural mash-up, Prevallet's version reads in part:

> The Supreme Court said that unless the Florida courts put in place even more protective measures to re-imagine the graphic image of abstract numbers, a position that is constitutionally impossible as the judges knew—they would have to account for the mangled wreckage of tiny grains of sand. . . . A place where nationally he had won to ensure their

breath, the Court said that hand recounts would "cast a cloud." From here came the weather over Bush's "legitimacy" that would harm the formation of planets. (24)

The poem splices the mundane and the lyrical, the sublime and the absurd to highlight the routinized syntax of "official" news, the doublespeak of politicians, as well as the absurdity of the whole situation (remember "hanging chads"?). This lyric infiltration of news stories lends an air of whimsy to the detached, detailed, and deadly serious record; by the same token, its parodic aspect makes one question the evidentiary value of that record and the institutions it legitimizes.

Prevallet does something similar in "Shadow Evidence Intelligence," from the 2006 book of the same title, by "mislabeling" aerial surveillance photographs of Iraq from 2003. "There are many ways to define proof," one photo is captioned. The original text in callout boxes is obscured and replaced with "A square iron box in the middle of a cornfield" and "Off-center, it defines the parameters of the cornfield" (23), as though Colin Powell were channeling the ghost of Wallace Stevens. Other callouts read, "Some people see bombs hidden here" and "(an arctic glacier)" (23); or again, "There are crows the size of crows" (24). Sometimes a cigar is just not a missile.

The work of Prevallet, Perez, Sand, and others from the 2000s is not "documentary" in the sense of offering a representational narrative as empirical evidence in support of an "expository" argument. In fact, a more accurate term than "documentary" might be Cole Swensen's term "research-based poetry." Swensen writes:

Language in such cases is more at the service of art, and its writers have devised ways of making the language of art even more aesthetically complex by augmenting it with the language of information. This shift is based on a shift in urgency. Such texts are not calls to action, but calls to reflection. Rather than wanting to get us out into the world doing things, they want us to reconsider, to think more deeply and they use poeticity to slow down our assimilation of language, to encourage us to take detours, to ponder alternatives. Such texts are often no less socially oriented, but they operate in a different time frame. (64)

Thus, as Prevallet puts it, "Language used to witness is simultaneously a witness of language" ("Investigating" 121). And these self-aware, socially conscious word-works may indeed "operate in a different time frame" than those with an unequivocal, univocal political message. Accordingly, any effects

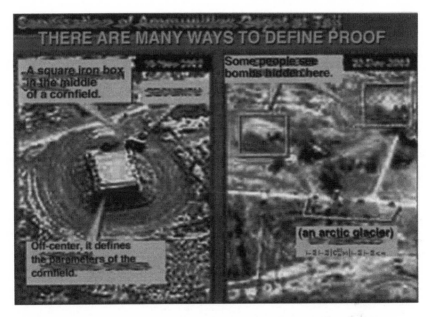

Fig. 3. Graphic from "Shadow Evidence Intelligence," by Kristin Prevallet. The Pentagon graphic of supposed missile sites has been "re-purposed."

to which poetry might contribute would be part of a very long-term cultural shift, rather than a short-term policy victory.

All of these books utilize quotations and research to represent some aspect of an historical topic. All of them employ mimetic language, evincing a *desire* for the truth of the past. But they also betray a *wariness* regarding that desire—or at least skepticism that it can ever be satisfied. Documentary poetry of the twenty-first century is thus more about inquiry, investigation, and interpretation than persuasive rhetoric. Jules Boykoff describes Sand's work as "eschewing the idea of poet as expert" in favor of the "poet as rigorous investigator" (223). The goal is not so much the presentation of data as a search for traces; it is not about presenting documentation so much as it is about the process of documenting and the documenting of process.

Accordingly, the political and social goals of documentary poets tend to be rather circumscribed. When I queried a number of well-known documentary poets about their motivations for producing the work they do, they cited personal and individual reasons—as ways to think, explore, or satisfy curiosity—rather than as ways to convince a phantom public of a coherent political position or philosophy. For Allison Cobb, documentary is a way to arrive at "an intuitive, felt understanding of our situation."[8] Narrating and reflecting on contemporary events, in particular, is for Cobb "a way of process-ing/countering/addressing all of the 'information' bombarding us all." Carol Mirakove says that poetry is "how I make sense of extreme things." Kathleen Ossip researches and writes documentary poetry "to see how the texts of the past could help me understand my emotional life"; she adds, "I think it would be too lofty to hope to contribute to a more public conversation." On a smaller, more immediate scale, the personal aspect of poetry can become interpersonal: Susan M. Schultz sees it as "a link between my experiences and those of others"; this impulse marks the beginnings of any popular politi-cal discourse, but only the beginnings. Poet-activist Stephen Collis wants to bring poetry "closer and closer into conversation with 'activism' . . . without having one obliterate the other (which they often do)"—and also, one might add, without conflating the two. Sand writes that "a poem's populace need not be mass, but unconventional contexts can afford new points of entrance" ("Affording" 320). In all of these responses, twenty-first-century practitioners distance themselves from the positivist, didactic, or instrumentalist strains in documentary art. They eschew not only linear narrative and definitive state-ment, but also the desire for a large audience.

Instead, as the quotations above indicate, the goal of the inquiry or in-vestigation is often to find an alternative method to construct a historical ac-count that differs radically in form and content from the dominant one. Pre-vallet writes that poetry "will not raise mass consciousness, although it will articulate new systems in which sources, language, lyric, document collage, and process come together as presentation of an alternative logic" ("Investi-gating" 128). This articulation may involve the reflexive move of questioning the status of history per se. Tony Trigilio is interested in "documenting the event while also questioning how we determine the truth of what we call 'his-tory,' . . . exposing the gap between our 'official' and 'unofficial' histories of an event"; he uses evidentiary sources while also questioning the status of evi-dence itself. Mirakove, writing her book *Occupied* in the wake of the U.S. occu-pation of Afghanistan, found that "publishing poetry with contradicting facts [to the "official version"] felt useful." But beyond the personal feeling, "The more instances of a statement or fact the more it sticks and documentary po-etry is empowering because it provides an opportunity to create one of those instances." Mirakove conceives of "poetry as media" and "art as dynamic documentation" in its own right. "If the journalists won't cover it, poets can" (Mirakove, message to author). While poets have a smaller circulation, they might produce work "that is more germane to activism," that can "engage our physical and virtual communities as sites of social change" (Mirakove, "Anxi-eties" 99, 112).

While this relation to activism is conditional and broad, it exists, for the poet, because of the counterdiscourse she produces. Or the aim may be "to get at the moment as it occurred," as Schultz says—simply to record an event that otherwise might be lost. Like many contemporary lyric poets, documentary poets talk about poetry as an "active thinking through . . . not arriving at an end-point," in Schultz' words; or, as Perez puts it, "a way to think about learning, remembering, memorializing, preserving, revitalizing, and recirculating native history, culture, politics, language, customs, and stories." A way to think about something is not the same thing as promoting or defeating it. For poets of the post-Reagan neoliberal era, it would seem, that would be asking too much of poetry; it is hard enough to tell untold stories or produce critical revisions of history. But doing so in a poem is a way of not only "getting the story" but also "getting at" its phenomenological feel and implications.

Given the goals and perspectives of today's "research-based" poetry, it makes sense that much of it is composed in mixed genres and media.[9] I would suggest that documentary writers create these texts in heterogeneous and sutured forms because of the conflict between a desire for investigative inquiry, on the one hand, and a mistrust of authoritative truth claims, on the other. In other words, this generic ambiguity or refusal of category may be part and parcel of twenty-first-century North American writers' and intellectuals' wariness of documents, documentation, and documentary generally. These have been used in service of repressive institutions, as the books described above make clear; they have been part of what poet Andrew Durbin calls "documentary surveillance culture." At the same time, such documents are the only way we know about that culture (ask Edward Snowden). As a way to negotiate this impasse, these books create multivocal counternarratives that make use of more than one generic epistemology.

This "undocumentary" impulse, expressed via heterogeneous forms, is a challenge to what German documentarian and theorist Hito Steyerl terms "documentality," that is, the process through which "forms of documentary truth production turn into government—or vice versa." As an example, she points to the very photographs Prevallet defaces:

The main statement was made by inserting interpretive written elements. Every indexical sign reference, which is traditionally regarded as a characteristic of documentary authenticity, was quite paltry in the pictures and charts and was mainly supported by "secret" sources. Nevertheless, this politics of truth prevailed over that of the weapons inspectors.

Steyerl asserts that documentary forms do not so much depict reality as produce it: "Documents . . . are supposed to first create the reality that is documented in them." But this critique of official documents raises a problem: on what epistemological foundation is your counterhistory based? This is the hermeneutic circle in which the postmodern "counterhegemonic" documentary poet finds herself, one in which ethics and epistemology seem at loggerheads. Steyerl, whose nation's historical actions have brought these questions into sharp focus, states the problem:

> On the one side [there is] the ethically absolutely necessary insisting on/ of a historical truth, which would still remain true, even if every evidence of it were obliterated; on the other side the insight that the perception of it can only happen within a construction conveyed through media (society, politics), which is therefore manipulable and opaque.

One must speak out; one cannot speak. Steyerl does not try to choose one way or the other or try to reconcile the two. As a test case, she uses the four surviving photographs taken by inmates of Auschwitz. As evidence, they are woefully imperfect. But they constitute documentation "in spite of"—they provide traces pointing to an inconceivable act—and also to the photographers' and accomplices' risking their lives to get the photos and then get the photos out. Rather than a pragmatist acceptance of the already-established rules of the epistemological game or a Foucauldian reduction of competing political positions to incommensurate desires, Steyerl's position is more a Kierkegaardian leap of faith, an imperative to document and a simultaneous mis/trust of the value of the document.

Today's docupoets appear to be acutely aware of this bind, which is why they are receptive to unconventional formal strategies. As Sand writes, "In terms of mixed genre, it seems like the openness of inexpert inquiry allows me to find my materials and form": the inductive, contingent, antiauthoritarian orientation of the poet ("the openness of inexpert inquiry") is precisely what leads her to a mixed-genre composition ("to find my materials and form") (message to author). Moreover, it is precisely that inexpert stance that "necessitates leaving the threads bare, the garment unhemmed," rather than tailoring it to a particular generic pattern (qtd. in Boykoff 248).

Thus documentary poetry, by moving beyond a traditional construal of "poetry," opens its documentary potential precisely by questioning it. If the lines between the author's voice, the voices of others, and other documents are made manifest, then the author has foresworn any attempt to co-opt others' stories or to naturalize a particular version of a particular history. She or he employs multiple ways of knowing via multiple genres. Unipolar and univocal narratives (such as those often employed by state and corporate actors) are exposed as just that, and the ethical stakes become palpable. While this strategy will not guarantee the work a mass audience, it may make for an engaged, even galvanized one.

Notes

1. I have elsewhere defined documentary poetry as "poetry that (1) contains quotations from or reproductions of documents or statements not produced by the poet and (2) relates historical narratives, whether macro or micro, human or natural." Unlike conceptual poetry, documentary poetry makes use of sources rather than simply reproducing them: it combines, paraphrases, and contextualizes them. Poet and critic Cole Swensen has added the category "research-based poetry" to describe that which uses source material in a manner that is neither expository nor tendentious. Tony Trigilio prefers the broader term "historical poetry," which could include poetry that relates historical events without directly citing documents. These are important and welcome modifications of my earlier definition. For instance, Camille T. Dungy's *Suck on the Marrow* (2010) is based on extensive research, which it weaves into the fictionalized voices of people held in bondage—individuals about whom nothing is known other than their names.

2. "John Grierson . . . coined the term 'documentary' by applying it to the work of the great American filmmaker Robert Flaherty's *Moana* (1926). . . . He defined documentary as the 'artistic representation of actuality'—a definition that has proven durable probably because it is so very flexible" (Aufderheide 3).

3. For more information on this work, including an audio recording, see "Dorothy Livesay and 'Call My People Home,'" on the *Historical Perspectives on Canadian Publishing* website.

4. The reflexive documentary was present from the beginning of documentary film, as in Dziga Vertov's *Man with a Movie Camera* (1929), in which the eponymous figure is seen taking shots that are then seen in the film. However, this approach was uncommon until the 1960s.

5. The *Cantos* is mentioned less often by practitioners of docupoetry; but then it is not the most self-critical example from the period, nor is its politics the most palatable. The early sections of Zukofsky's "A" would seem to be likely candidates (particularly section 8); these may have received less attention because they are only the early sections of that very long poem, which takes a very different direction after the 1930s.

6. As of July 2014, of the websites listed, one is a dead link; one has not been updated since November 2011; and the online petition in the third addresses "U.N. Secretary Koffi Annan and U.S. President George W. Bush." While the issue of "dated" poems may be a red herring or nonissue for many readers, as a practicality of organizing, the tactic of placing URLs in print books may be less than effective. However, the redeployment of those eight thousand U.S. troops seems to have been postponed and downscaled, as of this writing: "The troop movement—once envisioned to send more than 8,000 troops to Guam by 2014—now plans to send about 4,000 Marines to the U.S. territory, beginning in the early 2020s, officials told a news conference" ("Officials Update Guam, Okinawa Realignment Plans," *Stars and Stripes*, 3 October 2013, Web). So it is possible that the political exposure brought to bear by Perez and other activists may have made a difference here.

7. The entire book is unpaginated.

8. Except where otherwise noted, all quotations in this paragraph and the next are from email correspondence with the author. See works cited.

9. Or they are classified in more than one genre, as evidenced by "slash" designations of book covers: "Poetry / Labor History"; "Lyric Essay / Poetry"; "Poetry/Essay"; "Poetry/Biography/Memoir"; or even "Poetry/Literature" (!). Some docupoems seem to be classified as poems simply because there is no place else to put them. To be sure, there is documentary poetry that is lineated, in stanzas of equal length. But some of the best-known examples in the twenty-first century include expository prose as well as verse and prose poems, dialogue tags, "raw" reproductions of documents, graphics, and other devices that diverge substantially from the standard expectations of a volume of poetry. These would include, in addition to works by poets named in this chapter, books and projects by Jill Magi, C. S. Giscombe, Jena Osman, Brenda Coultas, Judith Goldman, Bhanu Kapil, NourbeSe Philip, Rachel Zolf, Claudia Rankine, Catherine Taylor, Christian Hawkey, Tan Lin, Dana Teen Lomax, David Buuck, Adeena Karasick, and others. Of course, this tendency was present here and there throughout the twentieth century as well: Muriel Rukeyser, Haniel Long, William Carlos Williams, and Charles Olson are obvious examples. But mixed-genre and -media documentary literature has become far more pervasive in the twenty-first.

Works Cited

Aufderheide, Patricia. *Documentary Film: A Very Short Introduction*. Oxford: Oxford UP, 2007. Print.

Boykoff, Jules. "Poets as Experimental Geographers: Mark Nowak, Kaia Sand and the Re-composition of Political-Historical Space." *Placing Poetry*. Ed. Ian Davidson and Zoë Skoulding. Amsterdam: Rodopi, 2013. 223–56. Print.

Briante, Susan. "Defacing the Monument: Rukeyser's Innovations in Docupoetics." *Jacket2*, 21 April 2014. Web. 30 May 2015.

Caldwell, Erskine, and Margaret Bourke-White. *You Have Seen Their Faces*. New York: Modern Age Books, 1937. Print.

Cobb, Allison. *Green-Wood*. New York: Factory School, 2010. Print.

Cobb, Allison. Message to the author. 24 and 25 May 2014. Email.

Cobb, Allison. *Plastic: an autobiography*. Ithaca, NY: Essay Press, 2015. Web. 24 January 2016.

Collis, Stephen. Message to the author. 25 May 2014. Email.

Collis, Stephen. *On the Material*. Vancouver: Talonbooks, 2010. Print.

Dungy, Camille T. *Suck on the Marrow*. Los Angeles: Ren Hen Press, 2010. Print.

Durbin, Andrew, Andrew Ridker, Ben Fama, and Dorothea Lasky. "Surveillance Poetics." *The Believer Logger*, 24 Jul, 2014. Web. 30 May 2015.

Harrington, Joseph. "Docupoetry and Archive Desire." *Jacket2*, 27 October 2011. Web. 24 January 2016.

Lai, Paul. "Discontiguous States of America: The Paradox of Unincorporation in Craig Santos Perez's Poetics of Chamorro Guam." *Journal of Transnational American Studies* 3.2 (2011), 24 July 2014. Web. 24 January 2016.

Livesay, Dorothy. *Call My People Home*. Toronto: Ryerson, 1949. Print.

Livesay, Dorothy. "The Documentary Poem: A Canadian Genre" (1969). *Contexts of Canadian Criticism*. Ed. Eli Mandel. Chicago: U of Chicago P, 1971. Print.

MacLeish, Archibald. *Land of the Free*. New York: Harcourt, Brace, 1938. Print.

Mirakove, Carol. "Anxieties of Information." *Traffic: A Publication of Small Press Traffic* 1 (2005–6): 72–114. Print.

Mirakove, Carol. Message to the author. 24 May 2014. Email.

Mirakove, Carol. *Occupied*. Berkeley, CA: Kelsey Street P, 2004. Print.

Nichols, Bill. *Representing Reality: Issues and Concepts in Documentary*. Bloomington: Indiana UP, 1991. Print.

Ossip, Kathleen. *The Cold War*. Louisville, KY: Sarabande, 2011. Print.

Ossip, Kathleen. Message to the author. 27 May 2014. Email.

Perez, Craig Santos. Message to the author. 26 May 2014. Email.

Perez, Craig Santos. *From Unincorporated Territory [hacha]*. Kāne'ohe, HI: TinFish P, 2008. Print.

Prevallet, Kristin. *I, Afterlife*. Athens, OH: Essay P, 2007. Print.

Prevallet, Kristin. "Investigating the Procedure: Poetry and the Source." *Telling It Slant: Avant-Garde Poetics of the 1990s*. Ed. Mark Wallace and Steven Marks. Tuscaloosa: U of Alabama P, 2001. 115–29. Print.

Prevallet, Kristin. *Scratch Sides: Poetry, Documentation, and Image-Text Projects*. Austin, TX: Skanky Possum Books, 2002. Print.

Prevallet, Kristin. *Shadow Evidence Intelligence: And Other Formal Disruptions*. New York: Factory School, 2006. Print.

Sand, Kaia. "Affording Entrance." *Placing Poetry*. Ed. Ian Davidson and Zoë Skoulding. Amsterdam: Rodopi, 2013. 201–22. Print.

Sand, Kaia. Messages to the author. 7 and 9 July 2014. Email.

Sand, Kaia. *Remember to Wave*. Kāne'ohe, HI: TinFish P, 2010. Print.

Sanders, Ed. *Investigative Poetry*. San Francisco: City Lights, 1976. Print.

Schultz, Susan M. Message to the author. 25 May 2014. Email.

Schultz, Susan M. *She's Welcome to Her Disease (Dementia Blog, Volume Two)*. San Diego: Singing Horse P, 2013. Print.

Steyerl, Hito. "Documentarism as Politics of Truth." *European Institute for Progressive Cultural Policies*. May 2003. Web. 30 May 2015.

Swensen, Cole. *Noise That Stays Noise: Essays*. Ann Arbor: U of Michigan P, 2011. Print.

Tichy, Susan. "Equal Meadows." *Evening Will Come*, 13 (July 2013). Web. 30 May 2015.

Tichy, Susan. *Trafficke: An Autobiography*. Boise, ID: Ahsahta, 2015. Print.

Trigilio, Tony. *Historic Diary*. Buffalo, NY: BlazeVox, 2011. Print.

Trigilio, Tony. Message to the author. 27 May 2014. Email.

FIVE

"Hands Off"

Official Language in Contemporary Poetry

Jeffrey Gray

"Take an object. Do something to it. Do something else to it," wrote Jasper Johns in his sketchbook sometime in the 1970s. As an artistic practice, the use of found materials is an ongoing phenomenon requiring ongoing explanations, its cultural meaning changing from decade to decade—variously playful, iconoclastic, subversive, and by now part of the cultural furniture, even while sometimes retaining the capacity to shock. If many literary texts amalgamated found language in the modernist era, many more did so in the last half of the twentieth century, as subjectivity in poetry began to be held in greater suspicion. The list is long and includes works by Kathy Acker, John Ashbery, Bernadette Mayer, Ted Berrigan, David Markson, Harry Matthew, and many more. Remarkable examples include Clark Coolidge's *Smithsonian Depositions* (1980), which draws on thirty different sources, ranging from Godard films to geology textbooks; Charles Bernstein's "Emotions of Normal People," deriving from an apparently random sampling of computer handbooks, direct-mail consumer surveys, catalog descriptions of *Poet's Market*, and other sources; and Walter Abish's *99: The New Meaning*, which, in the author's words, consists of "99 segments by as many authors, each line, sentence or paragraph appropriated from a page bearing that same, to me, mystically significant number 99."[1]

The practice of appropriation in U.S. poetry is even more widespread in the twenty-first century than it was in either the modern or postmodern eras; indeed, almost everything seems *found* now—both because of deliberate compositional strategies taught in writing workshops, now far more widespread (both the workshops, numbering nearly four hundred at present, up from perhaps a dozen in the 1960s, and the techniques) and arguably because of readers' growing awareness of language as shared, that is, as by *definition* unoriginal and recycled. But most of all, the ascension of found language from an experimental to a mainstream practice is a consequence of the repudiation— over several decades—of the self as an organizing principle in artistic prac- tice. Only twelve years ago Eliot Weinberger could complain—as others had done thirty years earlier—about the "autobiographical, anecdotal, therapeutic poems of the workshop," a characterization that today seems wildly inaccu- rate (and was largely inaccurate at the time). In our own time, against a spotty background of continuing personal and experiential poetry, explicit agency associated with the self is seen as suspect; moreover, from the artist's stand- point, retiring the idea of self allows other forces to emerge: linguistic, un- conscious, aleatory, and procedural.[2] In this way, found poems, contemporary documentary ("docupoems") or research-based poems, or the poetry of stuff, as David Wojahn has called it, may be seen as part of this general turn away from subjectivity and toward found materials of varying forms.

Though it has roots in early modernism, the demystification of the self was most explicit in the first wave of reactions to the personal/confessional poetry of the 1960s and 1970s, particularly in the Language poets. Robert Lowell was no doubt prescient in saying, "Everybody's tired of my turmoil" (18). But the displacement of the self, whether in literary criticism or as part of larger soci- etal ethos, owes something also to the mid- to late-century literary theory that tracked and to some extent also generated it—notably to Roland Barthes's "death of the author," Michel Foucault's positing of the "author function," and Louis Althusser's concept of a socially constructed subject. With respect to the first of these, "The fabled death of the Author," says Marjorie Perloff in 2012, "has in recent poetry finally become a *fait accompli*" (18), prompting one to reflect that, if we date the "fabled death" from Barthes's 1967 essay "The Death of the Author," it has taken almost fifty years for the author to die. Perloff herself has been instrumental, over several books, in tracing the continuity of non- or anti-subjective poetry from the beginnings of the twen- tieth century to the beginnings of the twenty-first. Psychological poetry, not only confessionalism but also surrealism, has been for Perloff merely an un- fortunate distraction from this more important artistic and historical current of modernism.

In this essay, I want first to consider the contemporary poetic practices I am describing and their frequent emphasis on neutral, inert discourse—in contrast, say, to Eliot's use of Dante and Baudelaire, or Pound's of Confu- cius and Li Po, or Ashbery's of Popeye or Daffy Duck—in the light of broader forces in contemporary Western culture, which they seem to parallel or pos- sibly even spring from. I will look at poetic strategy in several contemporary poets, to illustrate the degrees to which appropriation is practiced, and the significance of "impure" transcriptions—wherein found language is newly contextualized, juxtaposed with other language, or subjected to critique—and the purportedly "pure" transcriptions, as in much of the work of Kenneth Goldsmith.

★

Escape into the Real

The general repudiation of the self I have described in recent Western art and discourse is reflected in several ways in contemporary academic culture—notably, in the shift in literary scholarship away from interpretation and toward studies of material culture—that is, in contemporary books and articles about the lived specificity of, say, Henry James's or Edgar Allan Poe's time, the covers of the magazines where these authors published, the source of the pulp out of which the paper was made, or the economy of that pulp industry—rather than metaphoricity, linguistics, or hermeneutics. To interpret rather than to *present* data, whether data generated by personal experience or by found materials, is increasingly seen as retrograde in creative writing and unnecessary in scholarship.

Concurrently with this turn in literary criticism, a turn in philosophy has been advanced with regard to the radical inaccessibility of "the Real." I refer particularly to the "nonphilosophers" François Laruelle and Quentin Meillasoux, who repudiate philosophy's attempt to grasp the—for them—irreducible events of existence. Their approach—called both "speculative realism" and "object oriented ontology," is achieved, Meillasoux explains, by "absolutizing facticity" (60). "The Real," also known in Laruelle's writing as "the One" (xxii), is "a radically immanent identity" that is by its nature foreclosed to thought. Thus, to the question posed by Parmenides—why is there something rather than nothing?—Laruelle and Meillasoux respond: for no reason. No theory is offered; indeed, a theory is an impertinence when unreason is an absolute ontological reality: for these writers, as Herman Rappaport notes, there is nothing beyond the absolute gratuitousness of everything.

But the antihermeneutic turn is much larger than any particular movement in French philosophy. Pedagogy today is action-oriented, as it is in the social sciences, which have increasingly privileged information over interpretation. In psychology, to use a well-documented example, CBT (cognitive behavioral therapy) entails fixing a problem, not—as in psychoanalysis—understanding it. These empirical and forensic methods support fundamentalisms of irreducible fact. Alzheimer's, Mars exploration, rising tides, cholesterol, school shootings, or the hoarders on television—all are inexplicable in this context.

It is in this milieu of hermeneutical fatigue that scholars in literature departments may write about the glue used in Renaissance bookbinding, about furniture, clothes, and food, materials that can be described and cataloged but about which no ideas need be formed.

This shift in value and purpose from interpretation to information might seem to stand in ironic contrast to a turn in poetry toward engagement with public issues. But this is not necessarily an opposition. I would suggest that poetry is becoming engaged not *in spite* of an increased affinity for found materials but *through* those materials—that is, that poems get written and critiques get made by the process of writing through found discourse—often and especially suspect discourse—and through the resistance that discourse offers. The question then becomes: What does poetry look like when driven not only by inward forces (loss, love, contemplation), and public realities (mergers, mortgages, and wars), but also by discourse, especially, as I'll argue below, official, corporate, or bureaucratic discourse, the language circulating around us and in which we are embedded.

Through most of the history of twentieth-century poetry, appropriation took the form of allusion or quotation, or in more pronounced cases a continuous tissue of quotations marshaled to a poetic or thetic end, as in *The Waste Land*, arguably the founding document of twentieth-century collage (though visual collage practice preceded it). The more extreme instances, such as those listed at the beginning of this essay, had a somewhat marginal relationship to mainstream poetry until recently. The mainstreaming may have begun with Ashbery, in whose work it became more and more difficult, without extrapoetic commentary, to tell what was found from what was not (*Three Poems*, for example, often seems found but is not). Recent Ashbery poems seldom constitute appropriation *tout court*. Rather, the typical twenty-first-century Ashbery poem is a flotsam of miscellaneous lines held together only by grammar (he is usually grammatical) and the margins of the stanza. Occasionally, all lines are appropriated but seldom from the same source: this is the case with the cento "The Dong with the Luminous Nose" (in which every line is taken from a different poetic source) or, more recently, "They" (a list of movie titles). In most of the hundreds of Ashbery's free-verse poems appearing in magazines in the last two decades, unattributed found language drops into the poem more or less whimsically as suits the poet's ear, leading a recent critic, echoing a blockbuster movie title about U.S. military prowess in Iraq, to call the poet the "American Snipper" (Chiasson). This practice contrasts with the extreme appropriation of a conceptual poet such as Kenneth Goldsmith, who cuts and pastes entire texts without alteration or commentary. At this point, the writer becomes what Clark Coolidge calls a "sublime interceptor," transcribing entire texts, attributed or not.

*

Official Language in American Poetry Today

Contemporary poets tap into many discursive registers, most of them not, in our own time, literary. Indeed, many poets—Bernstein, Timothy Donnelly, Goldsmith, and others—seem to choose texts specifically for their affective flatness: instruction manuals, guides, catalogs, reference books, or the sort of scientific surveys and engineering descriptions that Marianne Moore admired. Of the various registers to which contemporary poetry is most attracted, I want to look particularly at the role of official, corporate, or bureaucratic language in poetry—whether this language is ironized, critiqued, or (on the face of it) unexamined. The reader's implication becomes more consequential where shared discourse, especially hegemonic or institutional language, is concerned. By these adjectives—"official," "hegemonic," "institutional"—I mean discourses characterized by a purported erasure of subjectivity, a projection of neutrality, and an unproblematic authority.

First, then, a number of poets of our time submit official language to scrutiny. In their recent work, Rae Armantrout, Brenda Hillman, Naomi Shihab Nye, and Maxine Kumin fall into this category. Their scrutiny sometimes takes the form of etymological inquiries, as in Kumin (who reinterprets and extends the meanings of the Pentagon's phrase "extraordinary rendition"), Brenda Hillman ("In a Senate Armed Services Hearing"), Nye ("Dictionary in the Dark"), or Robert Wrigley in his exploration of the engineering term "tolerance" in connection with the engineering of artificial limbs. Other poets fold snippets of received discourse into their poems, mixed with other materials—advertisements, popular songs, television programs, or personal narratives. In both of these techniques, in all these cases, an investigation is proceeding: When Armantrout, referring to state language in wartime, asks, "[How can] we process this deception and how is it processed for us by our popular culture?" ("Statement" 205), she seems to speak for such poets. Elsewhere, she writes, "I tend to focus on the interventions of capitalism into consciousness . . . in a society where perceptions are commodities, already shrink-wrapped" (*Collected Prose* 120).

Those who do not seem to present a critique of found language may nevertheless register their complicity with it insofar as this language is composed of components drawn upon by all who speak it. "We are like painters," writes Francis Ponge, "who, from as far back as can be remembered, would all have to dip their brushes in the same immense can in order to thin out their paints" (qtd. in Rubinstein). Far from parodying the language, such poets often depict experience as accessible only through already manipulated forms. As Ponge notes, no matter what we say, "The same sordid order speaks, because we have no other words at our disposal" (7). This latter awareness of the writer's embeddedness suggests that institutional discourse is the only discourse we have. Today's appropriation thus differs from modernist collage by revealing its materials not as defamiliarized or shocking, but as in fact familiar—constitutive of who we are at this moment in history. That it is possible to work within such constraints—perhaps like that vicious beetle that eats its way out from inside a still living animal—suggests some of the post-Foucauldian ideas one finds in critics such as Linda Hutcheon, who coined the phrase "complicit critique" to describe the practice in which one inhabits, is complicit with, and yet able to find a position within a discourse in order to destabilize it.

All the above are examples of poets explicitly *doing* something with official language, interlarding that language with other sometimes conflicting or interventionist materials. In the following, more extended examples, I will try to illustrate particularly how transcendent, even visionary language erupts in the fissures opened within or beneath hegemonic discourse.

Joel Brouwer's poem "Lines from the Reports of the Investigative Committees" concerns British Petroleum's Transocean Deepwater Horizon, the offshore oil drilling rig that drilled the deepest oil well in history, and whose explosion and sinking in 2010 resulted in the largest environmental disaster in history. The bulk of the poem consists of lines that sound as if issued from a committee. (At least five committees are mentioned in the poem's headnote, including British Petroleum's committee, the U.S. House of Representatives Committee on Energy and Commerce, the Subcommittee on Oversight and Investigation, and the Senate Committee on Energy and Natural Resources.) Much of the language is as disaffected and pedestrian as language can be, with sentences such as "Bank of America will offer limited foreclosure / deferments in affected communities" and

> care must be taken to ensure continued high
> reliability of the shuttle valve, since it is
> extremely critical to the overall disconnect
> operation.

But this language—bureaucratic in the first case, instrumental in the other—is at times adulterated with words that seem improbable coming from such depersonalized bodies, suggesting an insidious agency familiar from conspiracy movies: "Recommendation: Declare selected points on earth / invisible" (32) and "Recommendation: Prevent access to the invisible" (33). These attributions evoke a committee involved not only in godlike power but in access to the psyche, as the final lines of the poem suggest: "If the committee may offer an analogy, the death / drive resides at wholly dark depths of imagination / and fuel issues from a wound we've opened there. " The first lines cited above ("Bank of America . . .") are composed in the inert if not soporific language of business and bureaucracy. At the end of the poem this register changes violently, the cold, reasonable diction giving way to a visionary alliterative language of violence and trauma ("death / drive" residing at "dark depths"). The image of fuel burning underwater as it issues from a fissure thirty-five thousand feet below the sea surface, which millions watched for weeks on television in the spring of 2010 before a successful "plug" was fashioned and the leakage stopped, has here been transferred from the material world to the psyche, on which those broadcasts are imprinted. Inaccessible ocean depths are conflated with inaccessible depths of the unconscious and the Freudian "death drive." This conflation is not part of the language, much less the conceptuality, of the BP committee's reports but is familiar from science fiction novels in which advanced technology destroys its creators. The death drive in this scenario is traced to its psychic source in an image, provided by the news of a rupture, seen as if at the entrance to the magma chambers at the earth's core—metaphorically, the psyche's core.

Brouwer's prose commentary on "Lines from the Reports" raises an epistemological question central to understanding the appropriation of hegemonic writing. He introduces the idea of a "crew one," which cleans up after disasters, looks after the injured, distributes food and water, and contains the damage; and a "crew two," which consists of "various scientific, charitable, meteorological, journalistic, and academic institutions and authorities" ("Statement" 212). The job of this second crew is to construct "coherent narratives" (212)—that is, to alter our sense of what has happened, leading us to "forfeit at least a portion of the confusion which is our natural state" (212). To "forfeit" suggests a loss, but institutional narrations designed to promote the sanity of the populace are, according to Brouwer, not nefarious. Does a poet's quoting them, cutting and parsing them—sometimes but not always adulterating them—reinscribe the texts' self-interested and suspect sensemaking, or do the invisible quotation marks of the appropriated material, its being framed as poetry, invite us to examine it, to form an attitude (disdain, suspicion, amusement) toward it? These are questions one might ask of all official discourse: is it *other* enough for us to scrutinize, or is it woven so far into us that its services seem not only immediately acceptable but indispensable?

After getting all the news from meteorologists, the Red Cross, the mayor, and other sources, Brouwer now knows why the storm formed; he knows how best to help the victims; he knows just where the tornadoes struck—all necessary information. But he has sacrificed the lability and potential of not-knowing. In his commentary on this poem, he writes,

My actual experience of that afternoon—an opaque stew of ignorance, fear, tension, and excitement—was the purchase price of all this understanding. Was that a raw deal? Of course not. Only a narcissist would claim to prefer the experience of his private sensorium to the representations provided by crew two. (212)

Thus, one surrenders interpretive faculties in favor of a manufactured—not to say dishonest—version of reality that one can live with. This does not constitute an approval of the language of BP: the parodic element is plain in the very fact of the framing of the official language and—as we see in many of these examples—its mixture with other elements that undermine and expose it. The poem might be said to reveal the nature of the official discourse without suggesting that it can be any other way.

Generally, as I have suggested, the projected neutrality of state and corporate language gives the impression that it has emerged—as in the indistinguishable committees of Brouwer's poem—from a seat of authority with no individual features. In the case of Timothy Donnelly's "Dream of Arabian Hillbillies," however, it is not a matter of government or corporate policy announcements but of language charged even in its origins with point of view, with emotion (anger, humor, absurdity). The poem is made up of phrases taken, first, from Osama bin Laden's 1996 "Declaration of War against Americans Occupying the Land of the Two Holy Places," and second from the theme song of the 1960s TV show *Beverly Hillbillies*. The language of the former source is solemn, committed, and pitched at a level both (unintentionally) comical and dangerous; that of the latter is absurd, vulgar, (intentionally) comical, commodified, and perhaps comforting. Donnelly's poem does not represent here a shift from the neutral and bureaucratic language of earlier examples, but, as in those examples, a mix of conflicting discourses. Osama bin Laden's language is official, the language of an edict, high-toned in a way one does not find in political discourse of the West today but which formerly was found widely—consider Roosevelt's or Churchill's speeches or for that matter any local U.S. mayor's speeches from fifty to one hundred years ago.

This poem also introduces a compositional principle important to any study of appropriation, that is, that a complete transformation or redirection of materials is possible when the quoted units are small: the smaller the unit, the greater the possibility of agency; the larger, the more the passivity, the less room for ideological intervention—as we will see in the case of Kenneth Goldsmith—within the passage. As with bin Laden, so with the lyrics of the TV sitcom: often only a phrase or a single word at a time is quoted, and thus much more composition is required. At times the source is clear: The high diction and formality of "Cleanse the road to your destiny / of all idolaters" and (in quotation marks) "'To express hate and anger is a moral gesture / to the future'" obviously belong to bin Laden, whereas "y'hear," "y'all," "heapin'," and "kinfolk" are drawn, equally clearly, from the *Beverly Hillbillies*. Other phrases are not easy to attribute and probably derive from neither of these two sources. The rhetorical pattern of the poem is that of the curse (or blessing), Donnelly writes,

> May you journey in the security
> of a huge American truck. May your enemies come
>   to wither in front of this truck
>
> allowing you and your kinfolk to occupy
>   the avenue of personal interests. (40)

The poem moves, however, as Donnelly has said, "from drunken absurdity into an ironically clear-eyed rallying cry" ("Statement" 215). (Note the parallel shift at the end of the Brouwer poem discussed above.) The "drunken absurdity" lies largely in the non sequiturs and jarring juxtapositions resulting from two such different discourses. The ending is another matter:

> May you not cave in and weep deep. May wolves
>   not eat your wings. May your life
> not be a lifelong movie of your life
>   but a steadfast becoming other than that
>
> which you are: a slave to the power
>   fiddling among hills of fed clouds and shaken
> into wonderment like a shot horse barely
>   gathering will to lay down with it, y'hear? (40)

Except for the final "y'hear?," which undercuts the tone that precedes it, this is a passage one can read "straight," taking into account that it uses the resources of poetry—"fiddling among hills of fed clouds," for example, is at once pastoral, celebratory, musical, and surreal. One can account for the insertion of "y'hear" the same way one accounts for the jazzy or hip language that John Berryman used to insert into his poems as a nervous way of downplaying their "wisdom" dimension. The wishes (the "may you's") seem to issue neither from bin Laden nor Jed Clampett. The hope that your life be a life, not a trivial simulacrum but a liberation from servitude—this is the "rallying cry" that Donnelly describes, strangely not incongruous with the intermittent "drunken absurdity" of the rest of the poem. The poem is combinatory in other senses as well: both the dadaist impulse and the ludic "blank parody" of postmodernism are heavily qualified by the 9/11 *situation* of the poem and, beyond that, *by intention*: by the conflation of two discourses—each about oil, economics, and destiny, as Donnelly notes in his comments on the poem. The result is that the poem comments on both North American and Middle Eastern dreams: bin Laden as a narcissistic apocalyptical messiah, the Beverly Hillbillies as a kitsch send-up of down-to-earth Appalachians—the "hillbillies" of American folklore from Faulkner's Boon Hogganbeck to film's Ma and Pa Kettle.

My third example of an impure transcription illustrates more explicitly that a "neutral" appropriated language is not at odds with the transcendent. Brenda Hillman writes, on the one hand, that "the source material for several of these poems is the public record" ("Statement" 227), a record consisting of congressional hearings, as well as interviews with weapons and munitions sales personnel. But also, experientially, "Materials for the poems come from the unconscious. . . . I use trance techniques to visit the blue cave and the yellow tablets" ("Statement" 226). In Hillman's prose essay/poem "Reportorial Poetry, Trance, and Activism," which serves as a commentary on "In a Senate Armed Services Hearing," she writes that "meditative states can be used to cross material boundaries, to allow you to be several places at once, such as Congress and ancient Babylon" (102).[3] She thus connects the two modes explicitly; on the one hand transcription, which may seem merely passive, merely documentary; and on the other, vision, trance, altered states of consciousness. "I recorded notes in Washington while attending hearings and participating in actions to make the record collective and personal. Working with trance while sitting in Congressional hearings I recorded details in a notebook" ("Reportorial" 102).

Thus, appropriation and transcription need not be alien to a kind of poetics that we seldom see in the early twenty-first century, though it cut a wide swath in the 1960s, as it did also a century earlier: a visionary poetics, wherein, for Hillman, "the stuff of dream and reverie are tools that can be taken into the corridors of power," where "the dreamer meets official language" ("Statement" 226, 228). The official language appears in italicized phrases such as "*I don't foresee a long / role for our troops*" and "*General I'd be interested to know*" (103). The last lines of "In a Senate Armed Services Hearing" read as follows:

> The breath they used
> When saying °°°A°°° for *American Interests* made the A stand still,
>   it had a sunset clause,
> They tried to say °°°*Safety*°°° but the S withdrew,
> The S went underground. Would not

> Be redeployed. Refused to spell. Till all the letters stopped
>   In astral light, in dark love for their human ones. (104)

Language is presented here as unyielding to power, uncooperative with state projects, the "S" like a soldier going AWOL rather than be redeployed for the general's rhetorical purposes. But the reader knows that language in the real world is just as willing to provide as to withhold that support. That willingness is the reason for the vigilance suggested in the poem—at the human, animal, and molecular levels. Hillman's poem in this regard, unlike the others, not only deploys official language but *addresses* it and one's confused and changing relation to it: Viewing the hearing, the speaker remarks, "I forget who asked what isn't even / in the same syntax of this / language i'm trying to make no progress in" (103). The poem also addresses positionality, the first three lines reading, "From my position as a woman / i could see / the back of the General's head" (102). Many more such phrases occur as markers or structuring devices, every dozen lines or so: "From its position on the table the fly could then foresee," "From my position as the fly / i could foresee as letters issued / from their mouths," "from my position as a fly," "A voice beside my insect / ear said," "From my / position as a molecule" (103–4). Even with the poem's emphasis on altered states of consciousness, the poet states the responsibility to report, advising that "entering the public sphere [the poet] should bring notebooks and recording devices, for many officials and public servants care about how they are depicted" (228).

Most of all, in its infiltration and representation of the governmental "Hearing," Hillman's is a poem about the role of the poet in public life: advising how to behave, how to locate and confront power, how to combine critique with understanding ("these Senators all have their lives: kids with stuff to do, folks with cancer" [228]), how to compose, and how to deploy language that lends itself to both abuse and conscience.

★

"Silver Reflectivity": Kenneth Goldsmith

"To have done instead of not doing / this is not vanity. . . . Here error is all in the not done," wrote Pound at the end of Canto 83. Without reducing the discussion of appropriation in contemporary poetry to a moral difference, a strategic opposition might be helpful at this point: one between intervention and agency on the one hand, and passivity or perhaps promiscuity on the other— what the poet Kenneth Goldsmith calls the "hands-off" approach ("Conceptual Poetics"). Goldsmith has achieved considerable fame by arguing for and writing from this stance. His assessment of the relative merits of John

Cage and Andy Warhol is revealing in this connection. He writes that Cage, while seeming to open the windows to all the world's sound as "music"—highway traffic, neighborhood noise, sounds whether of nature, humanity, or industry—nevertheless had a moral filter that wouldn't have allowed, say, the popular music of his time through that window; by contrast, says Goldsmith, Andy Warhol let everything into his art. He was a "model of permeability, transparency, and silver reflectivity. Everything was fodder for Warhol's art. . . . Our world turned out to be Andy's world" ("Statement: Politics" 220).[4] In this juxtaposition, Warhol's is clearly the preferred practice. It is a suspect opposition since of course Warhol was not transparent; he made choices, as much as Cage did. (The selection process was carried out "according to taste," as Cage once wrote [qtd. in Perloff, "Unoriginal" 169].)

In his thirty-year career of transcribing found texts—traffic reports, weather reports, newspapers, and recently (at this writing) an autopsy report, all purportedly neutral, univocal, nonsubjective texts—Goldsmith has striven to achieve that "silver reflectivity."[5] But what if no direct transcription, no silver reflectivity is really possible? What if intervention operates even when quotation is wholesale and unglossed, when a poem is made up entirely of one found text? Perhaps, in short, there is no direct transcription but only the aspiration to it. Allen Ruppersberg's installation *The Picture of Dorian Gray* (1974) is a longhand transcription of Oscar Wilde's novel in its entirety over twenty large, square canvases, each resembling a page of a book. "I think the copy is the truth," says Ruppersberg. But hand-writing the novel on canvases—in impeccable script, with almost obsessively even lines—results in a completely different work, one that few viewers would consider reading (it is much easier to read the book) but which—not only the concept but also the resulting artworks—is pleasurable, even compelling to view.

Even in the programmatic practices of the Oulipo writers, once a formula is decided upon and the author has stepped aside, agency tempts from the sidelines: after all, why follow the rules? You follow them insofar as you make the first choice, as Goldsmith points out, providing the machine that will create the poem (ending each line with a reference to a kind of wood, or composing the poem without definite articles, say), but why not break them at least *some of the time*? Goldsmith's books No. 109 and No. 111, for example, were composed first by using a constraint, then by abandoning it where it suited the poet to do so.[6]

This is what Marjorie Perloff shows that Kenneth Goldsmith is doing in other works as well. He just *says* he's boring, unoriginal, and uncreative, Perloff claims. Behind the curtain, he is cooking the books, deciding that some utterances are more worthy than others (in his *Soliloquy*, for example, in which he decides to write every word he speaks during one week but leaves out words), or that, in *Traffic*, some traffic narration on the radio is more worthy than other. Raphael Rubinstein writes that "Goldsmith appears at first to be assuming a Warholian passivity to the world around him, but the rhythmic structures he establishes and the personal nature of his choices soon make the reader realize that even this extreme form of linguistic appropriation is permeated with personal vision."

Goldsmith pleads innocent to these charges, saying he has graduated from his early slips into intervention: "I *used to* feel that only some words were collectible, that certain words were better than others, but I've come to question that as the years have passed" (Perloff, "Interview"; emphasis added). He now favors a model as close to silver reflectivity as possible, as he says in an online response to the poet Reginald Shepherd:

> I feel the best critique of any language is to let it speak for itself. I feel that the interpretation of language is always subjective and no amount of arm-twisting will change anybody's mind, hence my hands-off approach. I find that language contains enough morality or lack thereof that we don't really need to do much with it; we're working with explosive material here. I'm not interested in a hierarchical approach to language; I'm not interested in judgments or moralizing.[7]

In adhering to such a poetics, Goldsmith sets himself apart from the more interventionist examples I introduced earlier, those in which language is *used*, played with, reframed, or critiqued—interventions that Goldsmith sees as moralizing or judging—claiming, instead, that the best thing to do is to "let it speak for itself." But this is where the binary of intervention versus passivity begins to collapse. Consider the books *Day* and *The Day*, Goldsmith's most famous works, in which he transcribes issues of the *New York Times* (respectively, September 1, 2000, and September 11, 2001) verbatim.[8] *Day* is the transcription of a newspaper published on a day deliberately chosen for its insignificance (September 1, 2000), and in this way it is a "neutral" book, says Goldsmith. *The Day*, on the other hand, transcribes the paper issued on September 11, 2001, which of course did not describe the events of that day (the following day did that); thus its transcription constitutes a deliberate irony: a paper announcing events that would never happen, sales that were canceled, events indefinitely postponed, and "top" stories forever after buried. Therefore, the difference between *Day* and *The Day* would seem to illustrate the two poles of passivity and intervention, even though both experiments are examples of "not writing." *The Day* would seem to reveal more design, more choice, and yet neither transcription is passive. In both cases, the artist sees the possibilities of what he has conceived. Goldsmith is, as Jaspar Johns proposed, doing something to the object.

What exactly is he doing? First, both *The Day* and *Day* look very different from the texts they have copied. The columns, fonts, designs, and of course the photographs—that is, all the machinery of newsprint hierarchy and order, the features that have trained us to see at a glance what is most and least important—have been surgically removed, with a result comparable to pasting a formatted pdf poem into a Word document, losing line and stanza breaks, and splitting up words. A random passage reads:

> But the competition for bleary eyes has grown more intense as media conglomerates have awakened to
>
> the idea that changing lives, heightened interest from advertisers and other factors have made the morning one of the few areas of growth in the
> television business. ("A1" 56)

Other sections are defamiliarized through form to an even greater degree:

> Mr. Lott said he would like to see
> Continued on Page A20
> Traced on Internet,
> Teacher is Charged
> In '71 Hijacking
> By C. J. CHIVERS (56)

Here Goldsmith retains capital letters, and he indents not where, or not for the reasons, the *Times* editors indented but rather, evidently, as a substitute for new columns, new articles, new sections of the page. In this way, despite his aspirations to be a machine—Warhol's stated ambition—Goldsmith is performing a formal practice: remediating the newspaper lines into the template of the typed page and in doing so draining them of the formal logic they originally possessed. On the one hand, this practice defamiliarizes in startling ways, removing the text's fiction of transparency; on the other, it inserts the element of abstraction. If Goldsmith had wanted to *copy* the *Times*, he could have photocopied it, or used desktop publishing or another such program to reproduce the look of the newspaper; it is that look that has been eliminated. The results of the typing, printing, and the binding into book form, taken together, do not "copy" the newspaper. They do not produce any resemblance to the newspaper other than the now-denatured "content," yet the result demonstrates that by looking, by noticing and remediating—as in the "observer effect" in physics—we change things.

In the long career of "uncreative" appropriation that is Goldsmith's, there are inevitably degrees of passivity and intervention. One notes, for example, the considerable appeal of Goldsmith's *Traffic*, where the voice *does* something with the material. Similarly, *Seven American Deaths and Disasters* is at times riveting: no one else had ever thought of transcribing not the events of the JFK or John Lennon assassinations (among others) but rather the nervous, erratic, error-ridden radio and television broadcasters' accounts of those events. Content is indeed important, as Goldsmith himself seems to say, in spite of himself, in his somewhat uncomfortable appearance on the *Colbert Report* in June 2013.[9]

In the context of a discussion of American poetry of appropriation, or even of American poetry at large, another important matter must be introduced, particularly when one remembers what an unpopular genre poetry (at least the reading of poetry in print) is, relative to prose genres. I refer to the fact of Goldsmith's celebrity—not only among poets and critics but at large, his visibility by far eclipsing that of the other poets I have discussed here. None of those poets, nor any of hundreds of others, were invited to the White House as Goldsmith was; neither Frank Bidart nor John Ashbery—to choose two famous poets who might conveniently be cast as the two poles of the contemporary poetry scene, the one psychological and experiential, the other experimental and disjunctive—will ever be, it is fair to say, interviewed on the *Colbert Report* or excoriated as "the end of civilization as we know it" on Michael Savage's radio show—for forbidding his students to "create," a charge to which Goldsmith happily pleads guilty. Nor will Bidart or Ashbery ever be poet laureate—the one poet too personal and transgressive ("*if you / give me enough money you can continue to fuck me*" [3]), the other too nonreferential, linguistic, and transgressive ("nicer things to be doing! . . . sucking each other's dicks is only one" [184])—as, for example, Robert Hass, Robert Pinsky, Rita Dove, or Ted Kooser have been. *But perhaps Goldsmith could.* He was a success at the White House. He is animated, provocative, sartorially expressive, public, and good with children. Goldsmith's career illustrates the fact that what the poet can do, as James Scully notes in *Line Break*, is not determined so much by the poet as by the cultural and political moment.[10]

The new centrality of Goldsmith's poetry is real and palpable. While not expressly *underwritten* by the state—as, say, Pollock and the abstract expressionist painters were, unwittingly, by the CIA—Goldsmith nevertheless approximates the quietism and formalist interventions of mainstream American poetry of, say, the 1950s. Is Goldsmith's work, then, symptomatic, and little more? Is it not even a reaction within the ideological formation, but just the formation itself? Is he simply a typist (as Truman Capote once said of Jack Kerouac)? Or is he background noise, like that other Kenny G (to whom Goldsmith seemed to allude on his radio show)? Elevator music? These comparisons suggest, variously, inertia, complicity, passivity. But transcribed texts need not be inert, though inertia, like the speed of light, can be approached. A writer like Goldsmith may *aspire* to passivity, but representation always involves transference, just as it always involves filtering. Significantly, nevertheless, Goldsmith's reception and his influence on other poets and on contemporary criticism suggest a taste for nonsubjective passivity and the preference for radical immanence of the kind I suggested earlier in this chapter.

A taste for quietism and leaving things alone was not part of the high modernist ethos. For Jasper Johns, as for Marcel Duchamp, the artist was to *do* something with the object. Duchamp's 1917 urinal was labeled "fountain," and it had a tag: "R. Mutt." A gesture was involved. Leah Dickerman, regarding the modernist exhibition at MOMA in New York in 2010, was speaking particularly of Duchamp's found objects when she wrote that "the ready-made was [always] a thing *plus* text." Why is that "plus" now under suspicion? While sentiment was suspect in early modernism, the poet's originality was not. Nor, clearly, was it in the postwar poetry that tilted so markedly toward the subjective. Nor even was it suspect, as Perloff documents in the first chapter of her *Unoriginal Genius*, in avant-garde and Language poetry. Why has happened then, in recent times, to change this?

One answer, as I have tentatively suggested, has to do with larger trends in Western culture. The other concerns the local world of U.S. poetry. The "larger trends" I have tried to indicate in my comments on the antihermeneutical turn in scholarship, both in the sciences and in the humanities. As for the local dimension, one need only reflect on the fact that "language" poetries were marginal in the 1970s and 1980s, that they increasingly began to inform (and then to enhance and sophisticate) mainstream American poetry, and that in the past twenty years, that mainstream has become as a result much more involved in procedural methods and found discourse. Swensen and St. John's *American Hybrid* serves as a good benchmark for the change. Rae Armantrout's winning of the Pulitzer Prize in 2012 is another: a "Language" poet who became—not because of any change in her own work but because of a change in the orientation or education of poetry's readership—a readable, personal, engaged poet.

Goldsmith's contempt for points of view, ideas, interpretations—which he sees as "moralizing" or "judging"—dovetails almost perfectly with the antihermeneutical trends I mention. The turn against affect (permissible, as Goldsmith notes in his introduction to Flarf poets in *Poetry*, only if it's not one's *own* affect but rather textual and appropriated), extends beyond the early modernist distaste for Victorian or Georgian sentimentality, and beyond the later Language poets' disapproval of first-person experiential or confessional poetry. It is a culmination of these antisubjective forces whose steam has built for one hundred years. In 1912, F. T. Marinetti argued the need to "Remplacer la psychologie de l'homme par l'obsession lyrique de la matière," to replace human psychology with the lyric obsession with matter.[11] It was too early to say so, since the science of psychology was just getting started, millions were fascinated by it, surrealism was just around the corner, and decades of personal poetry lay ahead—*after* all of which reality would catch up with Marinetti's words.

How, in a post-Kantian, post-Wittgensteinian world, do data manage to exist without gloss, without interpretation? Perhaps because they do not. I began by pointing up the difference between an engaged use of found materials—especially "official" discourse, emanating from agencies, governments, and committees—in order to contrast those strategies with the paradoxically flamboyant (for a result so deliberately staid) practice of an impresario such as Kenneth Goldsmith. I have suggested that just as there is no view from nowhere, there is no transcription without transference, without perspective, and without intervention. There is no "hands off."

Finally, if a repudiation of the Subject and an antihermeneutic intellectual environment really characterize our time, how do we account for engagement? The likely answer is that engagement increasingly works through that ethos, and it is precisely that ethos that shapes the new poetry and accounts for its interest and peculiarity. The poetry of found materials finds its voice through the other. (The real insight of "anti" subjectivity remains Rimbaud's "je est un autre.") There are perhaps too many reasons for the renewed and expanded turn to found materials to list here, but they certainly include the following: lack of belief in the validity of one's own discourse; the sense indeed that there is no "one's own" discourse; the reign of irony, the national distaste for sentiment and affect, and thus the discrediting of "naive" first-person expression; and finally the poet's sense that other discourses—especially the alien, commodified, or official discourses I have highlighted here—are intrinsically promising and provocative. Through this ethos, then, not in spite of it, these poets—whether interventionist like Hillman, Kumin, Donnelley, or Brouwer, or doctrinally "hands off" like Goldsmith—are finding ways to engage contemporary life. The practice of working through received discourse, and changing it in the process—like the paradigm of Cage's writing through *Finnegans Wake* in the 1970s—gives the work its interest, its credibility, and its potential for discovery and change.

Notes

1. See Rubinstein for many more examples.
2. In *Unoriginal Genius*, Marjorie Perloff traces the long history of this repudiation, from the early twentieth-century futurist admiration of machines to Kenneth Gold-

smith's recent references to conceptual poetry's "self and ego effacing tactics" ("Conceptual Poetics").

3. The visionary poetics Hillman describes was not alien to the modernists, especially that aspect of vision which entails crossing material boundaries, "to allow you to be several places at once." Consider the opening of Pound's Canto 81, which moves from Greece to Spain to China in four lines; or Frank O'Hara's "The Day Lady Died," meandering from Paris to Ghana to Manhattan; or Langston Hughes's "The Negro Speaks of Rivers," which visits rivers from Asia to Africa to the Americas. Jahan Ramazani discusses these examples in "Traveling Poetry."

4. Regarding the Warhol-Cage comparison, Goldsmith ignores the ironic relish in Warhol's soup cans, Maos, and Marilyns, and particularly Warhol's admiration of the commodified, the discovery of possibility in the reframing of what most perceived to be kitsch. Warhol's was not an oppositional irony, but there was a distance, and a choice. The can in the painting was never the can in the advertisement, much less the can in the supermarket.

5. The autopsy report was presented as a poem titled "The Body of Michael Brown," and it produced a great deal of reaction. See the coda to the chapter by Bob Pereleman, "Delivering Difficult News," in the present volume.

6. The organizing principle of *No. 111* is that every item has to end with the sound or the letters "er." The first item is one syllable, the second two syllables, and so on. The book ends with the entire text of D. H. Lawrence's story "The Rocking Horse Winner," which Goldsmith insists he has never read, since reading for content, rather than for the formal principle—the fact that the story ends with an "er" sound—would be to violate the principle of the project.

7. This passage appears as a response to comments on Goldsmith's 2008 "Conceptual Poetics" essay by the late poet Reginald Shepherd.

8. "With these two books, I wanted to show how the identical technique of not writing could produce two entirely different effects. So, in conceptual writing, it's the choices we make beforehand—the machine we construct—which determines the outcome of the writing we produce" ("Statement" 220).

9. Regarding Goldsmith's appearance on the *Colbert Report*, see Bob Perelman's "Delivering Difficult News" in the present volume.

10. Robert Archambeau suggests that as with Warhol, Goldsmith's medium is the career rather than the work of art. "Goldsmith might be on the cusp of making the creation of a career, rather than the creation of texts, his main art form." Moreover, the *idea* of Goldsmith is necessary; it would certainly have been necessary to invent him.

11. Quoted in Perloff's *Unoriginal Genius*. "For psychology, Marinetti insisted, we must substitute *matter*, specifically such categories as noise, weight, and smell" (54).

Works Cited

Abish, Walter. *99: The New Meaning*. Providence: Burning Deck, 1990. Print.

Archambeau, Robert. "Kenneth Goldsmith, or the Art of Being Talked About." *Samizdat Blog*, April 9, 2011. Web. 10 March 2015.

Armantrout, Rae. *Collected Prose*. San Diego: Singing Horse P, 2007. Print.

Armantrout, Rae. "Statement." Keniston and Gray. 205–6.

Ashbery, John. "The Dong with the Luminous Nose." *Notes from the Air: Selected Later Poems*. New York: HarperCollins, 2007. 226–27. Print.

Ashbery, John. *Flow Chart*. New York: Knopf, 1991. Print.

Ashbery, John. "They." *Planisphere*. New York: Ecco P, 2010. Print.

Barthes, Roland. "The Death of the Author." *The Rustle of Language*. Trans. Richard Howard. Berkeley: U of California P, 1989. 49–55. Print.

Bernstein, Charles. "Emotions of Normal People." *Dark City*. Los Angeles: Sun and Moon, 1994. 35–36. Print.

Bidart, Frank. *Watching the Spring Festival*. New York: Farrar, Straus and Giroux, 2008. Print.

Brouwer, Joel. "Last Lines from the Reports of the Investigative Committees." Keniston and Gray. 32–34.

Brouwer, Joel. "Statement: The Clean-up Crews: La Vérité, L'Âpres Vérité." Keniston and Gray. 212–13.

Chiasson, Dan. "American Snipper." *New Yorker*, June 1, 2015. 73–74. Print.

Coolidge, Clark. *Smithsonian Depositions*. New York: Vehicle, 1980. Print.

Donnelly, Timothy. "Dream of Arabian Hillbillies." Keniston and Gray. 38–40.

Donnelly, Timothy. "Statement." Keniston and Gray. 213–15.

Goldsmith, Kenneth. "A1 from *The Day*." Keniston and Gray. 54–61.

Goldsmith, Kenneth. "Being Boring." *American Poets in the 21st Century: The New Poetics*. Ed. Claudia Rankine and Lisa Sewell. Middletown, CT: Wesleyan UP, 2007. 361–66. Print.

Goldsmith, Kenneth. "Conceptual Poetics." *Harriet: A Poetry Blog*. Poetry Foundation, June 6, 2008. Web. February 20, 2014.

Goldsmith, Kenneth. "Statement: Politics." Keniston and Gray. 219–20.

Hillman, Brenda. "In a Senate Armed Services Hearing." Keniston and Gray. 102–4.

Hillman, Brenda. "Reportorial Poetry." Keniston and Gray. 102–4.

Hillman, Brenda. "Statement: Seed Materials." Keniston and Gray. 226–28.

Hutcheon, Linda. *The Politics of Postmodernism*. New York: Routledge, 2002. Print.

Keniston, Ann, and Jeffrey Gray, eds. *The New American Poetry of Engagement: A 21st Century Anthology*. Jefferson, NC: McFarland, 2012. Print.

Laruelle, François. *Principles of Non-philosophy*. Trans. Nicola Rubsczk and Anthony Paul Smith. London: Bloomsbury, 2013. Print.

Lowell, Robert. "Eye and Tooth." *For the Union Dead*. Farrar, Straus and Giroux: New York, 1960. 18–19. Print.

Meillasoux, Quentin. *After Finitude: An Essay on the Necessity of Contingency*. London: Bloomsbury, 2008. Print.

Perloff, Marjorie. "Barthes, Ashbery, and the Zero Degree of Genre." *Poetic License: Essays on Modernist and Postmodernist Lyric*. Evanston, IL: Northwestern UP, 1990. 267–96. Print.

Perloff, Marjorie. "A Conversation with Kenneth Goldsmith." *Jacket 2*, February 2003. Web. 20 March 2015.

Perloff, Marjorie. *Unoriginal Genius: Poetry by Other Means in the New Century*. Chicago: U Chicago P, 2012. Print.

Pound, Ezra. "Canto LXXXI." *Selected Poems of Ezra Pound*. New York: New Directions, 1957. 172–75. Print.

Ramazani, Jahan. "Traveling Poetry." *MLQ* 68.2 (June 2007): 281–303. Print.

Rappaport, Herman. "The Work of Art as Reality Principle." Lecture. Modern Language Association, Boston. 2012.

Rubinstein, Raphael. "Gathered, Not Made: A Brief History of Appropriative Writing." *American Poetry Review*, March–April 1999. Reprinted on UbuWeb. Web. 4 January 2014.

Ruppersberg, Allen. *The Picture of Dorian Gray*. Painting. 1974. Museum of Modern Art, New York City. 11 June–28 September, 2014. http://www.moma.org/collection// browse_results.php?object_id=165595. Web. 15 July 2015.

Scully, James. *Line Break: Poetry as Social Practice*. Willimantic, CT: Curbstone, 2002. Print.

Spahr, Juliana. "Contemporary U.S. Poetry and its Nationalisms." *Contemporary Literature* 52.4 (Winter 2011): 684–715. Print.

St. John, David, and Cole Swensen, eds. *American Hybrid: A Norton Anthology of New Poetry*. New York: Norton, 2009. Print.

von Hallberg, Robert. "Poets and the People: Reflections on Solidarity during Wartime." *Boston Review*, September 1, 2008. Web. 20 April 2015.

Weinberger, Eliot. "In Conversation with Kent Johnson." *Jacket*, March 16, 2002. Web. 20 July 2014.

SIX

Delivering Difficult News

Bob Perelman

Stephen Colbert [at his main desk]: Welcome back, everybody. My guest to-night has a new book called *Seven American Deaths and Disasters*. Hey! Seven's my lucky number! Please welcome Kenneth Goldsmith.

This is the beginning of a transcription I made in July 2014 of an Internet clip of Kenneth Goldsmith appearing on *The Colbert Report*. The firestorm surrounding Goldsmith's performance of "The Body of Michael Brown" in 2015 casts an unavoidably ironic light on what follows here, and I supply a brief coda reflecting on this.

The six-minute conversation, originally broadcast on July 23, 2013, contains a number of incommensurate situations: conceptual poet who skewers authenticity meets mainstream broadcaster with his own trickster agenda; avant-garde transgressor-poet appears on mainstream talk show to hawk his new book; talk-show comedian maneuvers avant-garde transgressor into asserting a Wordsworthian poetics of speech as well as the moral imperative of poetic witness; the rhythms of public entertainment-talk are forced to share airtime with the strikingly distinct rhythms of poetry. These are compressed descriptions of what I trust will become manifest via my transcript and comments. Ultimately, I'm suggesting we see Goldsmith and Colbert as enacting a comic, serious debate on how art can best face the glare of the present.

My transcript, in boldface, is in part documentary: this is what Goldsmith and Colbert said to one another, with pauses, half-words, and some cross-talk omitted. But verbal transcription can't catch the assertions and transactions that take place via the tones and microrhythms of conversation and via costume, posture, and gesture, though to a close observer these things say at least as much as the explicit words. Here, my bracketed additions, also in boldface, will be an attempt to say what the conversation looks like and sounds like, and what it feels like is happening.

Fig. 4. Kenneth Goldsmith being interviewed by Stephen Colbert on *The Colbert Report* on July 23, 2013

To the Internet-enabled reader, and assuming that the link is live, the appeal is to corroboration—at this moment doesn't it sound like Goldsmith is trying to change the agenda? and that here Colbert has stopped speaking in persona? For those without access to the clip, the following is meant as a script with stage directions. It is realist to an extent—"based on a true story," as they say—but at the same time it is an investigative allegory of poetics, in the form of a masque with simplified figures: KG (Poet) and C (Broadcaster). I should emphasize that KG and C refer only to the on-screen protagonists of the six-minute conversation; they are to be distinguished from the off-screen persons "Kenneth Goldsmith" and "Stephen Colbert." The readers of this script are invited to activate their mental theater and watch poetry in action.

I will be interrupting the script, turning off the boldface to offer what I'll call comps. In the real estate world a comp indicates a comparison where there's at least one element in common, even if much else is quite different. In the case of this script, ultimately there are no good comps—Goldsmith appearing on *Colbert* is a one-of-a-kind situation—but as an instance of mainstream-media-asking-scandalous-artist-for-an-explanation, their conversation can be comped to Mike Wallace grilling William Carlos Williams in Book 5 of *Paterson*. And Williams as a documentary poet (e.g., the Marcia Nardi letters in Books 1 and 2) is an obvious comp to Goldsmith, though a more frequent comp is the Charles Reznikoff of *Testimony*. But then again the breadth of Goldsmith's public reach (from *Colbert* to the White House) suggests the Gertrude Stein of the 1930s as a better comp than either Williams or Reznikoff.

As is already evident, my comps are interruptive, and often quite speculative. It's good to remember that while these comps come from my stopping the flow of the script and comparing things, the speakers had to be continuously performative. The boldface of the script is a reminder of how rigorously the conversation had to enact the present tense: it was six-plus minutes of airtime on *Colbert* where the bar was set high: no wasted half-seconds, things must be presented clearly and at the same time made comic. Consider how briskly C's opening salvo, quoted above, carries out both tasks. In between naming guest and topic the manic Colbert-persona pops up and makes itself perfectly audible: [Topic] "My guest tonight has a new book called *Seven American Deaths and Disasters*. [Manic C interruption] Hey! Seven's my lucky number! [Conclusion of intro] Please welcome Kenneth Goldsmith [guest]."

[C leaves main desk and runs across stage to the interview desk; as the camera follows him, it pans across KG sitting at one side of the desk. We see KG wearing a straw hat, solid pink blazer, pink-striped shirt, striped bowtie; his legs are crossed, revealing, above the black-and-white saddle shoes, one red and one green sock. After the initial pan, a second shot settles on C and KG seated across from one another, and we see KG only from the waist up.]

    C: **Hey, Mr. Goldsmith, thank you for coming on.**
    KG: **So glad to be here.**
    C [referencing KG's waist-up outfit]: **Later we can play some *Dixieland jazz*, or churn some fresh *buttermilk ice cream*. . .**

KG's whole ensemble down to the clashing socks signals an avant-garde/bohemian lineage (Mayakovsky's yellow shirt; Pound's green velvet pants), but its initial presentation flashes by quickly; the second shot, where we see KG with blazer, shirt, and bowtie as the sole costuming code, reinforces C's sudden recasting of KG in a parodically retro-Americana frame. Thus the interview begins at an absurd slant—absurd for KG, that is; buttermilk ice cream and Dixieland jazz are perfect props for C's hyperconservative persona. It is a powerful comic maneuver: C begins by misidentifying KG, addressing him not as a major new poetry-provocateur—which is of course why he's on the show—but as an example of Americana-shtick, like some character in *The Music Man* who has wandered onto the wrong stage set.

    KG: **[smiling at C's gesture] . . . or recite some poetry.**

KG deflects C's parodic frame and reasserts his position as a poet who is here to talk about his new book. By completing C's sentence with a third item of his own (Dixieland, buttermilk, poetry), KG enters C's frame on his own terms, equating poetic recitation to fresh buttermilk as an equally imaginary consolation.

> C: **We could. We could do that now.**
> KG: **We could do it together.**
> C: **Whaddaya got? Whaddaya want to start with?**
> KG: **Oh . . . how about "Oh! Susanna"?**

When I first watched the clip this seemed very much like a rehearsed turn in the conversation and that a plan to recite Stephen Foster had been agreed on backstage. But Goldsmith, when I asked him, said it was spontaneous. In any event, the choice of "Oh! Susanna" as the poetry to recite is apt both for C's parodic persona and for Goldsmith's poetic position, even though it means opposite things for the two. (Note my switch to Goldsmith; there will be more to follow about his difference from the on-screen KG.)

Goldsmith is an artist with a highly visible, charged position that he has been presenting over the last two decades. As a leading exponent of conceptual poetry, and thus of provocation and a narrative of avant-garde poetic advance, he has repeatedly been concerned to mark his separateness from many nonnew poetic traits: creativity, inspiration, and the recognizably "poetic." A corny old ditty like "Oh! Susanna" makes a good stand-in for the naive assertions of presence that conceptual poetry defines itself against.

For C's persona, on the other hand, what better opportunity to enunciate his parodic hyperconservatism than "Oh! Susanna": an antebellum song obliquely celebrating plantation life and making something spritely and amusing out of slavery.

> C: **[Declaiming, emphasizing each syllable] Oh, don't you [KG points his index finger at C in approval, begins to recite along with C] cry for me [audience laughs with recognition] / I come from Alabama / With a banjo on my knee.**
> KG: **Absolutely. It's a . . . [This is a gambit to return to the speech rhythms of conversation]**
> C: **[overriding KG's gambit, continuing the poetic declamation] I had myself a dream last night, / when everything was still [KG stops trying to recite; rapidly, he swivels sideways to C, crossing his legs and resting a hand against his head, the ensemble of gestures polite but signaling a half-patient impatience, waiting out C's recitation]. / I dreamed**

> that I saw my girl Susanne, / she was comin' round the hill. / Oh the buckwheat cake was in her mouth, / a tear was in her eye. / I said that I come from Dixieland, / Susanna don't you cry. [Audience whoops and cheers as the second stanza is completed.]
>
> KG: You know it [i.e., you know this obscure other stanza; KG points his index at C, laughs].

Here, it's as if C becomes "the poet" in some old-fashioned sense. After the initial stanza KG seems to have heard enough. (And who could blame him? If you get invited onto *The Colbert Report* to discuss your new book you want to discuss it, not spend the finite seconds of airtime reciting Stephen Foster.) C, on the other hand, seems tinged with the oracular, fulfilling a ritual obligation to recite.

When I first watched the clip, I found the second stanza very odd (crying while holding a pancake in your mouth?); if KG didn't know it, I certainly didn't and thought that C must be making it up without a break in the rhythm, which would have been an impressive bardic feat. But to my surprise, looking it up later, the words are Foster's.

> C: You are the poet laureate of the Museum of Modern Art. You've got ten books of poetry; you teach writing at the University of Pennsylvania, and you've got a new book called . . . *Seven American Deaths and Disasters*. [Holds up book.] Did you write this?
>
> KG: Absolutely not. I never write any of my books. [Audience laughs.]
>
> C: You didn't actually write this, you . . . *collected* it?
>
> KG: I *transcribed* it. [Laughter.]

KG presents himself as provocateur, instigator of new turns in poetic history: conventional poetry is *written* by conventionally inspired poets; my work is premised on breaking these expectations: I didn't *write* this book, I *transcribed* it.

But six minutes of airtime doesn't allow for the presentation of the long-range complexities of Goldsmith's work: the acts of high art *impossibilitas*; uncreative writing; the indifference to content; the commitment to avant-garde provocation and excitement; the productively unstable position between the art world and the scene of innovative poetry—there is no time to mention any of this.

Provocation; unreadability: "You really don't need to read my books to get the idea of what they're like; you just need to know the general concept" ("Being").

Provocation/excitement: *Day*—where Goldsmith retyped the September 1, 2000, issue of the *New York Times* onto nine hundred pages of uniform type size—is, for most readers, unreadable. But for the writer (and the writerly reader) it's a portal to avant-garde excitement. Goldsmith describes the writing process: "If it could be considered text, I had to have it. Even if there was, say, an ad for a car, I took a magnifying glass and grabbed the text off the license plate. . . . [I]t was the most fascinating writing process I've ever experienced" ("Being"). Outraging the staid reader and exciting the writerly mind: they aren't always two sides of the same coin, but often enough they are.

Content as a matter of indifference: "Most of us spend hours each day shifting content into different containers. Some of us call this writing" ("Being"). *Sports*, where Goldsmith transcribes a broadcast of the Boston Red Sox playing the New York Yankees, is a good example of poetically indifferent content. One comp here would be Mallarmé's call for a book about nothing. The anthology *Against Expression* that Goldsmith coedited with Craig Dworkin begins with a related gesture, Mallarmé's "falsified writings on fashion."

Differing histories of the art world and the innovative poetry world. In the (visual) art world, avant-garde scandal is pretty much a lost art; but imported into poetry it still has legs: "Art has long ceased to shock. . . . [T]he poetry world [is] so conservative, that we can still get people upset. . . . [Y]ou can still have a bit of a scandal" ("Against").

None of this is shown on-screen. The six minutes only allow for the KG we see in front of us, discussing this one book.

> C: **Because this book itself is actually transcriptions of real-time reporting of deaths and disasters, as they happened in the United States.**
>
> KG: **Absolutely.**
>
> C: **You start with JFK . . .**
>
> KG: **Absolutely.**
>
> C: **. . . and it's a little radio station in Dallas. [Looks down at the page in question.]**
>
> KG: **KLIF.**
>
> C: **KLIF, that's Dallas's news leader. And they are . . . it's just a morning in 1963 and they are talking about, Buy Hamm's beer, and you're going to want a nice turkey this Thanksgiving because we're talking November 22 here, and slowly it dawns on this guy that this little shooting downtown turned into one of our greatest national tragedies. Why did you want us to hear every word of this?**

The off-screen Goldsmith could have supplied a provocative answer: you *don't* need to hear *any* of it, the particular words don't matter, you just have to know the idea of the piece. But the onscreen KG says something quite different.

KG: Well because radio sounded so *different* back then than it does now. And that's what happens throughout the book: there are different eras in the last fifty years and every transcription has the mark of its own era on it. So this is a beautiful naive fantasy time that is punctuated by an assassination, or a shooting at that point, of a president. And it shatters the entire illusion of pre-Thanksgiving holidays.

Neither KG nor C is indifferent to the content of *Seven*; far from it. The unconsciously historical November 22, 1963, is the place where before and after meet, where the naive totality—"Hamm's beer and a nice turkey," in C's image, and "beautiful naive fantasy time," in KG's—is shattered by death and disaster.

KG: And so these guys that are broadcasting this are not prepared in any way for this to happen. And suddenly they are improvising; they are riding by the seat of their pants and they're making it up as they go along. And this happens again and again and again. The World Trade Center chapter of the book is remarkable in this way because these guys are a.m. morning shock jocks guys, who go into work that day figuring they're going to do their shtick and then a plane goes into a building. They're stuck in the studio narrating something that they have no idea about. And this is incredible, how they have to make it up as they go along. What's amazing to me is that there have been hundreds of books written about 9/11 and to my knowledge nobody went to listen to the way those events were described.

C: Maybe they listened to it, but then [slightly dropping his persona], they did additional work. [Audience laughs.]

KG: Well, that work . . . But, you see, artists are dumb.

C: Artists are dumb?

KG: Artists are dumb. We do things that you shouldn't do. What I'm doing is too *easy* for an investigative reporter to do. And by doing something that is *that* simple, we're uncovering something that no one else has actually ever thought of: the poetic quality of what was unfurling linguistically at that moment.

One comp for "the poetic quality of what was unfurling linguistically at that moment" would be Keats's "If poetry comes not as naturally as the leaves to a tree it had better not come at all." Clearly, KG is departing radically from Goldsmith's Duchampian position where, just as art shouldn't be retinal, texts shouldn't be read. In contrast, here KG focuses on how interesting *Seven*'s language is. The claim is that unaltered transcription, rather than a pro-

vocative aspect of uncreative writing, is a tool for displaying the natural elo-
quence of crisis-charged emergent popular language.

Perhaps KG's answer is so different from the *impossibilitas* of Goldsmith's
prior projects because *Seven American Deaths and Disasters* is itself fundamen-
tally different, containing seven short pieces that are quite readable—in fact,
engrossing.

In my initial compressed description I referred to KG proposing a Word-
sworthian poetics, celebrating the power of everyday speech. But that comp
only stretches so far: Wordsworth celebrated the long-lasting certainties of
an unruffled rural language ("the real language of men") while deploring
the daily shocks of news that bombarded urban centers: "For a multitude
of causes . . . are now acting . . . to blunt the discriminating powers of the
mind . . . reduc[ing] it to an almost savage torpor. . . . [T]hese causes [in-
clude] the great national events which are daily taking place, and the increas-
ing accumulation of men in cities, where the uniformity of their occupations
produces a craving for extraordinary incident which the rapid communication
of intelligence hourly gratifies." Long story short, Wordsworth loathes news.
KG, in contrast, is celebrating the real language of shocked broadcasters.

From this perspective, the deaths and disasters themselves have the qual-
ity of avant-garde breakthrough into a newly made present. Another comp for
KG's praise of *Seven*'s language would be Stein's "Composition as Explana-
tion." For Stein the opposition is stale routine versus the presentness of ge-
nius. Routine: "It [bad art; old-fashioned battle plans for World War I] is pre-
pared and to that degree it is like all academies it is not a thing made by being
made it is a thing prepared"; genius: "the few who make it as it is made." For
KG, the routine is the shock jocks who are "going to do their shtick"; in con-
trast, the genius of the present is "And suddenly they're improvising; they are
riding by the seat of their pants and they're making it up as they go along."

C: **You've got seven of these. It's the reporting on the death in real time
of JFK, RFK, John Lennon, the Columbine tragedy, September 11, the
Challenger disaster, and Michael Jackson's death. All these things,
these 7 different events, we know what's happening when we read
this. These people who are just livin' their lives, thinking it's an ordi-
nary day, don't know it's coming [out of persona here]. When I read
this I feel like I am some sort of time-traveling aesthete, who is com-
ing in to sample other people's shock and tragedy. I'm tasting their
disbelief and the way it's changing them forever. I'm tasting it while I
read it and it feels vampiric.**
[Slight pause.]
KG: Umm.

C: **Are you giving us a feast of other people's blood?**
[Audience and KG laugh briefly, thoughtfully.]

KG is here far from the Duchampian provocateur and instigator of the new. Goldsmith's work has been premised on indifference to content and to readerly identification. For a reader expecting to identify with what is written, Goldsmith has insisted on a basic displacement: I didn't *write* this, I *transcribed* it; this isn't poetry, you're not reading my eloquent thoughts and feelings, this is a transcript of the Red Sox playing the Yankees. Such displacements have been, up to now, the point of Goldsmith's work.

And C is far from his persona, which is built on a continuous dismissal of trauma (evoking it only to run roughshod over it: e.g., "*Seven American Deaths and Disasters* . . . Seven's my lucky number!"). Here, he has dropped the persona and is speaking earnestly of the vivid pain the book causes him. He finds this pain morally suspect: he's not joking when he calls *Seven* vampiric.

At this point, both KG and C are admitting that the trauma presented by *Seven American Deaths and Disasters* is all too real, and both are contemplating it.

KG: **These are the tragedies that mark our lives . . .**

KG counters C's charge of vampirism. I am not a time-traveling vampire ransacking the *past* for aesthetic pleasure: these disasters are part of our *present* condition.

C: **But must we go back to them? Why can't we just . . .**
KG: **We go back to them all the time. [Both voices are rising in pitch a bit, and the timbre and rhythm of exchange are more intense.]**
C: **. . . forget they happened, just forget they happened [dialing down the volume, fully back in persona], so we can move on to happy days again.**
KG **[not joining C's switch back to the conversational, still intense]: And then we have things like the Boston Marathon bombing, which could have made an eighth chapter on this book. They never go away.**

In fact, three months before this interview, Colbert had presented a quite eloquent, though still quite funny, response to the Boston Marathon bombing ("Boston Bombers").

C: **Of course they never go away so what's the point of going back to look at them? There's always going to be another one for us to experience.**

KG: Yeah, right. You know, why don't you write the next book of the next eight or nine of these that happen? This book can go on forever.

C: All right . . . [abruptly quite soft, acting out a faux-therapy mode]. You seem mad. [Pause; audience laughs at the quick switch.]

KG [still agitated]: I'm upset about it: we live in a . . .

C [continuing the faux-therapy voice, expanding his previous remark, softly ignoring what KG's saying]: You seem mad at my desire to not think about sad things. [Audience laughs.]

Again, we have C being "the poet," rhyming "mad" with "sad"—both negative words disavowed by C and applied to KG.

KG [still agitated]: You must think about sad things.

Rilke's "You must change your life" (181) is possible as a comp; but Pound's Hell Cantos are a better one.

Seven's JFK chapter has been described briefly on-air but no word of it has actually been read.[1] This can be explained by the six-minute time constraint, but it's also possible that C, who appears to have read *Seven* (at least some of it) and, as I say, seems to have been knocked out of persona by it, found the mentions of JFK too grossly real to read. The JFK that the KLIF broadcasters name is the real president, and it hurts to read about the actual assassination in such unfiltered form.

Pound's Hell Cantos are in this sense a comp. Lloyd George and Woodrow Wilson in Canto 14 are the prime minister and real president, and Pound's presentation is as gross as he can manage: ". . . . e and . . . . n, their wrists bound to the ankles, / Standing bare bum, / Feces smeared on their rumps, / wide eye on flat buttock, / Bush hanging for beard, Addressing crowds through their arse-holes" (Pound 61). But the Hell Cantos are cringe-worthy due to the childish violence of Pound's editorializing, and they foreshadow all too clearly his upcoming broadcast follies on Radio Rome, where his delusional pretensions to Dantescan powers of judgment are sadly obvious. "Poetry is news that stays news" may have been the slogan but, after World War I Pound registered contemporary events with paranoiac rigidity.

Another comp: "Wichita Vortex Sutra," where Ginsberg transcribes his own speech, peppered with occasional phrases from the car radio. The basic similarity to *Seven* is the transcription of real-time voices: both poets are showing how poetry can be expanded by use of new recording technologies. The basic difference is the politics. Ginsberg is denouncing LBJ and the Vietnam War as contemporary facts he wants to change; *Seven*, on the other hand, is inescapably elegiac. KG's "You must think about sad things" is proposing that his book and its method be considered a means of purified remembrance. Perhaps the better comp is "When Lilacs Last in the Dooryard Bloomed."

> C: **Why must you think about sad things?**
> KG: **Because sad things** *happen.*
> C [**in a rhythmic chant which makes the audience laugh**]: **"Put on a happy face."**

There's a familiar frame in which poetry is seen in a zero-sum position, defined against ordinary language use. Here, such a frame might show C as "winning," since his persona has reemerged, got the audience laughing, and knocked KG out of his initial position. But the conversation does not resolve into such a stand-off.

> KG: **People . . .**
> C [**arms outstretched, chopping hands marking the beat emphatically**]: oh susanna, oh don't you cry for me! [**KG, recognizing this as a conclusion, joins in at the end, reciting and hand-chopping somewhat tentatively. When the recitation is finished KG points his index finger at C in approving pleasure for the apt citation of the line; then C and KG clasp hands in rhythmic coordination.**]

Again, in the zero-sum frame this could be taken as the triumph of C's persona: let us forget the disasters and celebrate a transhistorical America; let the indestructible "Oh! Susanna" enunciate and erase slavery; let avant-garde hijinks yield to anodyne comedy.

But consider the physical actions of the moment: KG's immediately recognizing the wit of C's sudden citation of "Oh! Susanna," his joining in the recitation, his index finger pointing in appreciation at the end of the line; then KG and C reaching forward and clasping hands in rhythmically entrained fashion to signal the conclusion of the interview. The wordless total of these actions suggests that a zero-sum reading is shortsighted: the moment can be seen as KG and C both affirming a place for poetry in the present world. Over the course of the interview, they have agreed that there are disasters (quasi-unmentionable as they are), and here both are buoyed by their mutual recognition of the aptness and power of the citation. They are agreeing that poetry is one answer we can make in the face of unceasing disaster.

But what are they agreeing on as poetry? Do we have to choose between Stephen Foster's "Oh! Susanna" and Kenneth Goldsmith's *Seven American Deaths and Disasters*?

No: it's not a matter of particular items. As a start, let's say it involves basic displacement. Here at the end of the interview, a line from "Oh! Susanna" has been wrenched from its antebellum associations. But such displacement is only blurrily comped by the N + 7 method:[2] it is not a matter of the appearance of the unexpected; rather, multiple appropriateness is the point. "Don't you cry for me" works as the end of the interview and then there's a larger application: it's a stoic anthem to be chanted in the midst of ongoing, traumatic history, something like: "Pessimism of the intellect; optimism of the will." How can we talk about the disastrous present? With a buckwheat cake in our consuming mouths and a tear in our networked eyes? Possibly; but it's not a static content that counts, but rather the mutual recognition that the words have moved in order to speak to the present moment. It's a poetry of the present, using whatever's around: in the old Greek sense, poetry as *kairos*, where all vocabulary, to work, must be opportune, mutually audible, mutually enacted. Goldsmith and Colbert's rhythmically entrained handshake is as central to the poetic moment as the words.

Two last comp questions. First, is Kenneth Goldsmith a comp for KG? Or does what KG says about *Seven*—and the fact of *Seven* itself—signal a large departure from his poetics of the prior two decades?

Second: is C a comp for KG? Is C a conceptual poet? If both are poets—in the wordless sense enacted by the handclasp that I have just tried to articulate—then does that mean they are both poets of displacement?

Throughout the interview, C has demonstrated his quickness with displacement (the buttermilk ice cream moment, for example). As we have seen, Colbert's persona uses displacement continuously. But in addition to displacement, Colbert has developed a method that's more powerful: embedding—a species of exaggerated agreement, as opposed to the estranging effect of displacement. Does C's (and Colbert's) use of embedding rather than displacement give C a wider political articulation than KG?

Ten years after the U.S. invasion of Iraq, *embedded* remains a poisonous word for leftists: the propaganda relayed as if it were news by reporters "embedded" with the military continues to emit toxic consequences. The standard comp is Judith Miller, front-page reporter for the *New York Times* in 2003. It was only because Miller was embedded that *Times* readers were able to read up-to-the-minute dispatches from the search for WMDs, spurious as we now know those searches and dispatches were.

However, in a redeployed sense, embedding is an apt word for much of what Colbert does. The results are the opposite of those of reporters like Miller: it is impossible to miss his critique of what his character pretends to be praising. Many of his effects can only be achieved from an embedded position.

Saying the following to President George W. Bush at the 2006 White

House Correspondents' Dinner: "No matter what happens to America, she will always rebound—with the most powerfully staged photo-ops in the world. . . . Over tax cuts, W.M.D. intelligence, the effect of global warming: we Americans didn't want to know, and you had the courtesy not to try and find out" ("Stephen Colbert Roasts Bush"). Running for president; creating a super PAC; almost persuading the South Carolina Republican Party to accept the $400,000 the super PAC had raised in exchange for renaming the primary "The Stephen Colbert Super PAC South Carolina Primary"—such statements have wide political reverberations.

Perhaps Kenneth Goldsmith sitting across from Stephen Colbert is not so much displacing as beginning to embed.

C: **Kenneth Goldsmith. The book is *Seven American Deaths and Disasters*. We'll be right back.**

★

Coda

I wrote this piece in 2014; one year later, the situation of Goldsmith and conceptual poetry is markedly different, sparked by the outrage over his reading "The Body of Michael Brown" at a poetry conference (and the related outrage at Vanessa Place tweeting *Gone With the Wind* accompanied by racist imagery). The controversy is taking place via digital media, which will rapidly outstrip and outflank the slow-to-emerge, monologic print medium I am using. What I write here is emphatically time-bound.

Goldsmith read the poem at a conference in March 2015. It was a mostly verbatim presentation of the autopsy report on the police shooting of Michael Brown, on August 9, 2014, by the Ferguson, Missouri, police during a confrontation after he stole some cigarettes from a convenience store. In one sense, Goldsmith was doing much the same thing he did in *Seven*, transcribing public words that describe a terrible event; however, how he went about fashioning the poem was significantly different, and its immediate reception and the ensuing consequences were very different.

Beginning during the reading itself and spreading out exponentially, there was an eruption of comment on social media condemning Goldsmith's appropriation. His response was various. He has defended the piece on poetic grounds: he is a conceptual poet and has been doing such things for years. But his poetic claims have not stilled the storm of protest; comment has ranged from disapproval of a thoughtlessly invasive appropriation to accusations of simple racism. It wasn't literary appropriation that sparked the rejection (transcribing some official's prose); the plane of discussion has shifted to his actions: he is a white avant-gardist with major publicity privileges swooping in to a scene of maximum trauma; it is poetic ambulance chasing. Meanwhile, Place's tweets have kept the flames of outrage stoked.

To my knowledge, Goldsmith has not apologized for the poem, but in response to the general agitation he did donate his conference fee to the Brown family and has taken the clip of the reading—and thus the poem itself—out of circulation.

At the moment I'm writing, the reading-and-disappearing of "The Body of Michael Brown" seems to mark a watershed in Goldsmith's work.

Before, his figure was that of heroic innovator, dandy, trickster. Oscar Wilde's hostility toward what mattered to ordinary people ("a little sincerity is a dangerous thing, and a great deal of it is absolutely fatal" [118]); Duchamp's paradox pieces (this snow shovel, and only this, is an utterly advanced work of art); Warhol's stance of indifference to meaning—these would be comps. Before, Goldsmith was a very successful innovator; his CV-for-TV is that of a quasi celebrity: poet laureate of MOMA, teaches at Penn, ten books, new book (and we can add in his appearance at the White House). Before, Goldsmith's mode was emphatically open. His website *UbuWeb* had for decades hosted links to hard-to-find avant-garde work that it made available without asking for permission—the militant assumption was that a free avant-garde cultural commons was a greater good than copyright.

Afterward, much is reversed. *Seven* was thoroughly public and widely publicized; "The Body of Michael Brown" has been removed from circulation. Goldsmith's joke/provocation that his pieces needn't be read is now literalized; the poem can't be read and only circulates in anecdotal details. Where conceptual poetry had flaunted indifference to content, now it is the technique of rigorous truth telling.

Goldsmith's statement on Facebook in defense of the poem mixes elements of these before-and-after situations. On the one hand he writes that "The Body of Michael Brown" was like his other conceptual work: "Many of you have heard me read from Seven American Deaths and Disasters. This reading was identical in tone and intention. This, in fact, could have been the eighth American death and disaster." The verbatim nature of the appropriation is emphasized: "I didn't add or alter a single word or sentiment that did not preexist in the original text, for to do so would be to go against my nearly three decades' practice of conceptual writing." But the purity of conceptual appropriation is not kept up: "I altered the text for poetic effect; I translated into plain English many obscure medical terms that would have stopped the flow of the text; I narrativized it in ways that made the text less didactic and more literary" ("Body").

This signals a profound change in stance. Content, rather than a matter of indifference, is now something that has to be communicated. The end of Goldsmith's Facebook statement is emphatic: "Perhaps people feel uncomfortable with my uncreative writing, but for me, this is the writing that is able to tell the truth in the strongest and clearest way possible."

On its face, this sounds like Reznikoff's procedure in *Testimony*: lightly editing court transcripts to ensure legibility. But when Goldsmith writes that he "narrativized" the report, his phrasing obscures a major change that has become an infuriating detail for many detractors. Instead of copying the autopsy report sentence by sentence, he moved one sentence, which described Brown's genitalia as "unremarkable," to the end.

I am not privy to Goldsmith's intentions here, but I can imagine this ending was meant as critique: reactionaries in the United States are obsessed by fear of black masculinity; the tacit moral of the concluding sentence might be that each of us is merely human. But such an interpretation, in addition to being thoroughly universalizing, requires ironclad faith in the power of critique, as if terrible truth needs painful form in order to be communicated adequately.

Goldsmith is receiving no such allowance of critique. "The Body of Michael Brown" may have been presented as art, but it is being received as a gesture in an ongoing crisis, like something someone says at a rally, with many impatiently listening. The artfulness of the poem dissolved, in its reception, into the content of what the person reciting the poem was saying.

The poem has been a public-relations disaster for Kenneth Goldsmith; and among poetic communities it has galvanized aesthetic vigilance and been the occasion for high-ratcheted aggression. The poem may have been drastically weak for the forces it was trying to make palpable; but in response some of the outraged voices are exercising a depressing vigilance on the border between who speaks and what gets said.

Goldsmith's work expresses a lineage. It is part of a sequence of radical innovation, and it is all art. Thus it presupposes access to public space.

At the moment, certainly, many disagree. Goldsmith may have been a time-traveling aesthete on *Colbert*, but both C and KG tacitly agreed that JFK was a monumental figure at a temporal distance, needing to be properly mourned. There was no time travel, however, for the immediate audience for Goldsmith's poem and for its subsequent detractors, and the abysses between immediate social spaces were too painfully present to transcend: no visas were being granted for travel from MOMA to Ferguson. "The Body of Michael Brown" was not an eighth American death and disaster, nor was it part of any innovative series. It was heard in the context of a long series of acts of violence against people of color in the United States, an ongoing, crowded series:

Trayvon Martin (February 2012); Walter Scott (April 2014); Eric Gardner (July 2014); Michael Brown (August 2014); Tamir Rice (November 2014); Freddie Grey (April 2015); the nine members of the Bible study group at Emanuel African Methodist Episcopal Church (June 2015).

Notes

1. Unless we count the name of the Dallas radio station: KLIF.
2. An experimental method from the French group Oulipo, where a word is replaced by another word seven items distant in the dictionary: e.g., "morning" becomes "moron." Automatized comedy/estrangement.

Works Cited

"Boston Bombers." *The Colbert Report.* Comedy Central, April 16, 2013. Web. 14 July 2015.

Dworkin, Craig, and Goldsmith, Kenneth, eds. *Against Expression: An Anthology of Conceptual Writing.* Evanston, IL: Northwestern UP, 2011. Print.

"Francis Collins." Colbert, Stephen. *The Colbert Report.* Comedy Central, 4 April 2013. Web. July 14, 2015.

Ginsberg, "Wichita Vortex Sutra." *Collected Poems, 1947–1980.* New York: Harper & Row, 1984. 394–411.

Goldsmith, Kenneth. "Against Expression: Kenneth Goldsmith in Conversation." *Poets.org.* Academy of American Poets, 2011. Web. 14 July 2015.

Goldsmith, Kenneth. "Being Boring." *American Poets in the 21st Century: The New Poetics.* Ed. Claudia Rankine and Lisa Sewell. Middletown, CT: Wesleyan UP, 2007. 361–66. Print.

Goldsmith, Kenneth. "The Body of Michael Brown." *Facebook,* 15 March 2015. Web. 14 July 2015. https://www.facebook.com/kenneth.goldsmith.739/posts/354492771403205.

Goldsmith, Kenneth. *Day.* Great Barrington: Figures, 2003. Print.

Goldsmith, Kenneth. "Interview with Stephen Colbert." *The Colbert Report.* Comedy Central, 23 July 2013. Television.

Goldsmith, Kenneth. "Kenneth Goldsmith Reads Poetry at White House Poetry Night." Online video clip. *YouTube,* 11 May 2011. Web. 14 July 2015.

Goldsmith, Kenneth. *Seven American Deaths and Disasters.* New York: Powerhouse Books, 2013. Print.

Goldsmith, Kenneth. *Sports.* Los Angles: Make Now P, 2008. Print.

Goldsmith, Kenneth. *Uncreative Writing: Managing Language in the Digital Age.* New York: Columbia UP, 2011. Print.

Keats, John. "Letter to John Taylor." *Critical Theory since Plato.* Ed. Hazard Adams and Leroy Searle. New York: Thomson Wadsworth, 2005. 536. Print.

"Kenneth Goldsmith." *The Colbert Report.* Comedy Central, 23 July 2013. Web. 14 July 2015.

McGrath, Charles. "How Many Stephen Colberts Are There?" *New York Times,* 4 January 2012. Web. 14 July 2015.

Pound, Ezra. *The Cantos*. New York: New Directions, 1996. Print.

Reznikoff, Charles. *Testimony*. Los Angeles: Black Sparrow P, 2015. Print.

Rilke, Rainier Maria. "Archaic Torso of Apollo. *Translations from the Poetry of Rainer Maria Rilke*. Trans. M. D. Herter Norton. New York: Norton, 1966. 180–81.

Stein, Gertrude. "Composition as Explanation." *Poetry Foundation*. Web. 18 July 2015.

"Stephen Colbert Roasts Bush at 2006 White House Correspondents Dinner." *Political Comedy*. YouTube, 28 April 2012. Web. 14 July 2015.

Whitman, Walt. "When Lilacs Last in the Dooryard Bloomed." *The Norton Anthology of Poetry*. 5th ed. Ed. Margaret Ferguson, Mary Jo Salter, and Jon Stallworthy. New York: Norton, 2005. 1078–85.

Wilde, Oscar. *The Wit and Wisdom of Oscar Wilde*. Ed. Ralph Keyes. 3rd ed. New York: Gramercy, 1999.

Williams, William Carlos. *Paterson*. New York: New Directions, 1992. Print.

Wordsworth, William. "Preface to Lyrical Ballads." *Critical Theory since Plato*. Ed. Hazard Adams and Leroy Searle. New York: Thomson Wadsworth, 2005. 482–92. Print.

PART THREE

REDEFINING IDENTITY

/ SEVEN /

Frank Bidart's Poetics of Engagement

Steven Gould Axelrod

"... the disaster of our circumstance ..."
—Frank Bidart, "Introduction"

Frank Bidart initially entered into poetic discourse in the guise of a metaconfessional poet. He has said that "the great model" for his early poems was "of course" Robert Lowell's *Life Studies*, but "rather than try to replicate *Life Studies*, I was engaged in an argument with it" (Bidart, *Western* 236–37). Although Bidart's early poems such as "Golden State" (1973), "The Book of the Body" (1977), and "Confessional" (1983) adopted Lowell's autobiographical focus, they swerved from the precursor by dwelling on the anguished inner life of the speaking subject. Lowell, who was Bidart's mentor and friend, had made his speaking subject into an early Emersonian "transparent eye-ball" (Emerson, *Nature* 10), though focusing on the density of the social world instead of Emerson's natural world. Lowell's "I" mainly communicated his grief and anxiety through portraits of others. In contrast, Bidart, like the later Emerson of "Experience," located density in the speaking subject himself. Bidart's speaker and Lowell's speaker both, in Bidart's phrase, "feel too much" (*Book* 26); but whereas Lowell's "I" implies such feelings through family recollections, Bidart's "I" explicitly details his affective excess. Those rare moments of direct psychic representation in *Life Studies*—for example, the Miltonic admission, "I myself am hell" (Lowell, *Poems* 192)—became the basis for Bidart's reconceptualization of the confessional project, in which the speaker fully explores his very similar recognition, "this was hell" (Bidart, *Golden* 50).

How did Bidart develop from these confessional origins to his later poetics of engagement? Let's begin by positing that it was not a 180-degree reversal but rather a change of a few degrees. Recall that Lowell and his cohort did not generate the "confessional" term. It was the scholar M. L. Rosenthal who first referred to "poetry as confession" (30), citing Lowell as the exemplar. Lowell distanced himself from the label without quite denying all of its implications.[1] Bidart similarly ironizes it: "It implies helpless outpouring, secrets whispered with an artlessness that is their badge of authenticity" (Lowell, *Poems* 997). Perhaps the term "intimist," with its resonances in the history of painting and fiction, might be a more appropriate rubric for a poetics of psychic and spatial interiors. But whatever name one uses, so-called confessional poetry has always included public associations. The poems avoid triviality and acquire significance by means of such resonances. The Miltonic framing of the most confessional moment in "Skunk Hour" is just one obvious example. Lowell's *Life Studies* poems comment sardonically on such public issues as white privilege and class privilege; Plath's *Ariel* poems indict patriarchy. Early Bidart poems such as "Golden State" and "Confessional" illuminate the politics of family, gender, sexuality, and economic status. "Another Life" (the last poem in *Golden State*) evokes dreamlike images of John Kennedy and Charles de Gaulle as a way to epitomize "all the raging desolations / which I had come to learn were my patrimony" (*Golden* 50). Those early images forecast the more explicit meditations on political figures, historical events, and moral issues in the three recent poems I am about to discuss.

In the current century Frank Bidart has directly addressed the sorts of public issues that were always implicit in his earlier work. He has permitted unanticipated events—such as 9/11, the Iraq War, and Obama's election—to enter his textual world, generating something akin to the "occasional" poems of Andrew Marvell and William Butler Yeats, both poets whom he studied with Lowell at Harvard. Bidart has called Marvell's "Horatian Ode upon Cromwell's Return from Ireland" possibly "the greatest political poem in English" ("Statement" 207). He similarly invoked Yeats's "Easter 1916" as an exemplary poem by "the greatest twentieth-century political poet in English" ("Statement" 207). Inspired by such poems, Bidart writes his own political poems to illuminate "the usually terrible process" that is at the heart of public issues. More specifically, his poems explore the notion that "the great enterprise that was America in the beginning leads us into bewilderment." It is, Bidart concludes, "a terrible story. My 'political' poems . . . are little shards of it" ("Statement" 207).

Bidart's occasional poems aren't poems he planned to write. The public sphere itself produced the poems' urgency, and can therefore claim some of their creative agency. "Curse" (2005), "To the Republic" (2008), and "Inauguration Day" (2013) interweave the political discourse of the day with literary language and with the private monologue one carries on with oneself. Perhaps the strangest and most interesting feature of Bidart's engagement with contemporary history is that it also entails an engagement with literary and cultural texts of the past. As he once remarked, "I want my poems to include lots of levels of language—it's the only way to even begin to embody the nature of things" (Rathmann and Allen 73). Interweaving multiple linguistic practices, these three poems diagnose our communal disorders, our shared disasters. They participate in the return to political involvement that marks so much of this century's creative writing thus far. They construct a destabilized space where differential discourses of psyche and commons collide and alter—where mighty opposites contend, and where the Furies they provoke cross borders that once ostensibly protected the *oikia* from the *polis*.[2]

Although historical chance threw up the occasions for these three poems, they all share a preoccupation with the word "dead." The word appears in the first line of each poem. The word suggests the specific style of the poet's way of seeing, the thing he tends to notice everywhere, Eliot's "skull beneath the skin"—or perhaps it is the hidden nature or "mystery" of our time (Bidart, "Statement" 207). We might want to consider these poems Bidart's "dead" trilogy. They include other elements that tie them together as well: each of them concerns a specifically dated historical event, and each embeds the event in an oneiric web of repetition and pastiche. We need not posit that their author intended them as a trilogy. We can think of them, rather, as a postmodern trilogy, one constructed not by a godlike creator of self-enclosed stylistic systems but by readers who are collaborating to discover contingent meanings in the texts and their contexts. We can make sense of these poems by seeing them as a trilogy, or perhaps as the first three in a longer series that communal events will intermittently precipitate. Considering them together highlights the similarities and differences among them in a way that brings us further insight (though also blindness). It may help us to ponder the interrelation in poetry between personal and public, chance and design, dreams and reality.

*

It was the shock of 9/11 that propelled Bidart into the political arena, inserting him squarely into what Hannah Arendt called the space of "merciless exposure" (35), a cathected site for this most introspective and self-critical of poets. Bidart reflects Arendt's thinking in numerous poems,[3] and her meditation on public and private realms in *The Human Condition* seems to condition his own approach to public poetry. Reflecting the excrucation of crossing not simply from individual existence to common world, but to common world at its most horrific, "Curse" is a poem as uncomfortable to read as it must have been to write. As Jeffrey Gray has rightly observed, "I can think of no contemporary poem that requires more caution than ["Curse"], and it may be several years too soon to read it at all" (268). That being said, let's examine it anyway:

Curse

May breath for a dead moment cease as jerking your

head upward you hear as if in slow motion floor

collapse evenly upon floor as one hundred and ten

floors descend upon you.

May what you have made descend upon you.
May the listening ears of your victims   their eyes   their

breath

enter you, and eat like acid

the bubble of rectitude that allowed you breath.

May their breath now, in eternity, be your breath.

Now, as you wished, you cannot for us
not be. May this be your single profit.

Of your rectitude at last disenthralled, you
seek the dead. Each time you enter them

they spit you out. The dead find you are not food.

Out of the great secret of morals, *the imagination to enter*
the skin of another, what I have made is a curse. (Star Dust 25–26)

The speaker of this poem imagines bestowing on the perpetrators of 9/11 precisely the moral quality their act indicates they lack: that is, empathy. He tells us that "the great secret of morals" is "*the imagination to enter / the skin of another.*" In this formulation Bidart revises Shelley, who wrote in his "Defence of Poetry": "the great secret of morals is Love; or a going out of our own nature, and an identification of ourselves with the beautiful which exists in thought, action or person, not our own" (682). Bidart has thus reinterpreted Shelley's concept of love to be, as he later explained, "sympathetic identification with others . . . imagination of what is experienced as the result of your act" (Keniston and Gray 207).

Empathy, of course, can be a curse to those who possess it. Whitman's speaker in "Song of Myself," stunned by his devastating ability to enter into the suffering of others, shouts to himself, "Enough! enough! enough! // I discover myself on the verge of a usual mistake" (230). Bidart's entire career has been marked by his variously gratifying and disturbing efforts to step into the skin of others, in such poems as "Golden State," "Herbert White," "The War of Vaclav Nijinsky," and "Ellen West." In "Curse" he uses the tactic as an imprecation against a specific group of ideological zealots—and by implication, and by connection to "Inauguration Day," an imprecation against all true believers who resort to what Arendt called the muteness of "sheer violence" (26).

Bidart's speaker curses the 9/11 conspirators in five different ways, each one introduced by the word "may." Whether used in a blessing or a curse, "may" signals an appeal to supernatural or imaginative powers to fulfill a wish, to make the broken straight. The five curses amount to five fantasies of the same thing—that the murderers imagine the awareness of the other, see through the other's "eyes." The poem charges the conspirators not only with the failure of empathy but also with its corollary, the inability to employ the language of fantasy. And it imagines a Dantesque punishment that fits "the nature of the act" (Keniston and Gray 207). Ejected from their "bubble," the murderers are to spend eternity within an empathic fantasy, perpetually seeking out victims who reject them. This is a chilling vision of public loneliness that strips the conspirators of their group identity and places them in some lower circle of Dante's hell.

The trancelike effect of this poem depends on its insistent repetitions. Unlike the redundancy within the conspirators' sealed bubble, the poem's verbal repetitions are repetitive rather than repetitious. They invite us into another frame of thought, a deeper one than we use in everyday consciousness. The poem in a sense is a sorrow song without the music, leading us away from empirical understanding and into mystery. We encounter a plethora of repetitions from the title to the very last word: Curse/curse; dead/dead; slow/mo; floor/floor/floors; descend/descend; made/made; enter/enter/*enter*; rectitude/rectitude. Most important are the anaphora of May/May/May/May/*May* and the recurrence of breath/breath/breath/*breath*/*breath*. The repetitions are complicated by the changes in typeface. As James Longenbach suggests, alternations between italic and roman type in Bidart's poems indicate "an interplay of voices," with the lines in italic sounding particularly "otherworldly."[4] This disorienting combination of repetition and difference plunges us into new ways of apprehending a familiar and archetypally painful public event.

"Curse" troubles the soul in at least two ways. The first is the poet's willingness to empathize with the 9/11 conspirators. As in "Herbert White," the poet places himself and his readers in a spot we presumably do not wish to be. By doing so, he problematizes the binary distinctions between self/other and innocence/guilt. Empathy inevitably carries some degree of sympathy along with it. We are forced not only to occupy the conspirators' subject positions but also to pity them. It is not a welcome fate, to be continually spat out by victims who do not forgive. It is not a happy prospect to be alone and hated. In challenging readers to imagine what that feels like, the poem forces readers to form some kind of bond with the objects of their revulsion. We ourselves must enter the murderers' skin in order to feel the punishment we imagine for them. Once there, perhaps we can acknowledge that some version of the murderers was in us all along, that the difference between "us" and "them," and between "innocent" and "guilty" desire, is thinner than we pretend.

A countervailing and yet even more disturbing aspect of the poem resides in its very language of curse. Like Sylvia Plath, ending "Daddy" with the curse, "you bastard" (*Poems* 224), Bidart's speaker finds himself employing a vocabulary of vituperation not entirely dissimilar to the spirit of the individuals it would deplore. This paradoxical response to Arendt's "sheer violence," in which the voice of opposition becomes uncannily aligned with the aura of the oppressor, wends its way backward in time to such texts as Milton's "On the Late Massacre in Piedmont," which also expresses a wish for vengeance within a format of prayer or curse. In his anger, Bidart's speaker has refashioned his empathy into a curse; and readers must confront their impulse to do the same.

However well designed, a curse is still a curse. The discomfiting question Bidart's poem asks is whether we are all cursed by the act of violence committed on September 11, 2001. Did the curse include the U.S. government's subsequent institution of a torture regime at Guantánamo, Abu Ghraib, and secret renditions around the globe (Goldsmith; Greenberg; Mayer; U.S. Department of Justice)? Did it include the violence of the Iraq War, founded on a misreading of 9/11, and resulting in the deaths of many times more than the original three thousand?[5] "Curse" is a poem of many divergent threads. Pull one, and the text begins to unravel, and the righteous certainties that the 9/11 event reflected and precipitated unravel along with it.

★

Bidart returned to issues of political violence several years later, in "To the Republic," a poem that splices the battle of Gettysburg in 1863 to contemporary American history. This poem again meditates the dangers of cognitive bubbles, and again uses the lenses of Dante and Marvell to do so. Marvell's representation of the English Civil War in "Horatian Ode upon Cromwell's Return from Ireland," which itself borrowed from Lucan's poetry of the Roman civil war, yields an ambiguous portrayal Cromwell, with lines that may be read either straightforwardly as praise or ironically as critique. (Bidart, like most scholars, reads them as critique.) "To the Republic" uses a nightmarish vision of the soldiers slaughtered at Gettysburg to interrogate the war politics of the George W. Bush era. We know that this is a timely poem because it's dated at the end, unlike any other poem in *Watching the Spring Festival*. It specifically addresses the year 2005:

To the Republic

I dreamt I saw a caravan of the dead
start out again from Gettysburg.

Close-packed upright in rows on railcar flat-
beds in the sun, they soon will stink.

Victor and vanquished shoved together, dirt
had bleached the blue and gray one color.

Risen again from Gettysburg, as if
the state were shelter crawled to through

blood, risen disconsolate that we
now ruin the great work of time,

they roll in outrage across America

You betray us is blazoned across each chest.
To each eye as they pass: *You betray us.*

Assaulted by the impotent dead, I say it's
their misfortune and none of my own.

I dreamt I saw a caravan of the dead
move on wheels touching rails without sound.

To each eye as they pass: *You betray us.* (*Watching* 40)

Like the other poems of the "dead" trilogy, "To the Republic" achieves part of its effect through repetition and allusion. Lowell described his practice in *Notebook 1967–68* thusly: "I have taken from many books, used the throwaway conversational inspirations of my friends, and much more that I idly spoke

to myself" (159). "To the Republic" masters and extends this method of bri-
colage, quoting from poems, books, and songs, juxtaposing historical times,
and alternating (as all three poems of the trilogy do) between roman and italic
fonts. The poem moves backward as it moves forward, losing and recovering
ground, recursive yet purposeful. Whereas "Curse" repeats single words, this
poem repeats sentences and phrases: "I dreamt I saw a caravan of the dead";
"To each eye as they pass"; and the italicized *You betray us.*" The sad music
of these internal repetitions counterpoints the poem's recurrent intertextual
echoes.

The speaker of "To the Republic" dreams he sees "a caravan of the dead"
proceeding from Gettysburg, a Civil War battle site where eight thousand
men died in three days of furious warfare. The dreamscape harkens back to
Dante's first sight of the dead soon after his dream vision commences in *The
Inferno* (Canto 3). He too sees a long "train" or "caravan" of the dead, their
faces streaming with blood, and he reflects (in a line famously echoed by Eliot
in *The Waste Land*): "I should never have believed death had undone so many"
(Dante 23; Eliot 39). The first verse of "To the Republic" also evokes a myriad
of war poems, including Charles Hamilton Sorley's Great War sonnet that be-
gins, "When you see millions of the mouthless dead / Across your dreams in
pale battalions go, / Say not soft things" (79).

Although the caravan in Bidart's poem seems to "start out again," it's
important to recall that no such caravan historically occurred, so this is not
a dream reenactment of an actual event. Perhaps the phrase implies a re-
enactment of Dante's caravan of the dead. Or perhaps it conflates the rot-
ting corpses covering the battlefield (an image made famous in Timothy
O'Sullivan's photograph, *A Harvest of Death*) with the train journey of Lincoln's
body from Washington to Springfield for burial, its route lined with mourn-
ers. In reality, the stinking bodies of dead soldiers were quickly buried in shal-
low, makeshift graves where they fell. Two months later the Union soldiers
were dug up and reburied in more fitting graves in a "Soldiers' National Cem-
etery" constructed on the battle site. Lincoln's Gettysburg Address concerned
only those soldiers who had given "their last full measure of devotion" so that
our "nation might live" (536)—not the Confederate soldiers who had died
in the cause of secession. Eight years later, in 1871, many of the Confederate
dead were disinterred and transported to Hollywood Cemetery in Richmond,
Virginia. Other remains were sent to other southern cemeteries or remained
unnoted in their shallow graves at Gettysburg (Blog of Gettysburg National
Military Park). So the idea of a caravan in which "victor and vanquished"
are "shoved together" is a reconciliation fantasy all the way through. Rather
than reproduce any empirical train ride, it revives the memory of several half-
forgotten poems, such as Henry Wadsworth Longfellow's defiant meditation

on death, "Victor and Vanquished" (351) and another Charles Hamilton Sorley sonnet, "Such, Such Is Death," which includes the line, "Victor and Vanquished are a-one in death" (78). The brutalism of "shoved" exposes the fragile corporeality of those poor victors and vanquished.

The corpses of "To the Republic" become figures of prosopopoeia as they rise to condemn their twenty-first-century inheritors, who now "ruin the great work of time." That phrase echoes Marvell's Cromwell ode, in which the regicidal leader is also said to "ruin the great work of time" (55). If, in Marvell's view, Cromwell destroyed what preceding generations had built, Bidart's Civil War dead silently accuse the present generation of doing likewise. Though silent, each risen soldier has emblazoned on his chest the words, "*You betray us*,"[6] a detail the poem emphasizes through italicization and repetition. Rolling across America on a surreal train, the soldiers implicitly protest dominant features of 2005 public life, including wars in Iraq and Afghanistan, a program of torture at various "black sites," continued racial inequities, and a forgetting of the lesson that war is hell.[7]

At several different points the dreamer seems to absorb the death language of other poets. He tells us that dirt and time have bleached the soldiers' blue and the gray uniforms to "one color," echoing Lowell's comment in "My Last Afternoon with Uncle Devereux Winslow" that the colorfully dressed uncle would soon blend to "one color" in death, and his image in "For the Union Dead" of black and white soldiers interred together (*Poems* 167, 377). The dreamer's reference to "the state" repeats its prior appearance in two precursory war poems: Randall Jarrell's "The Death of the Ball Turret Gunner" (*Poems* 144) and Robert Lowell's "Fall 1961" (*Poems* 329). Similarly, the dreamer's description of the "the impotent dead" echoes a phrase spoken by Odysseus in Ezra Pound's Canto 1 to refer to spectral figures of the battle-dead who assail him: "I sat to keep off the impetuous impotent dead" (*Cantos* 4). Such imported phrases disrupt the text. We no longer listen to one all-powerful verbal inventor or to one continuous flow of language but to disparate signifiers inserted by force into a new structure that both supplants and recalls the originals.

Moving on from his various poetic and historical sources, Bidart's speaker finds his final verbal shard in a traditional cowboy ballad called "Git Along, Little Dogies," first published in Carl Sandburg's *American Songbag* (1927) and subsequently recorded by the likes of Roy Rogers and the Kingston Trio. The dreamer's dismissive comment about the dead, "it's / their misfortune and none of my own," alludes to the song's refrain: "Whoopee ti yi yo, git along, little dogies / It's your misfortune and none of my own."[8] The dreamer wishes to disregard the dead, as if they were cattle; he wishes to shelter himself in the twilight of his privacy, hiding from what Arendt called "the much harsher light of the public realm" (51). He wishes to remove himself from the presence of others to such a degree that he fails to be fully real. Yet the accusation that he deflects, "*You betray us,*" haunts his awareness and closes his poem.

How, exactly, do we betray the past? By negating Whitman's idea that an "enemy" is as "divine as myself" (453)? By refuting Lincoln's affirmation that "these dead shall not have died in vain"? Almost as if to deepen the uncertainty, Bidart's poem "Race" begins: "*America is ours | to ruin but | not ours to dream*" (*Metaphysical* 51), a play on Jarrell's assertion that "America is full of ruins, the ruins of hopes" (*Poetry* 221). "To the Republic" obviously does not dream the conventional American dream. Nor, despite quoting from the Pledge of Allegiance in its title, does it express unquestioning loyalty to the flag or to the republic. Rather, it suggests disillusionment. If Bidart's "dead" poems do indeed compose a sequence of sorts, "To the Republic" marks little change in the bleakness of "Curse." Only the final poem of the trilogy offers a renewal of hope.

*

"Inauguration Day" contemplates the inauguration of Barack Obama as the forty-fourth president of the United States. To emphasize its connections to political journalism, the poem is time-marked January 20, 2009 (Inauguration Day), and it originally appeared on that date on the online news and culture site *Slate*. Only several years later did it more conventionally appear in non-electronic form, in *The Metaphysical Dog* (2013). Like "To the Republic," "Inauguration Day" is the only dated poem in its volume, another indication of its association with news, its aim to be "news that stays news" (Pound, *ABC* 29). Using Bidart's characteristic techniques of citation and metalepsis, the poem collocates a variety of precursory texts that reflect on American institutions, history, and anxieties. It also incorporates two dialogic voices: one italicized, recursive, and employing a first-person plural voice; the other, speaking in first-person singular, but inhabited by ghostly echoes from the past. By these means, the poem continues the somber meditations begun in Bidart's earlier political poems and, without in any sense providing closure, gives a sense of pressing forward into the "mystery" at the trilogy's "moral center" (Bidart, "Statement" 207).

Inauguration Day

(January 20, 2009)

Today, despite what is dead

staring out across America I see since
Lincoln gunmen

nursing fantasies of purity betrayed,
dreaming to restore
the glories of their blood and state

despite what is dead but lodged within us, hope

under the lustrous flooding moon
the White House is still
Whitman's White House, its
gorgeous front
full of reality, full of illusion

hope made wise by dread begins again (Metaphysical 50)

Initially one might be struck by the strange, compelling music of the verse—music discovered, so to speak, in the dirt of contemporary politics and in the dust of inherited culture. The italicized, communitarian voice proceeds haltingly toward the completion of its assertion: "*Today, despite what is dead || despite what is dead but lodged within us, hope || hope made wise by dread begins again.*" This voice, reminiscent to me of the inhibited "diseuse" struggling to speak in Theresa Cha's *Dictée* (3–5), strives to articulate a difficult sentence whose kernel might be read simply as "*hope begins again.*" After the gloom of "Curse" and "To the Republic," this kernel sentence might be read as a peripeteia. Yet that kernel misses the experience of the hesitations, subordinations, and reiterations, the Steinian logic of "telling it again and again" that governs the italicized utterance (Stein 200): "*despite what is dead || despite what is dead but lodged within us*" and "*hope || hope made wise by dread.*" Focusing on the kernel sentence alone would force us to miss the anaphora of despite/despite, the alliteration of despite/dead/dread, the syntactic ambiguity of "lodged within us," the rich rhymes of "dead" and "dead" and "hope" and "hope," and the distant, chilling rhyme of "dead" and "dread." The obsessive, incestuous repetitions of "despite," "dead," and "dread" ultimately yield to the liberating consonance of "begins again," slant-rhyming within itself through its *g* and n sounds that have nothing in common with previous phonemes. The auditory singularity of "begins again" emphasizes its semantic import of possible escape from the oppressive cycle of dread and death in which the national symbolic has been caught.

This is a poem centered on the word *despite*. Despite the anger and despair of "Curse" and "To the Republic," hope has refused to die. Despite the deaths incurred in wars, the persistence of hatred, and the drumbeat of gun violence that that haunts the domestic scene, hope revives. The italicized voice dialogues with the voice represented in roman font. This second voice speaks in five-line stanzas that contain their own music of internal rhyme and slant rhyme, assonance and consonance: I *see*/fantasies, fantasies/glories, restore/ glories, blood/flooding. The r's and l's of both cinquains are briefly interrupted by two lines of aspirate w's and h's linking together an iconic White House with an equally iconic Walt Whitman. Every phrase in these stanzas resonates: "gunmen / nursing fantasies of purity betrayed," the White House "full of reality, full of illusion." The plurisignation of "blood" evokes the bloodlines central to white supremacy—what the poem earlier calls "fantasies" of racial "purity"—while at the same time suggesting the regular recurrence of bloodletting that punctuates American history. The conjunction of "blood" with "state" reinforces this latter significance, and the words also subtly bring the poem into conversation with "To the Republic," where war victims crawl through "blood" in the mistaken belief that the "state" will shelter them.

The cinquains of "Inauguration Day" have an unsettling, oxymoronic rhythm of naming and immediately undermining: gunmen nursing, purity betrayed, glories of blood, a national symbology full of reality but also of illusion. Just when you think this rhythm is generally (though not always) up-down—elevation followed by descent ("full of reality, full of illusion")— you arrive at the poem's startling italicized conclusion: "*hope made wise*" (elevation) "*by dread*" (descent) "*begins again*" (a second, unexpected elevation, reminiscent of Williams, who in *Paterson* III yearns to "begin to begin again" [*Paterson* 140] and who in in "Spring and All" describes the way nature and the imagination "begin to awaken" [*Poems* 183]). Bidart's last italicized line carries the poem's (and the trilogy's) final twist, as in the couplet of a Shakespearean sonnet. The communal italicized voice asserts that we won't be ruled by dread any longer, however apposite dread may still be, and however much a deadness of spirit remains lodged within us. Concluding an often angry or despairing trio of poems, this voice hesitantly appropriates what Obama called "the audacity of hope."

As we have seen, "Inauguration Day," like the two poems preceding it, achieves some of its power through a complicated structure of sounds, voices, typefaces, and interior repetitions. It also achieves power by echoing its two predecessors in the trilogy and by alluding to a variety of other texts touching on the politics and ethics of nation. Official inauguration poems have recently become a tradition in Democratic administrations, beginning with Robert Frost in 1961 and stretching through James Dickey, Maya Angelou, Miller Williams, and Elizabeth Alexander to Richard Blanco in 2013. However valuable this new tradition may be, it inevitably bears the burden of propriety. "Inauguration Day" belongs to a different tradition of unofficial poems that speak more freely about American history and institutions. Bidart's poem emphasizes exactly what the official lyrics suppress: a fear of civic disorder and racist hierarchies, and a disillusionment with the United States itself. Bidart suggests these transgressive feelings by revising earlier texts by James Shirley, Walt Whitman, Edward Kennedy, Allen Ginsberg, and Robert Lowell.

Bidart has commented that the poem's language "isn't all mine": "I'm just the ringmaster of all this. . . . Speech about such a public event feels as if it has to be collective" (Bidart, email). His self-deprecatory figure of the "ringmaster" perhaps alludes to Yeats's "The Circus Animals' Desertion," in which the poet's figures of speech are paradoxically troped as circus animals— paradoxically, because the speaker has claimed the loss of the figurative ability. Yet, like Yeats, whom Bidart considers the greatest modern political poet, Bidart is more than a ringmaster, and his tropes are different from animals. As in "Curse" and "To the Republic," the poet has reengineered the words of his predecessors, producing a poem that both quotes and alludes, and in so doing swerves. It reads the precursory texts so as to fill in their gaps and make the words mean in a new way.

In the initial cinquain of "Inauguration Day," the assassins who seek to restore "the glories of their blood and state" have incorporated in twisted form the moral rhetoric of James Shirley (1596–1666), the English playwright and poet. Although Shirley's once-popular works are now generally forgotten, his poem "The Glories of Our Blood and State" (1659) lives on, particularly as the lyric to a hymn composed in 1891 by Charles Hubert Hastings Parry.[9] It is also cited in Robert Frost's 1960 *Paris Review* interview, in which Frost calls Shirley's poem "splendid" and approvingly quotes the first line (879). The initial quatrain of the poem and hymn are as follows:

> The glories of our blood and state
>> Are shadows, not substantial things;
> There is no armour against fate;
>> Death lays his icy hand on kings.

Shirley's text questions the substance of earthly "glories" when divorced from "the actions of the just," dismissing such seeming "glories" as mere "shadows." Yet the first line, read in isolation, has the opposite meaning. Bidart's poem, by separating out that initial verse, reconfigures it into an expression of white supremacist cognition. The cinquain implies that this kind of Christian extremism can lead to murder just as easily as can the Islamic militancy evoked in "Curse," or indeed any equivalent variety of religious zealotry.

The second of Bidart's cinquains quotes from Walt Whitman's chapter "The White House by Moonlight" in *Specimen Days and Collect* (742), much as a blog might link to another blog. Whitman describes wandering around the president's house at night under the moonlight. Almost anticipating Bidart's presence and inviting him into his vision, Whitman calls it "the White House of *future* poems." He recalls "the gorgeous front . . . under the lustrous flooding moon, full of reality, full of illusion." In repurposing those words, Bidart omits surrounding passages of lyrical, dreamlike idealization: the white portico "spotless as snow," the building "so white, so marbly pure and dazzling, yet soft." Bidart's poem undermines Whitman's blissful mood by pruning such phrases, and he fosters an ambience of resistant witnessing by ending his quotation with Whitman's first and only truly critical phrase, "full of illusion."

Bidart's anxious tone captures something present but hidden in Whitman's text. Whitman concludes his rhapsodic description with a reference to the blue-uniformed sentries at the White House gates, "stopping you not at all, but eyeing you with sharp eyes, whichever way you move" (742). Here we see intimations of the surveillance state to come and of assassinations to come. *Specimen Days* goes on to contrast one of Lincoln's inaugural balls ("beautiful women, perfumes, the violins' sweetness") with a different scene Whitman witnessed days before while tending to the war wounded: "the amputation, the blue face, the groan, the glassy eye of the dying" (785). Later still, Whitman became transfixed with the figure of the fallen president, in his three major poems about Lincoln (especially "When Lilacs Last in the Dooryard Bloom'd") and in *Specimen Days and Collect* itself. Perpetually mourning "the greatest, best, most characteristic, artistic, moral personality" of his time (787), Whitman helped establish Lincoln's iconic status, which Obama has perpetuated. Bidart's observation that the White House is "still Whitman's" thus has many resonances. It suggests the physical continuity of the building's appearance; its continuing associations with Lincoln and assassination; and its metonymic relationship to the problematics of race and violence, and to the reality and illusions of American power.

In a related way, Bidart's poem also echoes and revises Senator Edward Kennedy's address at the 2008 Democratic National Convention in Denver. Kennedy's speech was widely thought to have legitimized a moral connection between Obama and the Kennedy legacy. In the speech, Kennedy referred explicitly to John F. Kennedy's promise that Americans would go to the moon, and he obliquely alluded to both John and Robert Kennedy by recalling his family's "happiest days" and "hardest days." Like Obama himself, he associated Obama's candidacy with hope: "For me this is a season of hope." He concluded by affirming, "The work begins anew. The hope rises again. And the dream lives on." In Bidart's reflection of this peroration, hope "begins again," but only "despite what is dead" and in a form "made wise by dread"—phrases that foreground Kennedy's own allusion to the "hardest days."

Finally, "Inauguration Day" invokes two of Bidart's immediate poetic precursors: Allen Ginsberg and Robert Lowell. Both of those poets invoked Whitman—Ginsberg most memorably in "A Supermarket in California," which portrays Whitman as his "father" and a "lonely old courage-teacher" (*Poems* 144), and Lowell in "Skunk Hour," which he claimed was based not on his own life but on a story Logan Pearsall Smith told "about Walt Whitman in his old age" (*Poems* 191–92, 1046, *Prose* 228). Because both Ginsberg and Lowell made a practice of citing predecessor texts, they seemed to be inviting their inheritor, Bidart, to do likewise. Bidart's phrase, "staring out across America," in addition to repeating two words from "To the Republic," also summons the Ginsberg of "Howl," "America," and "Wichita Vortex Sutra." One thinks, for example, of the poignant last line of "Howl," in which the poet imagines "the highway across America" and, incidentally, concludes by portraying himself "in the Western night" (*Poems* 141), the phrase Bidart chose as the title of both a poem and his 1990 collection, *In the Western Night*. Bidart's surreal line "Lincoln gunmen" also recalls Ginsberg's use of off-kilter noun compounds such as "hydrogen jukebox" (*Poems* 134). The nation that Bidart evokes in "Inauguration Day" resembles the one in Ginsberg's texts—a litter of dead machinery spotted with a few nodes of vitality. By 1992, however, a downcast Ginsberg was saying about American politics: "I don't think that hope is useful at all here" ("Politics"). Based on the election of the country's first African American president, and building on Kennedy's speech, Bidart's poem posits the reappearance of hope in the years since Ginsberg died.

Bidart's "Inauguration Day" is also hailed into being by Lowell's similarly titled "Inauguration Day: January 1953." Like Ginsberg during the Reagan and Bush administrations, Lowell saw little cause for hope in the Eisenhower era:

Cyclonic zero of the word,
God of our armies, who interred
Cold Harbor's blue immortals, Grant!
Horseman, your sword is in the groove!

Ice, ice. Our wheels no longer move.
Look, the fixed stars, all just alike
as lack-land atoms, split apart,
and the Republic summons Ike,
the mausoleum in her heart. (*Collected Poems* 117)

Bidart honors this earlier unofficial inauguration poem by borrowing part of its title; and he deepens its critique by putting it in circulation with other later Lowell tropes. Bidart's imagery of gunmen and blood condenses a history of what Lowell in "Waking Early Sunday Morning" called "fresh breakage, fresh promotions, chance / assassinations" (*Poems* 386). Bidart's imagery also evokes Lowell's depiction of race and violence in "For the Union Dead," *Benito Cereno*, "The March" 1 and 2, "Two Walls," and "For Robert Kennedy 1925–68."

Like Ginsberg, Lowell portrayed an American culture in which what is living vies with what is dead. Both precursors construct a binary that "Inauguration Day" initially replicates but ultimately destroys. In Bidart's lyric, the forces of destruction have the dream, whereas hope, when it finally does appear, has been complicated by its opposite, dread. Bidart's phrase, "*hope made wise by dread,*" recasts the final line of one of Lowell's sonnets about American violence, initially called "Violence" and later "Can a Plucked Bird Live?" Lowell's sonnet concludes, "Are there guns that will not kill the possessor? / Our raised hands—fear made wise by anger" (*Collected Poems* 545). Bidart modulates Lowell's bent epigram, "fear made wise by anger," into "hope made wise by dread," which is very nearly its opposite. For Lowell, writing during the Vietnam War and in the wake of the Kennedy and King assassinations, violence was "hellfire" (*Prose* 281). Like Ginsberg two decades later, he saw no help for this. Whereas Ginsberg blamed the political right, Lowell blamed human nature. Bidart, inheritor of these bleak imaginings, challenges their determinism, with help from Whitman and Williams.

Perhaps the difference between Eisenhower and Obama also had an effect. In Lowell's inaugural poem, "the Republic summons Ike." The bathetic descent from the capitalized "Republic" and the formal "summons" to the smiling stick-figure of "Ike," instilled in the national discourse through the campaign slogan, "I like Ike," tells you everything you need to know about Lowell's political pessimism. Obama's campaign, however, deliberately invited a renewal of hope, as epitomized in its slogan of "hope and change." Bidart's poem begins where Lowell's poem ends, Lowell's "mausoleum" prefiguring Bidart's "*despite what is dead.*" Bidart's poem changes Lowell's "fear" (in "Can a Plucked Bird Live?") to an existential "dread," and it crucially substitutes "hope" for Lowell's "anger," yielding a different balance—not the raised hands of defeat but the cautious rebirth of hope. "*Hope made wise by dread begins again.*" Is this a moment of wised-up hope, a vision of a new democratic vista? Or is it just another illusion, the start of another cycle of disasters? The poem leaves such questions open.

Bidart's trilogy of political poems is traditional in a postmodern way—a pastiche, a subversion, a cacophony of fonts and voices, a series made of fragments. The poems crisscross the boundary between appearance and hiddenness. They put dreams and reality into motion and watch them collide. The result is a subtly new kind of poetry, shaped by the intersection of public event with introspection, intertextuality, and language experiment. Bidart's poetry of engagement exposes the dark recesses of the private mind at the same time as it provides a critical witnessing of our disordered common world.

Notes

1. Although Lowell acknowledged that he based *Life Studies* on his personal "experience," he also admitted to having "invented facts" (Meyers 55, 94). He later revealed his distance from the term "confession" in a comment about another autobiographical sequence: "This is not my private lash, or confession, or a puritan's too literal pornographic honesty" (Lowell, *Notebook* 262).

2. That is, protected the privacy of the household from the agon of the city-state. See Arendt 22–78.

3. For example, Arendt's idea of *homo faber* (22), or man the creator or maker, appears in such Bidart poems as "Homo Faber" (*Desire* 12), "Advice to the Players" (*Star* 10–13), and "Lament for the Makers" (*Star* 22). It also appears at the end of "Curse": "What I have *made* is a curse" (*Star* 26). See also Bidart's interview with Adam Travis: "The whole book [*Star Dust*] is about making, how the desire to make is built into us, its necessities and pleasures and contradictions" (Travis 91).

4. Longenbach 70. Langdon Hammer makes a similar point (17–21).

5. There is no authoritative count of the casualties of the Iraq War and its aftermath. Wikipedia estimates that 4,491 Americans were killed in Iraq between 2003 and 2014 and that about 500,000 Iraqis died between 2003 and 2011. Iraq Body Count estimates the "total violent deaths" including combatants and civilians on both sides to be 195,000. Agence France Presse estimates that the death toll on both sides between 2003 and 2013 reached 500,000.

6. Possibly a metalepsis of the rhetoric of betrayal endemic in the Bush years. The era produced best-sellers titled *The Betrayal of America*, *The Bush Betrayal*, and *Imposter: How George W. Bush Bankrupted America and Betrayed the Reagan Legacy*, while MoveOn mocked a general with the satirical name General Betrayus and Rush Limbaugh mocked an antiwar senator with the satirical name Senator Betrayus.

7. The phrase "War is hell" originated in two speeches by Union Army general William Tecumseh Sherman (Lewis 34; Shapiro and Epstein 708). In 2003, the George W. Bush administration sought to downplay the pain of war by forbidding photographs of soldiers' coffins returning from Iraq to the Dover Air Force Base in the United States.

8. White 16. A "dogie" is a motherless calf.

9. First published as "Dirge" in James Shirley's verse drama *The Contention of Ajax and Ulysses* (1659), the poem has been reprinted as "Death the Leveler" but more frequently as "The Glories of Our Blood and State." The hymn to which it provides the lyric is also called "The Glories of Our Blood and State."

Works Cited

Arendt, Hannah. *The Human Condition.* Chicago: U Chicago P, 1958. Print.

Bidart, Frank. *The Book of the Body.* New York: Farrar, 1977. Print.

Bidart, Frank. *Desire.* New York: Farrar, 1997. Print.

Bidart, Frank. Email to Steven Gould Axelrod. January 19, 2009.

Bidart, Frank. *Golden State.* New York: Braziller, 1973. Print.

Bidart, Frank. *In the Western Night: Collected Poems 1965–90.* New York, Farrar, Straus and Giroux, 1990. Print.

Bidart, Frank. "Introduction." *New Film Stills.* By James Franco. New York: Pace, 2014. N.p. Print.

Bidart, Frank. *Metaphysical Dog.* New York: Farrar, 2013. Print.

Bidart, Frank. *The Sacrifice.* New York: Random, 1983. Print.

Bidart, Frank. *Star Dust.* New York: Farrar, Straus and Giroux, 2005. Print.

Bidart, Frank. "Statement." Keniston and Gray. 207. Print.

Bidart, Frank. *Watching the Spring Festival.* New York: Farrar, Straus and Giroux, 2008. Print.

Blog of Gettysburg National Military Park. "What Happened to Gettysburg's Confederate Dead?" https://npsgnmp.wordpress.com/2012/07/26/what-happened-to-gettysburgs-confederate-dead/. Web. July 10, 2015.

Cha, Theresa Hak Kyung. *Dictée.* 1982. Rpt. Berkeley: U California P, 2001. Print.

Dante Alighieri. *The Divine Comedy.* Trans. Carlyle-Okey-Wicksteed. New York: Random, 1950. Print.

Eliot, T. S. *Complete Poems and Plays.* New York: Harcourt, 1971. Print.

Emerson, Ralph Waldo. 1836. Rpt. *Collected Works.* Vol. 1, *Nature, Addresses, and Lectures.* Ed. Robert E. Spiller and Alfred R. Ferguson. Cambridge, MA: Harvard UP, 1971. 1–46. Print.

Frost, Robert. With Richard Poirier. "'Paris Review' Interview." Summer-Fall 1960. Rpt. *Collected Poems, Prose, & Plays.* Ed. Richard Poirier and Mark Richardson. New York: The Library of America, 1995. 873–93. Print.

Ginsberg, Allen. *Collected Poems, 1947–1997.* New York: HarperCollins, 2006. Print.

Ginsberg, Allen. "Politics, Poetry and Inspiration." *Mavericks of the Mind.* Ed. David Jay Brown. Web. 13 April 2010.

Goldsmith, Jack. *The Terror Presidency.* New York: Norton, 2007. Print.

Greenberg, Karen. *The Least Worst Place.* New York: Oxford UP, 2010. Print.

Hammer, Langdon. "Frank Bidart and the Tone of Contemporary Poetry." 2002. Rpt. *On Frank Bidart.* Ed. Liam Rector and Tree Swenson. Ann Arbor: U Michigan P, 2007. 7–12. Print.

Iraq Body Count. www.iraqbodycount.org. Web. 10 September 2014.

Keniston, Ann, and Jeffrey Gray, eds. *The New American Poetry of Engagement: A 21st Century Anthology.* Jefferson, NC: McFarland, 2012. Print.

Gray, Jeffrey. "Precocious Testimony: Poetry and the Uncommemorable." *Literature after 9/11.* Ed. Ann Keniston and Jeanne Follansbee Quinn. New York: Routledge, 2008. 261–84. Print.

Jarrell, Randall. *Complete Poems.* New York: Farrar, Straus and Giroux, 1969. Print.

Jarrell, Randall. *Poetry and the Age.* New York: Vintage, 1953. Print.

Kennedy, Edward. Democratic National Convention Speech. Denver, CO, 25 August

2008. "Transcript: Edward Kennedy's DNC speech—CNN.com." *CNN Politics.com.* Web. 13 April 2010.

Lewis, Lloyd. *Sherman: Fighting Prophet.* 1933. Rpt. Lincoln: U Nebraska P, 1993. Print.

Lincoln, Abraham. *Lincoln: Speeches and Writings: 1859–1865.* Ed. Don E. Fehrenbacher. New York: Library of America, 1989. Print.

Longenbach, James. *The Resistance to Poetry.* Chicago: U Chicago P, 2004. Print.

Longfellow, Henry Wadsworth. *Complete Works.* Cutchogue, NY: Buccaneer, 1993. Print.

Lowell, Robert. *Collected Poems.* Ed. Frank Bidart and David Gewanter. New York: Farrar, 2003. Print.

Lowell, Robert. *Collected Prose.* Ed. Robert Giroux. New York: Farrar, Straus and Giroux, 1987. Print.

Lowell, Robert. *Life Studies.* New York: Farrar, Straus and Giroux, 1959. Print.

Lowell, Robert. *Notebook.* New York: Farrar, Straus and Giroux, 1970. Print.

Lowell, Robert. *Notebook 1967–68.* Farrar, Straus and Giroux, 1969. Print.

Mayer, Jane. *The Dark Side.* New York: Anchor, 2009. Print.

Marvell, Andrew. *Complete Poems.* Ed. Elizabeth Story Donno. New York: Penguin, 2005. Print.

Meyers, Jeffrey, ed. *Robert Lowell: Interviews and Memoirs.* Ann Arbor: U Michigan P, 1988. Print.

Obama, Barack. *The Audacity of Hope: Thoughts on Reclaiming the American Dream.* New York: Crown, 2006. Print.

O'Sullivan, Timothy. "A Harvest of Death, Gettysburg, July, 1863." *Gardner's Photographic Sketchbook of the Civil War.* By Alexander Gardner. 1866. Rpt. New York: Dover, 1959. 70. Print.

Plath, Sylvia. *Ariel.* New York: Harper & Row, 1966. Print.

Plath, Sylvia. *Collected Poems.* New York: Harper, 1981. Print.

Pound, Ezra. *ABC of Reading.* New York: New Directions, 1934. Print.

Pound, Ezra. *Cantos.* New York: New Directions, 1970. Print.

Rathmann, Andrew, and Danielle Allen. "An Interview with Frank Bidart." *Chicago Review,* Fall 2001. Rpt. *On Frank Bidart.* Ed. Liam Rector and Tree Swenson. Ann Arbor: U Michigan P, 2007. 68–86. Print.

Rosenthal, M. L. "Poetry as Confession," *Nation,* September 19, 1959. Rpt. *The Critical Response to Robert Lowell.* Ed. Steven Gould Axelrod. Westport, CT.: Greenwood P, 1999. 30–37. Print.

Shapiro, Fred, and Joseph Epstein, eds. *The Yale Book of Quotations.* New Haven: Yale UP, 2006. Print.

Shelley, Percy Bysshe. *The Major Works.* Ed. Zachary Leader and Michael O'Neill. Oxford: Oxford UP, 2003. Print.

Sheridan, Kerry. "Iraq Death Toll Reaches 500,000 since Start of U.S.-Led Invasion, New Study Says." Agence France Presse. *Huffington Post,* 15 October 2013. Web. 10 September 2014.

Shirley, James. "The Glories of Our Blood and State." 1659. Rpt. *Representative Poetry Online.* Ed. Ian Lancashire. U Toronto Libraries. Also rpt. as lyric of "The Glories of Our Blood and State." 1891. Music by Charles Hubert Hastings Parry. Web. 13 April 2010.

Sorley, Charles Hamilton. *Death and Downs: The Poetry of Charles Hamilton Sorley.* Providence: Poet's Press / Yogh & Thorn Books, 2010. Print.

Stein, Gertrude. "A Long Gay Book." 1933. Rpt. *A Stein Reader*. Ed. Ulla E. Dydo. Evanston, IL: Northwestern UP, 1993. Print.

Travis, Adam. "Bookslut Interview with Frank Bidart." *On Frank Bidart*. Ed. Liam Rector and Tree Swenson. Ann Arbor: U Michigan P, 2007. 87–91. Print.

U.S. Department of Justice. *The Secret Torture Memos*. New York: Arc Manor, 2009.

Wikipedia. "Casualties of the Iraq War." Web. 10 July 2015.

White, John I., ed. *Git Along, Little Dogies: Songs and Songmakers of the American West*. Urbana: U Illinois P, 1985. Print.

Whitman, Walt. *Poetry and Prose*. Ed. Justin Kaplan. New York: Library of America, 1996. Print.

Williams, William Carlos. *Collected Poems*. Ed. A. Walton Litz and Christopher MacGowan. New York: New Directions, 1986. Print.

Williams, William Carlos. *Paterson*. Ed. Christopher MacGowan. New York: New Directions, 1992. Print.

Zoroya, Greg. "Return of U. S. War Dead Kept Solemn, Secret." *USA Today*, 31 December 2003. Web. 9 July 2015.

EIGHT

Beyond Katrina

Ecopoetics, Memory, and Race

James McCorkle

Natural disasters expose the vulnerability of much of African American experience, where the long history of neglect of African Americans by social and political systems parallels the degradation of the environment. The 1928 blues song "Florida Flood Blues" exemplifies this intersection of depredation and disaster. Credited to Ruby Gowdy, "Florida Flood Blues" records the windstorm and flooding caused by the 1928 Lake Okeechobee Hurricane, which was also depicted in Zora Neale Hurston's 1937 novel *Their Eyes Were Watching God*, where thousands of mainly black migrant agricultural workers perished:

> Water all around me, I ain't got no place to stay,
> Water all around me, I ain't got no place to stay,
> Hurricanes has been here, killed all the crops on my land.
>
> Blew down my log cabin, there's no shelter left for me,
> Blew down my log cabin, there's no shelter left for me,
> Food is all exhausted; I'm as weary as can be.[1]

While adhering to the format of the "weary blues," the song describes the environmental and economic damages caused by the storm: the hurricane breaks the soul, the singer laments, just as it renders her homeless. In Hurston's description of the hurricane's aftermath, African Americans were conscripted to bury the dead: whites were provided with coffins and marked graves, whereas African Americans were buried in unmarked mass graves. A year earlier, when the Great Flood of 1927 threatened the city of New Orleans, city leaders devised a plan to blow up a section of the earthen levee, so that the swollen waters of the Mississippi could be diverted into an area south of the city that was mainly rural and poor. As Jason Rivera and DeMond Miller note, at the time, "There were few concerns about the welfare of the African American population residing in the marshland used as drainage"; all told, in the Mississippi basin the flood displaced "approximately 330,000 African Americans who were subsequently interned in 154 relief ('concentration') camps where they were forced to work" (506–7). Such descriptions of the storm, the loss of shelter, and the sacrifice of ecologically sensitive areas evoke contemporary images of Hurricane Katrina, particularly those from New Orleans.

As Patricia Smith writes in her collection of poems *Blood Dazzler*, "Up on the roof, stumbling slickstep, you wave all your sheets and your blouses, / towels, bandannas, and denims, and etch what you ask on the morning: // *When are they coming to save us?*" (23), Hurricane Katrina reveals, not surprisingly, the erosion of the sense of humanness, perhaps even the impossibility of fellowship, as well as the simple recognition of a state of emergency. Katrina, as not only a natural event but also a human disaster, represents the violation of humanness, the resulting degradation of the environment, and the transformation of that environment into what Robert Bullard has called, in his landmark text on environmental racism, *Dumping in Dixie*, "sacrifice zones," the legacy of enforced spatial and social segregation (97). Smith's revoicing of a woman trapped on her roof after the levees burst evokes others trapped in those sacrifice zones. This chapter focuses on Katrina as both an environmental disaster and a way of defining deeper ecological deformations within the human community. It emphasizes the ways these issues are both documented and interrogated in recent poems that also exemplify and expand the concept of a distinctively black ecopoetics.

How do we begin to name or consider those who have been lost or injured by Katrina? Where does the hurricane's figurative wind-field end? Katrina can be seen as an antithesis to 9/11, though both have come to define George W. Bush's presidency. Katrina has largely evaded mythologizing, whereas, in the case of 9/11, humanizing narratives of those who perished were widely circulated, and forms of mourning were ritualized and monumentalized. The role of poetry, and of art in general, was to interrogate and, in the immediate aftermath of 9/11, to provide solace.[2] In contrast, the response to Katrina, particularly in terms of poetry, was comparatively quiet.[3] Both events were cast as spectacles on national media platforms, yet it is 9/11 that seems indelible. Perhaps 9/11 offers the clarity of intentions and the apparent unfolding of oppositional forces; the hurricane, in contrast, exposed deep structural flaws in the nation while resisting a compact moniker such as "9/11." Perhaps the difference also involves 9/11's visual conciseness: the collapse of the twin towers is containable within a moment, unlike the messy sprawl of Katrina. Perhaps the visual field is narrow in representations of 9/11, since most visual records are variations on a limited spectrum, unlike the representations of Katrina, whose geography encompasses the casino coasts of Mississippi and Alabama, New Orleans' Ninth Ward, the Superdome and French Quarter, and the barrier islands reaching far out into the Gulf. Katrina was a local event: the winds and floodwaters were felt chiefly by the residents, whereas 9/11 implicated the entire nation. Katrina, in its immediacy, was also a series of cascading events—not only the hurricane, but the failure of the levees, the failure of emergency preparations, and long-standing socioeconomic failures rooted, in part, in racism.

Though one can and should see it in the context of colonial legacies, 9/11 has largely become a consumable national narrative. It effectively introduced a reductive "good guys"/"bad guys" vocabulary, allowing the nation-state to slip into the dichotomous logic of us and them. The event brought into the national discourse the metaphors of "the homeland" and "the new normal." In many ways it further entrenched an already resurgent nativism and validated militarism. In contrast, Katrina jeopardized the notion of the "homeland" while it racialized militarism *within* the homeland. The question of how to respond adequately to such a situation persists even now. In part, 9/11 deflected the legacies of race and racism to the world outside the "homeland" and gave a new rationale to distrust based on race—that of "Islamophobia" and terrorism. "Katrina" undid that displacement.

Storms have swept into the Gulf of Mexico countless times, crossing southern Florida before reaching the northern Gulf coasts of Texas, Louisiana, Mississippi, or Alabama.[4] In her abecedarian "Siblings" from *Blood Dazzler*, Smith lists all the named hurricanes, from Arlene to Wilma, that have struck New Orleans:

Arlene learned to dance backwards in heels that were too high,
Bret prayed for a shaggy mustache made of mud and hair,
Cindy just couldn't keep her windy legs together. . . .
Wilma opened her maw wide, flashing rot. (75)

Katrina, however, is set apart: "None of them talked about Katrina. / She was their odd sister, / the blood dazzler." Even among hurricanes, and natural disasters in general, Katrina is exceptional. It has become a metonymy for the immediate governmental failures—from the lack of maintenance of the levee system, and the inadequate means of sheltering or escaping the storm, to the slow and ill-organized relief effort—as well as for deeper structural issues such as poorly funded educational systems, rampant police brutality, and lax environmental laws. Katrina has thus come to identify the shortcomings of the neoliberal state and its implicit racist underpinnings.

This chapter examines the work of Nikky Finney, Smith, and Natasha Trethewey as they interrogate the effects of Hurricane Katrina and the larger, encompassing concerns exposed by the hurricane, including those related to visibility, possession and dispossession, and the vulnerability of African American lives. These three poets develop a poetics that both challenges and moves past the role of the poet as witness or engaged environmentalist. Joseph Soyka, in "The Right to Write about It: Literature, after Katrina," asks how poets might provide an authentic response to such a complex disaster. What might be the role of poets, especially those removed from the immediate scene? In response, Patricia Smith argues that "if you're African-American, you were placed there in another way. . . . There is always the chance, no matter what you're going through, you will be abandoned to deal with it on your own" (qtd. in Soyka).

Thus, while it should be acknowledged that Katrina affected diverse communities, it has been largely and correctly depicted as having disproportionately affected African Americans. Smith's assertion implies that the event of Katrina names the precariousness of African Americans, and particularly African American women, within a personal, daily space and within history. In her *Precarious Life: The Powers of Mourning and Violence*, Judith Butler asks, "Who counts as human? Whose lives count as lives? And finally, What *makes for a grievable life?*" (20). These questions haunt the poems I discuss. The physical forces of the storm exposed how we think of nature and the natural, who belongs and who does not, and who is in possession of power, their own bodies, and language. Even as these poets provide histories of Katrina that are both personal and public, they examine the essential question of who counts as human and what defines a human ecology.

In the wider context of the environmental movement and environmental literature, African Americans have largely been invisible. This, of course, does not mean that African Americans have not been long engaged with their environment or environmental concerns, but that white culture and the mainstream, white-centered environmental movement have largely ignored contributions by African Americans as well as their lived spaces or environments.[5] Carolyn Finney, in her *Black Faces, White Spaces: Reimagining the Relationship of African Americans to the Great Outdoors*; Dorceta Taylor, in her *Race, Class, and Gender, and American Environmentalism*; and Haki Madhubuti, in his *Claiming Earth: Race, Rage, Rape, Redemption*, all raise the interconnected questions of who owns the earth, who belongs, and who is represented. The failure to include African Americans within the narrative of environmental consciousness perpetuates particular stereotypes—related both to environmentalism in general (which is then seen as a white, middle-class form of activism) and to African Americans (seen as having little interest in the environment). As Taylor argues, the failure to recognize how race, class, and gender have structured our environmental responses over time limits the efficacy of environmentalism as a political and social movement (40–41). Carolyn Finney puts it this way: "Representation and racialization sustain the way many Americans think about the natural environment in the United States, which informs our environmental policies, institutions, and interactions" (68).

In her *African American Environmental Thought: Foundations*, Kimberly Smith traces how early twentieth-century mainstream environmental thought centered on conservation and preservation. Mainstream environmentalism had "significant ideological and political connections to white supremacy," which relied on scientific racism, particularly biological determinism and evolutionary progression, to maintain its intellectual authority (2). White supremacy favored a dichotomous view of nature, in which the human world was distinct and independent from the natural world. The natural world was looked upon as *other* and its resources were there to be exploited, whether for the production of cultural objects or industrial and agricultural purposes. By the mid-twentieth century, the dynamics of the neoliberal state (market-driven, meritocratic, post-Fordist, with an economy based on contingency) emerged; embedded within that economy are continuing racial and environmental predations. In other words, the natural disaster exposes the human disasters of racism, poverty, dispossession, and dehumanization. The precariousness of human economies, particularly African American economies, dovetails with the vulnerability of the environment. Black ecopoetics offers an implicit critique of these conditions.

The definition of *ecology* I am using here follows that of Kimberly Ruffin, in her *Black on Earth: African American Ecoliterary Traditions*: "Humans are indeed 'natural'; humans have developed a powerful and distinct culture within nature; and cultural definitions of 'humanity' influence an individual's experiences among humans and with non-human nature" (18). The poet Ed Roberson emphasizes the inclusion of African Americans in "the living":

> We exist in the midst of living as other living [sic]. We have words for our existence; but after enough words, we come to the limits of—if not our living—our knowledge of the nature of human living. There is, however, no humanly containable limit to living Nature; there is no outside of Nature. (Qtd. in Dungy 3)

Roberson implies a radical inclusiveness—but one informed by the specific historical experience of African Americans. Ruffin emphasizes the importance of historicizing the connection between nature and the human: the long history of scientific racism, as well as earlier metaphysical arguments for racial hierarchies in support of slavery, are always embedded in the social and political structures that Trethewey, Finney, and Smith interrogate in their writing on Katrina. Ruffin reminds us that within the "dual experience of societal exploitation and cultural conceptualizations of nature that include human beings, people of African descent have been aware of human beings as natural facts even while their status as human was questioned" (19). While "ecology helps illuminate how African-American authors understand human beings as part of the natural world," Ruffin argues it also reflects the effects of social systems upon the whole ecology (20).

Unlike conventional environmental literature, the work of Finney, Smith, and Trethewey is centered neither on the theme of human predation nor on the Romantic idealization of nature; the environment is not considered at a remove from the human but is intimately intertwined with it. The contemporary ecopoem, writes Christopher Arigo in "Notes towards an Ecopoetics," "does not merely reference 'nature' or the 'natural world'—the contemporary ecopoet is far too savvy, far too aware for such simplistic reductionism. The contemporary ecopoem is self-aware of itself as a construct, and of the larger role of the poet/poem/poetics in the context of the larger ecosystem of literature and the outside world." Ecopoetics, Arigo argues, "must not be seen as a return 'back to nature,' but rather as a reminder that we never left." Black ecopoetics further elaborates the political resistances that Arigo claims as inherent to ecopoetics, from the earliest works, including the poems of Phillis Wheatley,[6] to contemporary poets such as Will Alexander, C. S. Giscombe, Claudia Rankine, Ed Roberson, and those under consideration here. The work of Finney, Smith, and Trethewey challenges not only the racialized space of North American environmental literature and ecopoetics, but also the predominantly masculine voice of those canons. Hurricane Katrina as a phenomenon of nature exposed the dominant or mainstream logic (itself manifested in the history of white superiority)[7] that defines blackness as having "an essential and fixed quality," which, in the case of Katrina, is defined by "criminality and poverty" (C. Finney 67). As it contends with the event of Katrina, the work, both poetry and prose, of Finney, Smith, and Trethewey examines the environment as racialized space.

To develop the idea of a black ecopoetics that invests in understanding our humanness (and the question of who counts as human), we need to recognize the context of environmental history, replete with its marginalization of the African American presence. A black ecopoetics negotiates African Americans' positions in the environment as well as the discourses that enable its investigation. Natasha Trethewey's volume *Beyond Katrina: A Meditation on the Mississippi Gulf Coast* is part memoir, part local history, and part reflection on environmental conditions; it is a prose text infused with discrete poems. Her poem "Liturgy" illustrates both her position and a series of possible rhetorical responses to it:

> This is a love letter to the Gulf Coast, a praise song, a dirge,
> invocation and benediction, a requiem for the Gulf Coast.
>
> This cannot rebuild the coast; it is an indictment, a complaint,
> my *logos*—argument and discourse—with the coast.
>
> This is my *nostos*—my pilgrimage to the coast, my memory, my
>   reckoning—
>
> native daughter: I am the Gulf Coast. (66)

Trethewey challenges the idea of the Gulf Coast—how exactly can the coast be not only black but also female? What arises when this space is defined from the position of an African American, when it is claimed as "my *logos* . . . my *nostos*"?

Furthermore, a black ecopoetics reflects how the conditions of language validate citizenship and humanness within the *ecology*, by which is meant the community or the space of belonging. In other words, black ecopoetics addresses a racialized space, and investigates the conditions of racism within the aesthetics of environmental awareness. A part of reading the environment involves reading and responding to racist ideologies. Thus, a black ecopoetics is not so much an argument as an offering of alternative frameworks for the reading of poetry and the environment.[8]

Finney, Smith, and Trethewey write against the dehumanizing discourse that names, infects, and inflects Katrina. Four days after Hurricane Katrina struck New Orleans and brought devastation across the mid–Gulf Coast, Michel Brown, President Bush's director of the Federal Emergency Management Agency (FEMA), was interviewed by Jim Lehrer for PBS's *News Hour*. Brown responded to Lehrer's questions about the efficacy of FEMA by stating:

> The second part of my answer, Jim, which, I think, again, the American people understand how fascinating and unusual this is—is that we're seeing people that we didn't know exist that suddenly are showing up on bridges or parts of the interstate that aren't inundated. (Qtd. in Ishiwata 32)

As Eric Ishiwata notes, Brown's comments, while significant for their insensitivity, are perhaps more revealing in that "the abrupt emergence of the 'Other America' evinces the degree to which a large segment of Katrina's victims had, to the point of the disaster, been cast as *personae non grata*—citizen-subjects rendered invisible by the reigning neoliberal ideology of a 'colorblind America'" (33). Brown's statement fuses the semantic with the sociopolitical and ethical. Questions about who is seen, who is included in the terms "we" and "the American people," and who exists as a person are embedded in Brown's statement. Judith Butler's questions—"Who counts as human? Whose lives count as lives?"—are relevant not only to Brown's comments, but also to much of the reporting on Hurricane Katrina and its displacement and brutalization of the poor and preponderantly African American population in New Orleans.[9] The government's response to the effects of Katrina demonstrated, to borrow Butler's words, "a diffuse set of strategies and tactics . . . . to dispose and order populations, and to produce and reproduce subjects, their practices and beliefs" (52). Importantly, the responses to Katrina revealed the intersection of environmental injustice and racism. Equally important, black ecopoetics—as critically reflected in the lines "I see / what this language does" (Smith, *Blood Dazzler* 5)—offers another means of interrogating political positions, at the same time registering the erosion and contamination of language.

Nikky Finney's response to Katrina places the disaster in the context of institutional racism, where betrayal, neglect, bureaucracy, and immiseration have replaced the outright racism of the Jim Crow era: "Regulations require an *e* be at the end / of any *Pleas e* before any national response / can be taken" (Finney, *Head Off & Split* 14). A later edition of Finney's collection *Head Off & Split* ends with her 2011 acceptance speech upon receiving the National Book Award for this collection. In that speech she immediately grounds her work within a historical context by quoting the 1739 Slave Codes of South Carolina: "A fine of one hundred dollars and six months in prison will be imposed for anyone found teaching a slave to read or write, and death is the penalty for circulating any incendiary literature" (Finney 101). Literacy, as she here reveals, was central to emancipation. The narrative of racism promulgated the uneducability of African Americans; the national narratives of white superiority and privilege still revolve around stereotypes of intelligence drawn from the long history of scientific racism. With her acceptance speech, Finney situates her poetry in a history of critical literacy as resistance, the need to inscribe the agency of "I" to assert one's right to exist, to have presence.

The drama of Finney's poem "Left" hinges on the apprehension of literacy:

> The woman with pom-pom legs waves
> Her uneven homemade sign:
>   Pleas Help Pleas

and even if the *e* has been left off the *Pleas e*

do you know simply
by looking at her
that it has been left off
because she can't spell
(and therefore is not worth saving)
Or was it because the water was rising so fast
there wasn't time? (14)

Finney addresses the spectacle that television viewers across the nation witnessed: New Orleanians trapped on rooftops surrounded by turgid floodwaters. But the mere recording of suffering does not necessarily result in either empathy or knowledge, Finney contends:

The low-flying helicopter does not know
the answer. It catches all this on patriotic tape,
but it does not land, and does not drop dictionary,
or ladder. (14)

Finney exposes the cruel absurdity of the rescue efforts in New Orleans and the media's racially driven shifting of the focus from the woman and her urgent plea for assistance to the derision directed at her spelling. While it may be argued that Finney repeats the media's voyeurism, her interrogatory discourse challenges the media's consuming gaze and implicitly ours. Indeed, the *plea* names her cry; to insist on *please* is to place her in a position of subservience.

Working as a broken refrain, the children's rhyme "EeneeMeneeMainee Mo! / Catch a—" fractures, stutters, and resists uttering the derogatory term as it skips to "My mother said to pick / The very best one!" The children's rhyme satirizes the rescue process: those who are most vulnerable are belittled and all but called "nigger" (which is the implicit and common rhyme, not placed in print by Finney, but soundlessly present) by those who have power to effect rescue and, more significantly, by those watching the difficulties often faced by rescuers and victims from safety. The rhyme also reflects the childhood mnemonics that teach one not only how to read but how to read those around us and how to value or devalue others. Part of the cultural topography leading up to Katrina was the Department of Education's implementation of the No Child Left Behind Act (2001), which essentially disassociated education from socioeconomic contexts, in effect deepening the disparities of access to education, and shifting educational reform to entrepreneurial control:

What else would you call it,
Mr. Every-Child-Left-Behind.

Anyone you know
ever left off or put on
an *e* by mistake?

Potato Po tato e (15)

Dan Quayle's 1992 spelling blunder, when in an elementary school spelling bee he altered William Figueroa's spelling of "potato" to "potatoe," is not only an ironic twist, but one that suggests more insidiously that neoliberalism has dismantled an already fragile public educational system. It is not so much Quayle's ignorance but his act of de-educating that in effect became Bush's mandate some nine years later. As the key means of maintaining hierarchies in nature, language is a tool for devaluation and dehumanization. Finney's poem offers resistant witness to this process as it unfolded—and was re-exposed—in the wake of Katrina. As both a form of resistance to and an interrogation of these segregating hierarchies, Finney's poem exemplifies the political aspect of black ecopoetics.

Finney also links the events of Katrina to war and the visual history of war when she writes,

Three times a day the helicopter flies
by in a low crawl . . . the cameraman and pilot who
remembers well the art of his mirrored-eyed
posture in his low-flying helicopter: Bong Son,
Dong Ha, Pleiku, Chu Lai. He makes a slow
Vietcong dip & dive. (13)

By listing place-names that were also sites of combat in the 1960s in Vietnam, Finney weaves two histories together. The recovery mission in New Orleans was militarized, with the National Guard ordered to "shoot to kill" by Governor Kathleen Babineaux Blanco: "These troops are fresh back from Iraq, well trained, experienced, battle-tested and under my orders to restore order in the streets" (qtd. in Robertson 274).[10] The images of poverty and dispossession—like those of burning children and executions of Vietnamese—are images we were not "supposed" to see. The images from New Orleans and the surrounding Gulf Coast communities disrupted our sense of "racial progress" and the ability to manage disasters; this disruption may have effected a sense of shock and outrage, much as the war photography did during the Vietnam War. Yet

Finney's poem suggests otherwise. "Left" locates Katrina as a part of ongoing political contexts. In her visual representation of Katrina victims stranded on a rooftop, Finney sets us both uncomfortably in that observation helicopter hovering overhead and *with* those suffering the storm's deprivations. The poem's visceral anger points to empathy's failure to initiate social or political change in the storm's national audience: instead of conveying the vulnerabilities of those affected and in turn recognizing the spectators' role in the formation of many of those vulnerabilities, the images that emerged from the reportage of Katrina instead reify the victims' inhuman otherness and cater to social voyeurism.

By failing to acknowledge black space and presence—or in Michael Brown's words, not knowing "those people exist"—or by segregating otherness, we as viewer/readers lose our own selves; or as Butler writes, "I become inscrutable to myself. Who 'am' I without you? When we lose some of these ties by which we are constituted, we do not know who we are or what to do" (22). Finney's poem's title, "Left," defines the victims of Katrina as left behind, left out, stranded not only in the putrid floodwaters but in the decades of neglect. The title also recalls conservatives such as the then House Speaker, Republican Dennis Hastert, who after the storm stated that New Orleans "could be bulldozed" and that spending on recovery "does not make sense to me."[11] Or as Finney concludes, "After all, it was only po' New Orleans, / . . . Who would / be left alive to care?" (16). Here Finney amplifies Butler's ethical cautions: the breakdown of human relations, of the putative human community, is already our own dehumanization.

Black ecopoetics, then, in Finney's example, fuses the natural event with a political critique of the systematic neglect that enabled it, and it does so from the position of the dispossessed. Evie Shockley is helpful here in suggesting the import of *blackness* in black ecopoetics:

> "Black" . . . is not meant to describe the characteristics or qualities of the texts, nor does it refer specifically to the (socially constructed) race of the writer. Rather it describes the subjectivity of the African American writer— that is, the subjectivity produced by the experience of identifying or being interpellated as "black" in the U.S.—actively working out a poetics in the context of a racist society. (9)

In this sense, there is no checklist of characteristics or particular compositional strategies that either identify or motivate these texts; rather, as in Finney's work, black ecopoetics is defined by its commitment to the process of "working out a poetics in the context of a racist society."

Unlike Finney's "Left," which deploys a rhetoric of resistance even as it enacts witnessing, Patricia Smith's *Blood Dazzler* is a form of public conjuration—an assembling of voices or summoning, but also testifying and oath taking. Smith traces a series of voices, ranging from that of the hurricane to Michael Brown to thirty-four dead elders who drowned in their nursing home in St. Bernard Parish during the storm after being abandoned by their caregivers. Smith does not merely assemble different voices, but rather she arranges them to provide a choral chronology of Katrina's path. Each voice or figure comes to name her- or himself and, in turn, offers witness: "My name Earline / and I'm gon' say you my life" (54). As voices surface, so does the need to name, to recover one's own name, or to be tagged with a name in order to escape an anonymous death:

> Now her fingerprints slide away with the skin
> of her fingers. Five days in the putrid water
> have doubled her, slapped the brown light
> from her body. She could be anyone now,
> pudged, eyeless, oddly gray. (74)

Smith's graphic depiction of the recovery of an anonymous bloated body reveals that in the violence (of the storm, but also of war, for example) the individual's body does not belong to the individual. Instead, our bodies are public—"She could be anyone now"—and we are all vulnerable to the violence "she" suffered. The body is always public, subject always and already to violence, and given over to others. In Smith's poems, as in Finney's "Left," the body's physical exposure both to the elements and to the eyes of the media raises ontological questions: Who is real? How could this be real? How could those we did not know exist be now so present.

The act of naming as remembrance moves beyond the local in the 9/11 memorials, Maya Lin's Vietnam Veterans Memorial, the countless war memorials erected in cities after World War I and II, and in Yeats's iconic "Easter, 1916" (with its self-imposed command to name, "I write it out in a verse"). However, with Katrina the process of remembering has remained essentially communal and local, or as Trethewey notes in *Beyond Katrina*, "Rituals of commemoration serve to unite communities around collective memory, and at the second anniversary of the storm people gathered to remember—some at church or community centers, others at locations that held more private significance" (61). Smith's collection might best be seen as a dramatic form of public conjuration that moves toward catharsis and healing. In this way, the collection should be read as a dramatic whole, one that contains many voices and, through the process of voicing, tames the disaster in all its manifestations.

Of the voicings that Smith creates—or channels—none is as evocative as that of the personified Katrina, who voices her own creation:

A muted thread of gray light, hovering ocean,
becomes throat, pulls in wriggle, anemone, kelp,
widens with the want of it. I become
a mouth, thrashing hair, an overdone eye. How dare
the water belittle my thirst, treat me as just
another
small
disturbance,

try to feed me
from the bottom of its hand? (1)

The line break at "I become" signals self-birth and self-naming, which moves the poem from description to dramatic monologue. Juxtaposed with this self-birthing and naming is the technocratic observation of the reconnaissance aircraft that a tropical storm was forming from a low-pressure area. Smith's evocation of Katrina as a woman—"every woman begins as weather, / sips slow thunder, knows her hips" (1)—suggests depictions of the Yoruba orisha Oya, who, as Judith Gleason describes, manifests

> herself in various natural forms: the river Niger, tornadoes, strong winds generally, fire, lightning, and buffalo. She is also associated with certain cultural phenomena among the Yoruba people (the first to worship her), notably with masquerades constructed of bulky, billowing cloth— ancestral apparitions—and with funerals. . . . More abstractly, Oya is the goddess of edges, of the dynamic interplay between surfaces, of transformation from one state to another. (1)

This cyclonic deity, as Gleason describes her, combines transformations and acts as a harbinger of change. Natural forces of wind, water, and lightning are also cultural forces. West African cultural formations and identities have been carried across the Atlantic on the slave routes from West Africa to the New World, and the waves of low pressure that are nascent hurricanes track the slave routes, marking both the furies of the African Diaspora and its cultural exchanges, resistances, and continuities. The evident parallel between the manifestation of Oya and Smith's invocation of the hurricane suggests that black ecopoetics may also draw upon African cosmologies.[12] In Smith's chorally voiced collection, the mythopoetic—the evocation of Katrina and the supernatural force—reveals itself in passages such as the following: from "5 P.M., Tuesday, August 23, 2005,"

> I will require praise,
> unbridled winds to define my body,
> a crime behind my teeth
> because
>
> every woman begins as weather,
> sips slow thunder, knows her hips. Every woman
> harbors a chaos, can
> wait for it, straddling a fever.
>
> For now,
> I console myself with small furies,
> those dips in my dawning system. (1–2)

In answer to the storm, the poet offers these praise poems, in which she dons the mask of Oya/Katrina, fusing sexuality with the forces of the storm. Rather than invoking a passive nature, this fusion gives agency to sexuality and enables it to bring about change: "every woman begins as weather. . . . Every woman / harbors a chaos." Katrina as Oya is both disruptive and dancing, generative and destructive. Traditionally, Oya conceals lightning under her tongue and often is reconfigured in the human world as a steel machete (Gleason 66). In the same way, Katrina's enunciation revisions and empowers her. As the storm builds, in "11 A.M., Wednesday, August 24, 2005," Katrina claims,

> The difference in a given name. What the calling,
> the hard K, does to the steel of me,
> how suddenly and surely it grants me
> pulse and petulance. (3)

Smith traces the development of Katrina as she makes landfall in Florida—"I see / what this language does / and taste / soil on my tongue" (5)—and then emerges in the Gulf as a Category 5 storm: "For days, I've been offered blunt slivers / of larger promises" (11). Smith here seems to argue that nature, as part of our ecology, should be praised, whereas human failings should not be ascribed to nature.

Katrina, as she emerges and defines herself in these poems, revisions female creativity. Adrienne Rich, in her 1975 essay "Vesuvius at Home: The Power of Emily Dickinson," comments that "active willing and creation in women are forms of aggression, and aggression is both 'the power to kill' and punishable by death" (174). Dickinson's "My Life had stood—a Loaded Gun," the subject of Rich's essay, is an analogue to Smith's Katrina in that, in Rich's terms, as the poet/narrator/cyclone "experiences in herself . . . energy and potency[, she] can also be experienced as pure destruction" (174), an ambivalence that goes unresolved. In the volume's penultimate poem, "Katrina" (the second of two poems using that title), the destructive hurricane fuses with her own victims' desire: "All I ever wanted to be / was a wet, gorgeous mistake, / a reason to crave shelter" (76). In these lines, Katrina has an intimate connection with those sheltering at the Superdome or on Danziger Bridge: Nature *herself* is a dispossessed outsider.

Here, too, it is worth recalling ecology's root: "eco" or *oikos*, house or vicinity, shelter, community. Katrina thus names her own poetics, turning herself inside out, becoming the craving of those she has drowned and those she has made destitute. The natural world, as represented by Katrina, becomes part of the human ecology as Katrina reveals the needs and vulnerabilities of those who have remained invisible to the state.

In these poems, Smith considers the world as fully animate, with each element, not only the hurricane, capable of voicing its history and what it has witnessed. In "Superdome," the superdome speaks as witness:

I did not demand they wade through the overflow from toilets,
chew their own nails bloody in place of a meal.

I didn't feed their squalling babies chewing gum,
force them to pee out loud in gutters,
or make them lick their own sweat for healing salt. (40)

The physical site itself witnesses and memorializes. It also seeks to exonerate—"I did not demand they wade through the overflow from toilets"—as well as implicitly to ask who "demand[ed] they wade" through excrement, who was responsible for this dehumanization. "Glittering and monstrous," the Superdome's "coiled" and "tight musculature" mirrors the transgressive structure of Katrina; both are environments within which humans define themselves and reveal their own vulnerability, as well as their own propensity for violence. In giving voice to the Superdome, itself a panopticon, Smith states, "I was defined by a man's hand": the human environment, as mapped and built, mirrors the soul of its builders.

Katrina's devastation in New Orleans was amplified by two general conditions: first, the combined effects of destruction of the delta's barrier islands by dredging, reduction of replenishing silt from the Mississippi, and rising sea levels; and, second, the construction of extensive levee systems, which were built not as protection but in order to facilitate shipping—in particular, the transport and production of petrochemicals—and which were ill maintained. Natasha Trethewey reflects in *Beyond Katrina: A Meditation on the Mississippi Gulf Coast*, "The future of the Mississippi Gulf Coast's environment is tied to the stability of the wetlands, the possibility of rising tide levels—due, in part, to global warming rates—and the potential impact of humans and development along the coast" (58). Trethewey draws an explicit parallel between this threatened coastline and Katrina's destabilization of the social fabric. Her brother, for example, knows of only one person who now "lives in an apartment where the landlord didn't raise the rent by the roughly 70 percent that was commonplace in the months following the storm" (59). With affordable housing both metaphorically and physically washed away and people displaced after the storm, Trethewey's brother laments that his social network "has all but disappeared" (60). In *Beyond Katrina*, Trethewey creates a personal memoir that is also a social history. "Names are talismans of memory, too—*Katrina, Camille*. Perhaps this is why we name our storms," writes Trethewey (63). By naming, histories are reified, as Trethewey notes at the beginning of her "journey home—my *nostos*": "not until *after* Katrina did I come to see that the history of one storm, Camille—and the ever-present possibility of others—helped to define my relationship to the place from which I come" (2).

As a precursor to Katrina, Trethewey's "Providence," originally published in her *Native Guard* and reprinted in *Beyond Katrina*, describes Hurricane Camille, which struck the Mississippi Gulf coast in 1969:

> What's left is footage: the hours before
>   Camille, 1969—hurricane
>   parties, palm-trees leaning
>   in the wind,
>   fronds blown back (29)

The poem hinges on images of the storm and afterward, the "fronds blown back, / a woman's hair. Then after: / the vacant lots, / boats washed ashore" (29). This "footage" is almost banal; in fact, it is all that is left. Even memory is jeopardized as the poet recalls that the storm's aftermath has loosened the foundations of identity: "our house . . . seemed to float / in the flooded yard: no foundation / beneath us, nothing I could see" (29). If that sense of property and shelter becomes destabilized, the sense of self-identity does as well: "In the water, our reflection / trembled, / disappeared / when I bent to touch it"

(29). The storm has underscored the vulnerability of the poet and those she is connected to (it is "our house" and "our reflections").

The poem may also be read in the context of other poems in the earlier volume; immediately preceding it is "Incident," in which Trethewey describes a cross-burning in the front yard of her family's home:

> We tell the story every year—
> how we peered from the windows, shades drawn—
> though nothing really happened,
> the charred grass now green again.
> We peered from the windows, shades drawn,
> at the cross trussed like a Christmas tree,
> the charred grass still green. Then
> we darkened our rooms, lit the hurricane lamps. (*Native Guard* 41)

Taken together, these two poems address specific histories, familial and intimate ones; yet they also define a national history that has been dislocated so it does not implicate white America with its own violence. In "Incident" the experience becomes scarred over: "No one came. / Nothing really happened. / By morning all the flames had dimmed. / We tell the story every year" (41). Trethewey raises the question of how violence is remembered, what language one uses to recall one's own dehumanization, and whether such re-membering reinvokes that initial event of dehumanization. Is there such an originary moment if the story is told every year? How many stories are embedded in or precede the current story? As implied in Smith's "Siblings," quoted above, there seems no beginning or end to these racial storms. Trethewey's refrain, "We tell the story every year," applies to her subsequent insertion of "Providence" in her book *Beyond Katrina*. Trethewey suggests that the conditions have not changed; just as hurricane season is a fact of life, racism is an ingrained condition in the United States, always exerting its pressures on the poet.

It should be noted that neither Trethewey's prose nor her poetry—the book mixes the two—could be considered "innovative" in the sense, for example, that Claudia Rankine's prose poems or Ed Roberson's poetry are. With this volume Trethewey has, instead, created an album of previously published poems, family photographs, letters from her brother, and various forms of prose recollection. In this mix of memoir, reflection, and history, *Beyond Katrina* combines meditations on race and the environment, as Trethewey journeys back to her home in North Gulfport, Mississippi, to salvage her own memories, local African American history often rooted in family stories, and the story of her brother's incarceration for drug possession two years after the storm. For Trethewey, "Katrina" describes not only "New Orleans," but also the Gulf Coast of Mississippi and Alabama, thus widening the geography of history. The storm and its aftermath illustrate the layering and slippages of narratives as they move from the particular and often disruptive to the normative and dominant:

> Between the two [the narratives of Camille and Katrina], there is the suggestion of both a narrative and a metanarrative . . . how intricately intertwined memory and forgetting always are.
>   This too is a story about a story—how it will be inscribed on the physical landscape as well as on the landscape of our cultural memory. (11)

There are competing narratives of remembering; Trethewey recounts, "I know that a preferred narrative is one of the common bonds between people in a time of crisis. This is often the way collective, cultural memory works, full of omissions, partial remembering, and purposeful forgetting" (20). To illustrate her point, Trethewey recounts a conversation with a young African American woman named Alesha who was evicted from her Gulfport apartment so that the white owners, who had lost their home, could have shelter. Alesha claims, "Everyone helped each other. People shared what they had, were even friendlier" (20). But what does she mean by this, when she has been forced to leave her only shelter? The statement reveals that she has become subsumed in the narrative of community insisted upon by the state and disseminated by the media. Particular stories are dislocated and displaced, much as whole populations are, especially when they involve issues of race.

The slippages, dislocations, and renamings within personal narratives are also carried out institutionally: after Katrina, "developers have acquired land in the community for commercial purposes—as the city [Gulfport] has redistricted homesteads as commercial rather than residential property—many elderly citizens have lost their homes. Higher property taxes have forced people out even as property values have declined" (86). The landscape becomes renamed and reinscribed while, simultaneously, the community is destroyed. As Trethewey writes, "Instead of replacing all of the low-income housing lost in the storm, the state of Mississippi found ways to divert those funds for such things as the refurbishment and expansion of the Port of Gulfport" (89). Human ecology names the household, the sheltering, of humans: what Katrina has named is the destruction of the household.

With the storm's destruction and the consequent dismantling of the physical community, human connections are severed. The ruins are not only of a public past but also of a personal one: "Everywhere I go during my journey, I feel the urge to weep not only for the residents of the coast but also for my former self: the destroyed public library is *me* as a girl, sitting on the floor, reading between the stacks" (63). Trethewey continues this cumulative sentence, moving from landmark to landmark, drawing in not only her childhood connections but also those of her mother and grandmother: "My mother also stood in line, at the back door, for the peanut gallery, the black section where my grandmother, still a girl, went on days designated *colored only*, clutching the coins she earned selling crabs" (63). These memories of place evince an awareness of historical injustices, particularly the ubiquity of Jim Crow laws. The erasure of memories and the landscape that housed those memories began long before Katrina. The rise of the casino economy along the coast did not address the history of racial oppression; rather, it displaced that essential but constantly deferred dialogue. While people were excited by the prospect of the new jobs brought by the casinos, they "also feared an erosion of the coast's cultural heritage, the depletion of wetlands, the transformation of the character of the beach road and surrounding neighborhoods, and a variety of social ills" (13). Trethewey traces the relations between the collapsing landscape and social oppression, revealing that the former is thoroughly and historically implicated in the latter.

Trethewey's text is ultimately elegiac and personal, a record of the disappearance of primary figures. The last prose section ends with her brother disappearing from the courtroom, back turned and hand raised "as if he were pointing to a destination, some place not far up the road" (123). Her brother's incarceration is an aftereffect of Katrina in that the collapsed economies disproportionally affected African Americans. Trethewey's narrative arc begins with her responses to Katrina but ends with her brother's letters from prison and his final sentencing. While Trethewey's brother's incarceration reflects the larger social and political trend of imprisoning minorities, it also prompts Tretheway to reflect on culpability, including her own:

> I was not unlike those people content to look around certain areas of the post-Katrina landscape and praise the state for its remarkable recovery, while ignoring the dark underbelly reflected in the ongoing devastation of the lives of some of the poorest, least visible victims of the hurricane (107–8).

Trethewey records her own genealogical weaving into the environment of the Mississippi Gulf Coast, in the sixth section of her poem "Congregation":

> Once, I was a daughter of this place;
> daughter of Gwen, granddaughter
> of Leretta, great of Eugenia McGee.

> I was baptized in the church
> my great-aunt founded, behind
> the drapes my grandmother sewed. (79)

Trethewey also finds, post-Katrina, the conditions of loss and exclusion: though the poet "wanted to say I have come home / to bear witness . . . I wanted to say I *see*, / not I *watch*," the distance of years, and the storm, prevent her from returning (81). She cannot reenter the space of her past, this baptismal space:

> I got as far as the vestibule—neither in,
> nor out. The service went on. I did nothing
> but watch, my face against the glass—until
> someone turned, looked back: saw me. (81)

Trethewey as witness cannot return. Autobiographically, she is estranged, reenacting that peculiar American condition Thomas Wolfe describes ("you can't go home again"); yet onto this condition the effects of Katrina are added. What can one recover from Katrina, from storms, from profound ruptures? How is it that Trethewey—now a successful poet and educator—no longer belongs to this community? That this particular poem, "Congregation," with its implicit allusion to collectivity, ends with the atomistic "me" implies the loss of the "beloved community" and of that evocative term *oikos*, the sheltering ecology.

Mtangulizi Sanyika notes that one of the first rules of recovery after a disaster requires reaching a consensus about the future rebuilding by all stakeholders; this, however, "never happened in New Orleans because the elites attempted to impose their vision of a smaller, whiter, richer city on the body politic" (104). Finney, Smith, and Trethewey respond to this repetition of a history of imposed abjection through their depictions of the storm and its aftermath. Among the narratives circulating after Katrina was that of the storm as retribution, as Trethewey illustrates:

> The young waiter serving our table had been listening off and on to the story. . . . He's from Louisiana, and he moved to the coast for restaurant work in the casino. "What's different now is that the new generation respects the hurricanes, unlike the folks before. It needed to happen." When I ask him what he means, he replies vaguely: "to teach us something" and "a cleansing, that's what it was." When he turns to attend to another table, I feel uncomfortable thinking about what he might have meant, particularly after hearing some people opine about New Orleans

and who was turned out: the poorer, working classes—overwhelmingly African American—all lumped together with supposed criminals that the city would rather not see return. (27)

These discourses shape our perceptions, and they become, or can potentially become, policy: Speaker Hastert's comments broached the possibility of not assisting New Orleans, an option that was then allowed to materialize. This situation returns us to Judith Butler's series of questions: "Who counts as human? Whose lives count as lives? And finally, What *makes for a grievable life?*" To count some as human and others as outside our touch and sight ("We're seeing people that we didn't know exist") is to assert our own autonomy and deny our vulnerability. The waiter, like Hastert, refuses to mourn. What are the costs of this refusal to grieve? "When we think ecologically," writes Kimberly Ruffin, "we can appreciate the magnitude of our own fragility and recognize that people experience humanity in innumerable ways" (164). Black ecopoetics expands the range of imagination, in part by uncovering deep originary ecologies. This recovery enables the mourning of what has been lost—that which has been intertwined, the human and the natural worlds.

A black ecopoetics, at least as expressed in the work of Trethewey, Finney, and Smith, is investigative and resistant; it insists on agency and the presence of both the poet and audience. It embraces, in Ruffin's words, "cross-cultural aid and fellowship" as much as it claims a voice of resistance. Notably, both Trethewey's and Smith's collections end with expressions of healing: Trethewey's with "Benediction," providing a blessing for her brother, who enters, perhaps as we all do, at least figuratively, the carceral world after his own world collapses; and Smith's with "Voodoo VIII: Spiritual Cleansing & Blessing." Here, Smith, ambivalently, evokes the image of cleansing rain:

There's no deception like the world after rain.
Suddenly God is everywhere,
winking from dumpster rivers,
using the insistent perfume of plain water
to scrape funk from alleyways and men.
In the seconds after storm,
we sign on for brash little resurrections. (77)

The world appears changed; the processes of healing seem to have begun. Smith's tone, however, interrogates and disrupts that assumption: Katrina may have exposed what was invisible, at least to whites, but what then? What have previous "storms" revealed and changed? Is a conjured healing possible? Trethewey, in "Benediction," takes leave at the threshold of prison and dispossession. Smith's summary list of storms in "Siblings" suggests little has been resolved. Rather the storms continue to haunt us with their recurring betrayals and violences. The closing prose-like verse paragraph of Finney's "Left" recasts that haunting as a rhetorical question;

> After all, it was only po' New Orleans,
> old bastard city of funny spellers. Nonswimmers
> with squeeze-box accordion accents. Who would
> be left alive to care? (16)

Ironic as Finney's question may be, it needles us in its apparent banality and sentimentality—of course we care, but we should be asking, particularly in view of positions of privilege that many of us occupy, how do we care? May not our past senses of "care" persist in being inadequate? And more ominously, when communities—black communities in particular—are ecologically, in the most encompassing sense of that word, marginalized, who is "left alive" to grieve or offer solace? The repercussions of our actions, Finney suggests, are indeed matters of life and death.

Notes

1. Cited in Luigi Monge's "Their Eyes Were Watching God: African-American Topical Songs on the 1928 Florida Hurricanes and Floods." Monge notes that in addition to four field recordings available at the Library of Congress, Ruby Gowdy's was the only commercially available song about the 1928 Lake Okeechobee Hurricane. He notes that it was cut in New York City, on September 28, 1928, about seven weeks after the storm. The original 78 rpm was on Gennett 6708, and then released on Champion 15613 and Conqueror 7265. (This disc is credited to Martha Bradford.)

2. In the *New Yorker*, for example, immediately following the 9/11 attacks, Adam Zagajewski's poem "Try to Praise the Mutilated World" appeared; in the following months, W. S. Merwin's "To the Woods," Deborah Garrison's "I Saw You Walking," and C. K. Williams's "War" addressed, both directly and obliquely, the attack. Many other poets, including Amiri Baraka, Frank Bidart, Kamau Brathwaite, Louise Glück, and Yusef Komunyakaa, had their own, often controversial, responses.

3. Aside from the poets directly discussed in this chapter, poets such as Peter Cooley, Yusef Komunyakaa, Brenda Marie Osbey, and Brad Richard have addressed the effects of Katrina in individual poems. Nicole Cooley, Katie Ford, Raymond McDaniel, Alison Pelegrin, and Martha Serpas offer book-length mediations or long sequences of poems on Katrina and its aftermath.

4. Katrina has few literary parallels. The closest is the 1928 September storm that swept across south Florida from the Atlantic, described by Zora Neale Hurston in *Their Eyes Were Watching God*. While it has been estimated that twenty-five hundred perished, many bodies were washed into the Everglades never to be retrieved, counted,

or named; as most were agricultural workers, including Caribbean migrant workers, there was little documentation. What is apparent is the invisibility of the victims, particularly, if not explicitly, if they were of African descent.

5. For example, the anthology edited by Bill McKibben, *American Earth: Environmental Writing since Thoreau*, includes only one work by an African American writer, an essay by Alice Walker. This anthology, like many others of its kind, begins with an 1837 entry in Thoreau's *Journals*. That same year in New York, John S. Taylor published Charles Ball's slave narrative, *Slavery in the United States: A Narrative of the Life and Adventures of Charles Ball, a Black Man*, which includes extensive passages describing the ecologies, agricultural practices, and intersections of the slave economy and the degradation of the environment. Ball's work, like that of many other African Americans, is seldom included in anthologies of environmental literature or theory.

6. Consider Wheatley's "On Being Brought from Africa to America" (1773), where the allusions to the indigo and sugar plantation economies are alluded to in conjunction with race and humanness, in the lines "Some view our sable race with scornful eye, / 'Their colour is a diabolic dye,' / Remember, *Christians*, *Negroes* black as *Cain*, / May be refin'd and join th' angelic train." North American environmental literature and nature writing, as collected in anthologies, generally begins with Thoreau, a decision that implicitly grounds this writing in a particular, arguably masculine, framework.

7. See, for example, Allen, F. Michael Higginbotham, and A. Leon Higginbotham for discussions on racism and the structure of white supremacy.

8. Evie Shockley's reading of the work of Ed Roberson in her *Renegade Poetics: Black Aesthetics and Formal Innovation in African American Poetry* is illustrative of black ecopoetics. Shockley argues that Roberson's intention "was explicitly to challenge the racism underlying both the view that African American experience could not be effectively mapped onto the 'universal' theme of nature and the view that African American poetry was 'simple,' as opposed to being multilayered and, moreover, containing levels of philosophical abstraction" (152).

9. Sanyika offers a succinct discussion of the conditions of black New Orleanians before and after Katrina.

10. The issue of the militarization of police forces has returned to national prominence with well-publicized police shootings of multiple African American men in 2014 and 2015.

11. Hastert's September 2, 2005, comments were expanded on by various commentators; see, for example, Jack Shafer's "Don't Refloat: The Case against Rebuilding the Sunken City of New Orleans."

12. While Smith has not herself mentioned a connection between Oya and Hurricane Katrina, her depictions of Katrina may exemplify an act of unconscious cultural recollection that underscores cultural continuities across the African Diaspora, as Robert Ferris Thompson has argued.

Works Cited

Allen, Theodore W. *The Invention of the White Race*. New York: Verso, 2012. Print.

Arigo, Christopher. "Notes toward an Ecopoetics: Revising the Postmodern Sublime and Juliana Spahr's *This Connection of Everyone with Lungs*." *HOW2* 3.2 (2008). Web. 5 September 2014.

Ball, Charles. *Slavery in the United States: A Narrative of the Life and Adventures of Charles Ball, a Black Man*. New York: John Taylor, 1837. Print.

Bullard, Robert. *Dumping in Dixie: Race, Class, and Environmental Quality*. 3rd ed. Boulder, CO: Westview P, 2000. Print.

Bullard, Robert, and Beverly Wright, eds. *Race and Environmental Justice after Hurricane Katrina: Struggles to Reclaim, Rebuild, and Revitalize New Orleans and the Gulf Coast*. Boulder, CO: Westview P, 2009. Print.

Butler, Judith. *Precarious Life: The Powers of Mourning and Violence*. New York: Verso, 2004. Print.

Carney, Judith A., and Richard Nicolas Rosomoff. *In the Shadow of Slavery: Africa's Botanical Legacy in the Atlantic World*. Berkeley: U of California P, 2009. Print.

Cooley, Nicole. *Breach*. Baton Rouge: Louisiana State University Press, 2010. Print.

Dungy, Camille, ed. *Black Nature: Four Centuries of African American Nature Poetry*. Athens: U of Georgia P, 2009. Print.

Finney, Carolyn. *Black Faces, White Spaces: Reimagining the Relationship of African Americans to the Great Outdoors*. Chapel Hill: U North Carolina P, 2014. Print.

Finney, Nikky. *Head Off & Split*. Evanston, IL: Triquarterly Books, 2011. Print.

Ford, Katie. *Colosseum*. St. Paul, MN: Graywolf P, 2008. Print.

Gleason, Judith. *Oya: In Praise of the Goddess*. Boston: Shambhala, 1987. Print.

Higginbotham, A. Leon. *Shades of Freedom: Racial Politics and Presumptions of the American Legal Process*. Oxford: Oxford UP, 1996. Print.

Higginbotham, F. Michael. *Ghosts of Jim Crow: Ending Racism in Post-racial America*. New York: New York UP, 2013. Print.

Hurston, Zora Neale. *Their Eyes Were Watching God*. Urbana: U Illinois P, 1980. Print.

Ishiwata, Eric. "'We Are Seeing People We Didn't Know Exist': Katrina and the Neoliberal Erasure of Race." Johnson. 32–59.

Johnson, Cedric, ed. *The Neoliberal Deluge: Hurricane Katrina, Late Capitalism, and the Remaking of New Orleans*. Minneapolis: U Minnesota P, 2011. Print.

Madhubuti, Haki R. *Claiming Earth: Race, Rage, Rape, Redemption—Blacks Seeking a Culture of Enlightened Empowerment*. Chicago: Third World P, 1994. Print.

McDaniel, Raymond. *Saltwater Empire*. Minneapolis, MN: Coffee House P, 2008. Print.

McKibben, Bill, ed. *American Earth: Environmental Writing since Thoreau*. New York: Library of America, 2008. Print.

Monge, Luigi. "Their Eyes Were Watching God: African-American Topical Songs on the 1928 Florida Hurricanes and Floods," *Popular Music* 26.1 (January 2007): 129–40. Print.

Pelegrin, Alison. *Big Muddy River of Stars*. Akron: U Akron P, 2007. Print.

Rankine, Claudia. *Citizen: An American Lyric*. Minneapolis, MN: Graywolf, 2014. Print.

Rich, Adrienne. *On Lies, Secrets, and Silence: Selected Prose, 1966–1978*. New York: Norton, 1979. Print.

Rivera, Jason David, and DeMond Shondell Miller. "Continually Neglected: Situating Natural Disasters in the African American Experience," *Journal of Black Studies* 37.4 (March 2007): 502–22. Print.

Robertson, Linda. "How Shall We Remember New Orleans? Comparing News Coverage of Post-Katrina New Orleans and the 2008 Midwest Floods." Johnson. 269–99.

Ruffin, Kimberly N. *Black on Earth: African American Ecoliterary Traditions*. Athens: U Georgia P, 2010. Print.

Sanyika, Mtangulizi. "Katrina and the Condition of Black New Orleans: The Struggle for Justice, Equity and Democracy." Bullard and Wright. 87–111.

Serpas, Martha. *The Dirty Side of the Storm*. New York: Norton, 2007. Print.

Shafer, Jack. "Don't Refloat: The Case against Rebuilding the Sunken City of New Orleans." *Slate*, September 7, 2005. Web. July 10, 2015.

Shockley, Evie. *Renegade Poetics: Black Aesthetics and Formal Innovation in African American Poetry*. Iowa City: U Iowa P, 2011. Print.

Smith, Kimberly K. *African American Environmental Thought: Foundations*. Lawrence: UP Kansas, 2007. Print.

Smith, Patricia. *Blood Dazzler*. Minneapolis: Coffee House P, 2008. Print.

Soyka, Joseph. "The Right to Write about It: Literature, after Katrina." *Quarterly Conversation* 17 (Fall 2009). Web. August 13, 2014.

Taylor, Dorceta. *Race, Class, Gender, and American Environmentalism*. Portland, OR: U.S. Department of Agriculture, Forest Service, Pacific Northwest Research Station, 2002. Print.

Thompson, Robert Ferris. *Flash of the Spirit: African and Afro-American Art and Philosophy*. New York: Vintage, 1984.

Trethewey, Natasha. *Beyond Katrina: A Meditation on the Mississippi Gulf Coast*. Athens: U Georgia P, 2010. Print.

Trethewey, Natasha. *Native Guard: Poems*. Boston: Houghton Mifflin, 2006. Print.

Wheatley, Phillis. *Complete Writings*. Ed. Vincent Carretta. New York: Penguin, 2001. Print.

Whitmont, Edward C. *Return of the Goddess*. New York: Crossroad P, 1982. Print.

NINE

Claudia Rankine and the Body Politic

Elisabeth A. Frost

Using text and image in dialogue, Claudia Rankine's Don't Let Me Be Lonely: An American Lyric (2004) investigates how we understand the contemporary world's media onslaughts, immersing us in a still version of the inundation of information we process daily. Black-and-white photos, photo-collages, and drawings (often fictionalized images of TV news broadcasts) cohabit the page with blocks of prose at once analytic and lyrical. Extensive notes expand upon, cite sources for, and ironize the content, providing a countertext to the book's first-person, seemingly confessional, narratives, and linking Rankine's work to the recent reemergence of documentary poetics. Don't Let Me Be Lonely creates its own archive to meld cultural criticism, prose poetry, and visual art to explore what it means to inhabit an individual body—and a social body. I argue that Rankine illustrates our lack of understanding of what constitutes corporeal experience in a world gone virtual—a world-as-spectacle.

In the years after the publication of Don't Let Me Be Lonely, Rankine extended her artistic practice into time-based media. In collaboration with the artist John Lucas, she has created a series of video essays called, simply, "Situations." Like Don't Let Me Be Lonely, these scenarios create tensions between their verbal and visual elements, in order to provoke reflections on civic violence captured in specific moments in time. Rankine's most recent book, Citizen: An American Lyric (2014), extends this urgent work of witness by focusing on race not only as a social construct but as embodied experience. Rankine explores the lived realities of how race functions as a visible sign in our culture. Most fundamentally—and the reason this book has garnered extraordinary attention—Rankine documents the daily experience of violence inflicted on raced bodies, from micro-aggression to murder. In Citizen, six of the "Situation" videos appear as sections, identified as scripts and adapted to the page, revealing that her practice, no matter the medium, is a seamless one of social critique. I will examine several of Rankine's works—Don't Let Me Be Lonely, two of Rankine and Lucas's "Situation" videos, and several passages from *Citizen*—to show how Rankine explores, both formally and conceptually, bodies in crisis, and the crisis about bodies, seeking a remedy against a world of disembodied information and all-too-quotidian violence. In *Don't Let Me Be Lonely*, scenarios that focus variously on illness, mortality, and the lived experience of violence—especially racism—dramatize the confusions, inconsistencies, and denial that comprise our "understanding" of corporeality in contemporary America. Here Rankine's work strives toward an elusive but crucial goal: to replace spectacle with sensation and affect, with lived, embodied experience. In *Citizen*, the danger and vulnerability of that embodiment come into dramatic relief. I argue that throughout her genre-defying work, Rankine strives toward textual embodiment—a practice of writing, reading, and experiencing that seeks to bring the corporeal into, and through, the work of art.

★

An epigraph from Aimé Césaire provides this potent warning at the start of *Don't Let Me Be Lonely*: "most of all beware, even in thought, of assuming the sterile attitude of the spectator, for life is not a spectacle, a sea of grief is not a proscenium, a man who wails is not a dancing bear." Despite continual self-consciousness—through its endnotes, the work alludes repeatedly to its medium and breaks the "fiction" of its own narrative present—it becomes evident quickly that Rankine experiences no postmodern sublime. To the contrary, *Don't Let Me Be Lonely* is an extended lament over the state of the world's body, overtaken as it is by the spectacle Césaire cautions against.[1]

Emblematic of that spectacle is a recurring image of a television set with a staticky screen. Although there is no narrative through-line in the book, there are series of prose poems and photo-collages, each of which is demarcated by a full-page divider on which the static on the TV screen suggests a blank between programs, a disconnection from the metaphorical airwaves—a moment of no reception.[2] Renditions of media events appear in photo-collages on the same TV set—simulacra of simulacra. The effect is of supreme isolation: the TVs suggest the loneliness of Rankine's title, as well as a stark opposition between how we live now (screen-to-screen, rather than face-to-face) and a lost materiality of flesh. In fact, the well-being of bodies is Rankine's primary subject, surfacing both in the TV images and in the stories recounted within the text (or its notes). In tension with its self-consciously poetic subtitle, "An American Lyric," *Don't Let Me Be Lonely* is a predominantly narrative and discursive work, but although Rankine employs the first person, hers is a kind of fictional autobiography, conveying fragments of larger stories in the manner of confessional poetry on the one hand and TV talk show culture on the other.

Whether depicted on TV or recounted by the narrator, what happens in the book is almost always conveyed second- or thirdhand, far removed from lived, embodied experience. Many of the scenarios focus on illness or bodily traumas. In one sequence, the narrator responds to a friend with a newly received breast cancer diagnosis; another friend grapples with the sudden death in a car crash of her sister's family; someone's decline from Alzheimer's disease poses irresolvable emotional challenges; and another friend struggles with a clinical depression that is witnessed by the puzzled, ineffectual narrator. Periodically, we are also reminded of the narrator's work as a writer and her current project: a study of hepatotoxicity or liver disease, an ironically ineffectual effort to understand the body. At the same time, the speaker grapples with the news, bringing into the book's orbit the wider concerns of the public sphere, from the late 1990s through the U.S. invasion of Afghanistan. The narrator reflects on it all—the spectacle of the death of Princess Diana; the police killing of Amadou Diallo, and the police torture of Abner Louima, both in New York City; the execution of the Oklahoma City bomber, Timothy McVeigh; the events and aftermath—including war—of September 11, 2001. The voice remains oddly disembodied, as if poised between two unsavory possibilities: the agonized lived experiences of bodies and the agony of not being able to feel at all. Through these narratives we witness the paradox of our culture's dual obsession with disembodied image on the one hand and the medicalizing of bodies and emotions on the other. We engage with the vicissitudes of the entire social body, revealed by way of metonymy—in myriad individual stories.

From a theoretical vantage point, I would suggest that both the text and the images of Don't Let Me Be Lonely dramatize ongoing cultural conflicts about embodiment. As a writer of her generation—a writer committed to social justice—Rankine inherits a legacy of identity politics that proposes a knowable, empirical, often positivist, sense of bodily integrity and import. At the same time, she grapples with a post-Enlightenment (posthumanist) sense of the contingency of all corporeality on cultural codes, discourses, and belief systems. Rankine explores the tensions between these philosophies, evident not only in the stories she tells but also in the restless formal experimentation of the work. Linda Martín Alcoff asks questions similar to Rankine's: "How do [racial and gendered identities] relate to subjectivity, lived experience, and what a given individual can see and know? And what are the implications of a fuller understanding of these identities and political practices?" (8). In her response to narrative and lyric poetic traditions, as well as to visual culture, Rankine shares Alcoff's desire to explore fundamental questions about bodies and politics—even as she dramatizes the challenges of doing so.[3] Perhaps most fundamentally, Rankine asks, in phenomenological terms, how we know when (whether) we are "alive" in our own bodies. All too often, she suggests, we don't know—the assaults of contemporary living have dulled our senses and emotions. Rankine's reality is that of Lauren Berlant's "crisis ordinariness," in which traumatic experiences are routine rather than exceptional, and their "affective impact" results in new forms of mediation and adaptation: "In the impasse induced by crisis, being treads water; mainly, it does not drown" (10). For Rankine, all being is fragile, and the line between life and death impossible to draw. "What do we mean to each other? / What does a life mean?" one sparsely written page asks (62). Posing such basic questions, Rankine suggests that often we simply do not know.

In one sequence, for example, the narrator records a dialogue: "I thought I was dead," the exchange begins. Soon a second voice asks, "You'd let me be lonely?" To which the first repeats, "I thought I was dead" (16). Externalizing the uncertainty of existence, the speaker distances herself from the other, from herself, and from all affect. Even when asked, "Did you feel dead?" the first speaker resists identifying any emotional state within herself, resorting to another externalization: "I said, God rest me." The recounting of this speech act—a prayer—leaves unanswered the interlocutor's question, just as it leaves uncertain the "aliveness" of the speaker. The brief, repetitive dialogue circles back to the first assertion, with which it closes: "I thought I was dead." The speaker avoids both emotional and sensory experience, repeatedly taking recourse to the cognitive—to "thought." Rankine illustrates here that our own knowledge of aliveness is never sure because of our inadequate understanding of emotional and corporeal existence; all epistemic systems have failed. In this surreal, anti-Cartesian exchange, it's not just that the concepts of life and death are unclear; in a reverse tautology, the lived experience of life is no evidence of its existence (or one's existence).

Our empirical traditions have left us bereft of innate knowledge, even though—as Rankine's ubiquitous TV sets suggest—we are overwhelmed with information. Rankine's page space performs this media saturation: white space tends to correspond in the book to text when it appears "alone" on the page, while those pages that contain images are more often crowded to the margins, saturated, as if they would be "lonely" without that media input. We receive confirmation of this tendency in the narrator's description of her use of the TV in her daily life: "I leave the television on all the time. It faces the empty bed. I don't go into the bedroom during the day once I've dressed. Sometimes . . . I go in there and people are conversing" (15). Loneliness is captured in the image not only of the staticky TV (not just a screen but rather the whole set—the complete medium) but also in a Google search screen, an adhesive-backed prescription label, and the almost quaint-looking highway billboard that appears on the cover and within the volume. Even in duress,

TV trumps lived experience, as when an Alzheimer's patient struggling with language poses a seemingly metaphysical request to "see the lady who deals in death"—perhaps in this way showing "insight into his own mortality." Instead, the narrator realizes, in a moment of bathos, he wants to watch *Murder, She Wrote* (18).

As a product of such endless mediation, the bodies in *Don't Let Me Be Lonely* are not just unknowable but uncanny, illegible. To demonstrate how little we comprehend of our own being, Rankine focuses on the body's gray areas: emotional and somatic phenomena like tears; the mysterious condition of sleep; the soft tissue of the body-mind intersection. Whether through a commercial for Paxil (29), a series of visuals of prescription labels (30, 32, 68), a lengthy list of pharmaceutical companies (115), or the speaker's oft-referenced history with legal drugs from aspirin to Prozac, we are led to wonder where the physiological ends and the psychological begins. Can London's Museum of Emotions really help anyone quantify the grief so many experienced at Princess Diana's death? More to the point, the speaker asks, aren't the millions of mourners "simply grieving the random inevitability of their own deaths?" (39). How do we know when public mourning lapses from a socially acceptable phase into a form of group hysteria or medical disorder—somatic, emotional, spiritual, or all of these? Such questions are hard to answer not because of what we don't know but because of what we supposedly *do* know—because of the scientific bodies of knowledge that discount embodiment as such. In *Lonely*, Rankine reminds us, with Judith Butler, that bodies are of course material, but they're also "bound up with signification from the start" (30). Or, as Elizabeth Grosz puts it, bodies are "both biological and psychical . . . a hinge or threshold between nature and culture" (9). Rankine's focus is this corporeal "hinge or threshold."

Given such complexity, self-knowledge remains elusive. Rankine parodies the ways in which our culture claims we look inside ourselves—in the positivist tradition, we take pictures and analyze the results. Rankine uses the MRI machine as her figure, since it provides images of what is least defined in a body, such as its soft tissue, which can be especially subject to nonspecific symptoms (muscle pain, headache, nerve damage). The MRI is also used for difficult diagnoses, including cancer. In one sequence, the narrator receives news of a friend's diagnosis—breast cancer. A large image of a mammogram dominates the first page in this series, its curved lines and bright spots (indicating, perhaps, the cancer itself) nearly overwhelming the three short paragraphs that appear above and below it. The narrator points out that because the lump was missed the year before, misdiagnosed, death has become even less knowable: "when does her death actually occur?" she wonders. Rankine parallels the inability to interpret the clinical image—the mammogram—with the narrator's and the friend's incredulity: "Do you believe this? Can you believe this? Can you?" the friend asks (8). The search for knowledge and control through an intrusive, medicalized gaze has resulted in no enlightenment; there is clearly nothing now to "believe" in, certainly not in the sense of either faith or scientific clarity. Rather, the misreading of the evidence culled from the body has resulted in a shock—the shock of mortality. And within the system of Western medical science, feeling is inaccessible: as in the other narratives in *Don't Let Me Be Lonely*, this one presents the narrator as avoiding any expression of emotion. She moves instead, a page or so later, to a discussion of the film *Magnolia*, whose plot also includes a cancer diagnosis. The narrator sits by the friend's bedside—the friend dying now—talking about a movie.

In the same way that the mammogram represents our culture's ineffectual efforts to look inside ourselves, the narrator's attempt to do just that is also parodied. Consider the speaker's project of writing a book about hepatotoxicity: liver failure. The liver is critical to "living": it filters toxins, a metaphor for the toxic information we ingest daily. Studying the liver, the narrator is attempting to "read" the body. But in a scene between the narrator and her editor, meeting to discuss the project, we find the narrator taken off-guard. The speaker is in fact not a good reader, even in the face of easy questions, as in the editor's request to tell her "exactly what the liver means to me." The narrator can't begin to answer. We enter the realm of theory, an ironic set of writerly questions: "she wants . . . an explanation of the mysterious connections that exist between an author and her text," she writes defensively (54). But more to the point, a column of text appears alongside a pseudo-anatomy chart: "Why do I care about the liver? I could have told her it is because the word *live* hides within it. Or we might have been able to do something with the fact that the liver is the largest single internal organ next to the soul, which looms large though it is hidden." In the accompanying graphic, that soul is a map of the United States, an organ located somewhere in the Midwest of the torso.

The image constitutes a metonymy in reverse, a people lurking within a single body, a body politic lost in its own individuality. The end of this section—with its allusion to César Vallejo and the assertion that knowledge can be a prescription against despair—gets us as close as we ever can to interiority. "In truth," the narrator asserts, "I know the answer to [the editor's] question, but how can I say to her, *Understand without effort that man is left, at times thinking, as if trying to weep.*" Naturally, "she couldn't really use it for ad copy" (55). In this anatomy of melancholy, the writer would like the liver to siphon out toxins, to do what used to be a sacramental function. The absurdity here is less the editor's—of course none of this is good for ad copy—than the narrator's. The graphic "embodies" this disjunction alongside the stream of text: trying to read the body, the speaker mistakes the soul for an organ.

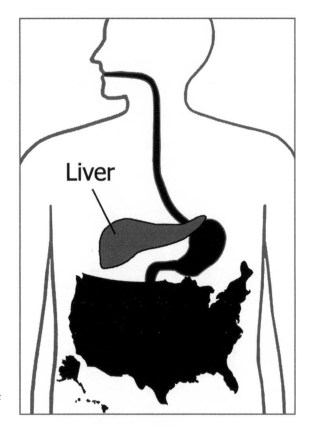

Fig. 5. Liver graphic, *Don't Let Me Be Lonely*, p. 54

Another series of pages displays the body as doodle. If the previous collage breaks the textual fiction (after all, who within the text could have "made" that graphic image?), in this instance, the body as doodle is perfectly naturalistic. In this brief scene, the narrator's mother tells her that she needs a "readable" life (a text to be glossed, an MRI result to be analyzed). The mother seeks not a happy, fulfilled, or even socially acceptable life, but a *legible* one. Again the speaker withdraws from the moment, this time distancing herself by doodling, an ironically embodied form of unconscious expression. We see a cartoon-like drawing of the mother's mouth, expressing nothing—there is no speech or even a thought-bubble attributed to it. Both anatomy and signification fail, opaque even in the act of speech. The narrator turns "inward," but her inner life is no more than a mimicry of the nonstop queries of TV ads: "As I watch my mother's mouth move, I ask myself: Am I often troubled by constipation?" There is an aptness here, of course. If the mother suffers from "diarrhea of the mouth"—and that pun does indeed underlie this scene— then the daughter suffers from the opposite condition (40). It is a moment

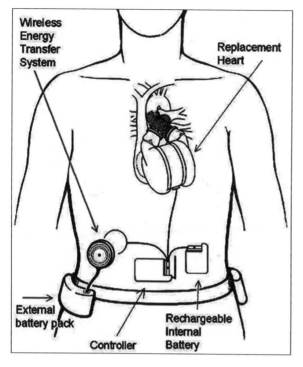

Fig. 6. Graphic of "Mr. Tools," *Don't Let Me Be Lonely*, p. 70

of noncommunication, of the daughter's anger at being judged. The mother's body is, to the narrator, as illegible as the narrator's life is to the mother. Rankine pushes further into parody: "Have I ever vomited love or coughed up blame?" She might well ask such a question—when *does* the psychic "bleed" into the somatic? When do we make ourselves sick with rage? When does love sour into blame? The doodle in the center of the page allows the narrator to parody the mother, even as the personal impasse—the lack of connection and communication—remains.

Rankine's tracing of cultural discomfort over bodies is perhaps epitomized by "Mr. Tools." A schematic diagram, centered on a left-hand page, faces two paragraphs of text. The line drawing of a torso—ending at neck and hips—displays a large cylinder labeled "Replacement Heart," a smaller one labeled "Wireless Energy Transfer System," and a series of battery packs at the figure's waist and abdomen. "Mr. Tools," the first paragraph begins, "for a while the only person in the world walking around with an artificial heart, said the weirdest thing was being without a heartbeat" (71). As paratextual confirmation, we are informed by a note that a man whose name really was Robert Tools survived a heart transplant and that his artificial heart, the only one at that time existing in a human body, made a "whirr" instead of a beat. He was for this reason a "lonely singularity" as long as he lived (71). The sound of his own living—the language of his body—no longer matched that of the rest of humanity, and no longer was it a familiar somatic sign to him of his own existence. Of course, all contemporary bodies are both permeable and contingent; Rankine illustrates our unacknowledged status as cyborgs, continually revamped, just like Mr. Tools, by technological interventions, from eyeglasses to synthetic hips.[4] But more fundamental to Rankine's vision is loneliness—Tools's corporeal singularity, which Rankine evokes through the irony of his name and the overdetermined metaphors associated with the heart: "Mr. Tools had the ultimate tool in his body. He felt its heaviness. The weight on his heart was his heart." With the metaphor of a heavy heart made a material reality, Tools experienced the ultimate alienation from his own body. In this, and despite his singularity, Mr. Tools may well have been the quintessential contemporary human. Rankine suggests through such examples that without the language for what we used to call unironically the *soul*, we don't know what it means to exist. What could be more lonely?

Don't Let Me Be Lonely concerns the status of bodies. But as these examples also make clear, Rankine is concerned above all about the explicitly political nature of bodies. In fact, all of Rankine's unknowable or illegible bodies are in need of sanctuary. Like Paul Celan, whose work has influenced her own, she attempts somehow to put flesh into text—to embody experience, sometimes unspeakably violent experience, in material words. In an autobiographical statement (in 2000, during the composing of the book), Rankine wrote:

> I think sometimes I am too private, too lonely in my heart, but my mind rows constantly as if involved in a public disturbance. When poet Paul Celan writes "pray Lord, pray to us, we are near," I feel he speaks of me and I with him in talking to God. There are some of us who are constantly mending our hearts, I write into that mending, my writing is that mending. (*African American Literary Book Club*)

Lonely performs that mending, stitching together individual corporeal experiences into a textual fabric. Rankine has stated that she is interested in "allow[ing] the field of the poem to be open to all the ways we are domestically and globally intertwined" (Flescher and Caspar), and she speaks of living in a "bruised world," seeking to articulate "felt experience" (*African American Literary Book Club*). For Rankine, poetry must meet its responsibility to attend to the mending of the social body, not just by bearing witness through language, but also by getting as close to textual embodiment as artistic expression allows—giving back to wounded and media-saturated bodies their very flesh.

In particular, Rankine performs this witness for racialized bodies—overexposed in mass media, rendered invisible as objects of projected national fantasies, continually at risk of being brutalized. In this sense, in both *Don't Let Me Be Lonely* and *Citizen*, Rankine builds on—and renders complex—the legacy of identity politics. She focuses on what Alcoff calls "visible identities"—assuming that "one's specific social identity is where one lives, or where one does one's living" (125), or, in concert with Sekou Sundiata, "It all depends on the skin you're living in" (cited by Alcoff 125). Rankine's depictions of racialized bodies, and of the atrocities in our contemporary American moment, combine with her formal breakages—from the use of images to the use of notes—to make us aware of the media in which she works, aware of the work's status as a representation. As she explores "media and mediation" (Flescher and Caspar), then, she can at once move beyond the positivist assumptions of identity politics and still bear witness to "ways in which we are being wounded that we shouldn't forget" (Hoover).

This quotation about "being wounded" refers to the torture of Abner Louima. Here Rankine is describing "the violence that happens to black men in this culture" and her effort to "still" such moments in order to "keep them present"—to keep them in the national memory (Hoover), as she does by including an image of Louima in *Don't Let Me Be Lonely*.[5] Perhaps the central performance of such witness in the book concerns the killing by dragging of James Byrd, Jr., an event the narrator juxtaposes with media coverage of the national disgrace of the 2000 presidential election. At the time that Rankine was writing *Don't Let Me Be Lonely*, the passage of the Matthew Shepard and James Byrd, Jr. Hate Crimes Prevention Act was still nearly a decade away: the act was signed into law by Barack Obama in October 2009; in fact, Obama himself was not even a national political figure at the time of the publication of the book in 2004.[6] Rankine seeks redress, then, for the national forgetting of an all-too-typical atrocity. Rankine describes this section of *Don't Let Me Be Lonely* as an example of her effort to illustrate "the inherent political condition of the black body," citing the artist Mark Bradford, who stated that any black body in public space is, by definition, political. Accordingly, Byrd's body, by its visual identity marks alone, became a target—the very reason that Rankine must "redirect the discussion back to Byrd's body" ("Statement" 245–46).

This sequence begins, however, not with bodies but with a theoretical notion: "Cornel West makes the point that hope is different from American optimism" (21). It's a notion that would later be articulated by Berlant, whose concept of "cruel optimism" entails a mass effort to "manage the incoherence of lives that proceed in the face of threats to the good life they imagine" (10)—a life that will forever elude them. In Rankine's vision of such misplaced optimism, we ironically shift to the seemingly never-ending news coverage of the 2000 election, the "counting" and "recounting" of ballots in a travesty of democratic process. All of this is a distraction from George W. Bush himself, who, the narrator points out, cannot remember whether it was two or three men who were convicted of Byrd's murder—in his own home state, of which he was governor. Bush's forgetting is no accident. We are told that it is an act of will, of not caring enough to remember. And since part of poetry's function is to re-member, it is necessary to attend to bodies, to embodiment.

In fact, in dialogue with the narrator's reflections, we also experience the beginnings of that embodiment. We start with an *absent* American body—the trace of a body (perhaps, metaphorically, that of James Byrd) in the amorphous form of a photo featuring pool of blood; these abject remains stand in for the invisible, "uncounted" body of a murdered man who has been forgotten. The bystanders here too lack bodies (let alone identities), as we see only their feet and legs: they are more gawkers than witnesses.

On the following page, we encounter two more images. The first is of a crime scene; it reads almost as conceptual art: "Head," it says, where there is no head, further emphasizing the *absence* of a human body. In the next image, though, we move from this empty, symbolic reference to a kind of presence: a portrait of James Byrd, Jr. in which his body—his selfhood—is given place.

Byrd's eyes meet our eyes. His gaze back at us is inescapable. In this photo, then, he is re-presented, perhaps even re-membered, in a gesture of healing of the mutilated body and the forgotten particularity of his life, which at the time of Rankine's writing had all but disappeared from the national discourse. And since the "memory" of this text is performed in its notes—not only establishing Rankine's archive but also creating a complex and layered paratext—we learn the source of the photo: the website of the civil rights group NAACP. This knowledge clarifies something else about what we see in Byrd's picture. It *must* be a coincidence that the cap Byrd wears bears Rankine's initials, C. R. Nonetheless, the shared initials can be read as an emblem of identification, recognition, connection—not just between Rankine and Byrd but perhaps also between ourselves and Byrd. The notes for this page, then, serve as an intertext for something that we may already know but have quite possibly suppressed, engaged in our own acts of forgetting and denial, not dissimilar from Bush's.

Two items of news are juxtaposed in Rankine's notes, reading as follows: "On December 12, 2000, Vice President Al Gore conceded the presidential election to George W. Bush, bringing an end to the election dispute that began on November 7 of that year. Gore said he wished to 'heal the divisions' created by the disputed outcome" (135). And the next item:

Fig. 7. Photo, *Don't Let Me Be Lonely*, p. 21

On June 7, 1998, 3 men: John King, Lawrence Brewer, and Shawn Berry, offered James Byrd a ride home in Berry's pickup truck. Byrd was walking along a road in Jasper, a rural town in East Texas. He was returning home from his niece's bridal shower. Instead of bringing him home, the men brought him to a clearing in the woods where they beat him and chained him to the back of the truck. They then sped along a road just east of the town. Byrd's shredded torso was found first, and then his head, neck, and right arm were found about a mile away. Police said a trail of blood, body parts, and personal effects stretched for 2 miles. (135)

This account is an insistent act of witness to the body of James Byrd—most especially because of the unspeakable juxtaposition between the supposed "healing of divisions" in a spurious national election with the "shredded" body of one of its citizens, one of the many who "never counted" in the first place. This act of documentation, this grounding in the historical record, is critical to the restoration of James Byrd's mutilated body, and although there is no pretense here of "healing," there is an effort to recognize a body rendered invisible—and to *feel* as well as to see, beyond the screen.[7] Significant to the process is not only that the text bears witness to James Byrd's body but

Fig. 8. Photo of John Byrd, *Don't Let Me Be Lonely*, p. 22

also that, as spectators and readers, we look James Byrd straight in the eyes. It is that human connection—that spark of recognition and affect—that Rankine seeks and finds all too rarely.

A quieter episode conjures a similar kind of embodiment, exploring what Alcoff describes as "the microinteractions in which racialization operates," the "everydayness of racial experience" (183). The scene presents a dialogue, and it is one of the few times we are made aware that the narrator is a person of color.[8] The narrator and a taxi driver converse "in his rearview mirror," intimating at once connection and distance—the exchange takes place at a remove, via reflection. The driver asks whether she's noticed that "these white people, they think they are better than everyone else." "Have I noticed? Are you joking?" she responds. She learns he is from Pakistan and understands: "I see," she offers. "It's only a few months since 9/11. They think you're al Qaeda." He shows the superior knowledge of the subaltern—"the things they say to me. They don't know anything"—at which she reflects, "Be happy you can't read their thoughts." But rather than speaking at all, she simply "smile[s] into the rear view mirror" (89–90). It's a moment of contact, if only a reflected one, as their eyes meet via the mirror. Such fleeting instances reveal that it remains possible to connect within the public sphere. Such connection requires recognition—here, a shared gaze, an embodied exchange.

*

Despite its emphatic acts of witness and its efforts at textual embodiment, there is a lack of optimism about the American public sphere, and especially about race, which *Don't Let Me Be Lonely* conveys through its narratives. Nonetheless, Rankine's more recent work, including both her video collaborations with the artist John Lucas and the volume *Citizen*, continue to explore not only mass media but also how we might better understand corporeality in concert with notions of community, urging her audience toward embodied awareness.

The first of the videos, *Provenance*, concerns the aftermath of 9/11, exploring the anxiety, vulnerability, and exhaustion that together create complex emotional, embodied responses in public spaces. *Provenance* is a montage of imagery with two voice-over texts. We see a series of stills: sleeping passengers aboard an airplane, heads slack, bodies relaxed, eyes closed. There is nothing remarkable here. In response to this familiar visual cue, anyone who has traveled on board a plane will likely recognize, with discomfort or chagrin, the exposure that results from sleeping near strangers—the vulnerability of the unconscious body, merged with the at-once privileged and disempowering experience of being in an airplane. The video opens without any sound other than the recognizable drone of a jet's ambient noise, as still images capture one passenger after another. These stills continue, as the scene is augmented with a voice-over text. The only eventual motion on screen is that of clouds passing swiftly inside a stylized window adjacent to one or another sleeping passenger.[9] The world outside is small and literally framed—yet this minimal area affords the only motion in play. Sharply focused, the clouds appear to flit by in their oval frame of bright blue sky—the scene is clearly a montage of digital images, not an actual filmed scene. For this reason, the world outside seems dreamlike, stylized, a contemporary version of a classical motif, like a Vermeer window. Although we register that the plane is flying (we hear the noise of engines and ventilation systems), all is still within it; the bodies are unmoving.

The voice-over text, then, ambiguously suggests internality and externality at once, rendering unclear its relationship to the bodies we see: are we hearing an omniscient voice commenting on the scene or a "transcript" of one passenger's consciousness? Where are we located, and where is the inner life of each of these still figures? The text, moreover, is about exhaustion, about nodding off, being released into unconsciousness and the ultimate vulnerability of sleep: "Despite your once-acute awareness," Rankine's voice intones, "your once-attentiveness, you fuse to trust. The nod. The eventual nodding off." In image and text alike, then, the people figured here hold no agency. They are solely the objects of our gazes and the subjects of the author's meditative text.

But another sound-text, indecipherable at first and perhaps confused with the ambient noise of the plane, slowly becomes audible. Eventually we notice that it consists of emergency calls to 911. Then we might start to discern that the 911 calls are those made from the World Trade Center on September 11. The "main" text, Rankine's voice-over, never wavers. It continues, smoothly, soothingly, while the "other" voices gradually become louder, more insistent. All the while, the passengers remain asleep, unmoving (literally so, as the video seems to contain stills montaged together, rather than actual film). I would suggest that the 9/11 tapes are a plea for complexity, for a slowing down or diminution of narrative in favor of an embodied moment. This is the same sort of complex thinking/feeling that the speaker in Don't Let Me Be Lonely laments as having been eroded by 9/11: "It strikes me that what the attack on the World Trade Center stole from us is our willingness to be complex. Or what the attack on the World Trade Center revealed to us is that we were never complex. We might want to believe that we can condemn and we can love and we can condemn because we love our country, but that's too complex" (91).

What is complex in Provenance is the combination of an embodied moment with a political, racialized moment—a search for an elusive sanctuary. The trusting bodies submit to time and place, the conscious self extinguished; the scene evokes at once the anxiety of that hijacked group of passengers on the planes used on 9/11, the "hijacking" of any person traveling in a confined space that has no exit, and the near-miraculous triumph of bodily necessity over anxiety. Provenance bears witness both to a historical event and to a collective experience—a shared confusion of the senses—as consciousness "succumbs," as the text has it, to vulnerability. The voice reflects: "Isn't this confidence? Isn't this the completed life, the body its own conclusion, the only prayer? You exposed, all your doors open, in the stillness of the moment . . . your body there . . . utterly convinced, utterly asleep." The body is "convinced" to let go. Sleep requires "trust," "confidence," the sense of safety that the scene ironically undercuts through our awareness of the violent deaths it references.

At this point, the clamor of the 911 calls (the background to our inner soundtrack of cultural anxiety) has increased and abruptly disappeared. The final sentences of Rankine's lulling voice inform us: "In the air, this happened, of drifting into nothing. The clouds going fast, the clouds going faster, the wind." The video ends on a highly lyrical, even pastoral, note. Through those tapes, and despite the video's avoidance of narrative, Provenance is a plea for an ideal community. Ambiguously, the text offers a deixis whose reference will never quite come clear: "this happened, *of drifting into nothing.*" Perhaps this "nothing" that has "happened" is 9/11 itself, annihilation (crash, implosion). But more literally, consider what we have experienced: the undramatic "nothing" that is people sleeping on a plane. The "drift" into unconsciousness is a relief, a release, in a time of exhaustion and anxiety, and we all share it, precisely because of our shared experience of flesh. In its skillful tension between emergency and banality, *Provenance* asserts a desire for embodied experience and, ultimately, for community.

Like those passages in *Don't Let Me Be Lonely* that seek textual embodiment for raced bodies, especially those rendered invisible through overexposure in the media, Rankine and Lucas's video *Zidane* engages directly with the politics of visible identities.[10] The video captures the few seconds leading up to the infamous head-butt during the 2006 World Cup by the legendary soccer player Zinedine Zidane against his Italian opponent (and former teammate) Marco Materazzi. It happened in overtime, and Zidane had already announced that this would be his final game. The fifteen seconds of documented time was watched live by literally billions of people. Zidane's personal story merges with the public event, and, as in *Provenance*, time slows down; we witness a series of freezes, frame by frame. In this sense, the six-minute slow-motion video inhabits that most familiar of mass-media genres: the instant replay.

But, as in *Provenance*, a subversive voice-over challenges the seeming simplicity of the visual imagery of bodies, with an intrusion of history, theory, and raw feeling. Here, in Rankine and Lucas's search for complexity, the image of a racialized and reified body—the oversimplified image of a great athlete in play—is transformed through the addition of a collage of texts by writers ranging from Frederick Douglass, Frantz Fanon, and Homi Bhabha to Zidane himself. These texts allow Rankine and Lucas to dissect the moment in time and thicken it. As in *Provenance*, we are asked to ask ourselves what happened to this body, and how our embodied selves are implicated in this scene, its "situation" in time and space. Of course, in this case, the episode generated versions of such questions from both fans and the media. But throughout the reporting on the incident, the longer line of history was absent, as was the institutionalized racism in which Zidane's body was ineluctably situated. Specifically, exactly what was said never came out, since neither Zidane nor Materazzi would specify. So the built-in tension between the picture and the words spoken provides Rankine and Lucas with a means of meditating on at least two aspects of this event: the racialized moment that ended Zidane's career in disgrace (with its interpretive impasse of not knowing what was said), and the passage of a body through time itself, a countdown to an instant that seemed at once inexplicable and inevitable.

Understanding the incident requires knowing the ways in which Zidane's

Algerian origins and extremely poor childhood as an immigrant in Marseilles helped make him a national hero, as well as a symbol—a kind of wish fulfillment. Zidane's status came to represent the fantasy of a postcolonial France recovering from trauma and even beginning to heal, despite the atrocities committed in Algeria and the xenophobia that shaped the entire French twentieth century. Did Materazzi utter a racial slur? A sexist taunt about Zidane's sister or his mother (who, the public later learned, was hospitalized at the time)? In the parody of delving for the truth that followed, one of the more grotesque aspects was the hearing world's annexation the otherwise-invisible ranks of "lip-readers" (or speech-readers) to decipher this unheard dialogue—despite the known limits of the technique.[11]

The importation of lipreading as empirical evidence—along with the privilege of able-bodied ignorance—is not overtly critiqued here; nor is the standard, clichéd sexism of possible insults to Zidane's sister or to the "sacred" mother, as Materazzi put it in denying that he leveled such slurs against unprotected femininity. Rankine and Lucas focus on race and colonialism and the language of racist assault: "Big Algerian shit. Dirty terrorist, nigger," as supposedly "seen" by lip-readers. Although the video doesn't fully engage the sexism and ableism the moment also brought forward, the implication Rankine and Lucas draw is a powerful one. As if spiraling out from Materazzi's unknowable speech, the text converts the media's prurient questions into analysis of affect and historical reflection. The intervention they make is to provide context—the very complexity that the mass media remain resistant to. The work literally slows down the incident so that Rankine and Lucas can open space for the most relevant, and most dangerous, awareness: that "there is no black who has not felt, briefly or for long periods . . . simple, naked and unanswerable hatred; who has not wanted to smash any white face he may encounter in a day" (Rankine and Lucas).[12] Further, we are asked to understand, as in *Provenance*, the lack of agency that can overcome a person: in Zidane's words, "Do you think two minutes from the end of a World Cup final, two minutes from the end of my career, I wanted to do that?" What happened, in the video's rendition, is that Zidane tried to follow Fanon's advice—"When such things happen, he must grit his teeth, walk away a few steps." Indeed, we see this take place, but according to Zidane, Materazzi repeated his words a second and then a third time, at which Zidane snapped or, in the words of Frederick Douglass, "resolved to fight." What happened in an instant, Rankine and Lucas imply, took generations of violence to create.

Throughout the media coverage, and implicit in *Zidane*, is the gap between the supposedly surefire evidence of one's senses (the empiricist approach to materiality) and the elusive power of the unknown words (the social and symbolic contexts for that corporeality). In that gap the video seeks to intervene, to slow time down, challenge the empirical evidence of the documented sound and image. The opening of Rankine's theatrical work called *The Provenance of Beauty*—a bus tour of the South Bronx with live and recorded text—captures the concerns with embodied understanding that both of these "Situation" videos explore: "Identity is time passing. Every moment of what we call life is life in the shadow of choice, some fact of your consciousness hesitating before me." It is that hesitation, that possibility or occlusion of "choice," that Rankine and Lucas bear witness to as an embodied moment our culture continues to oversimplify and deny, most blatantly in its racist politics. Delving into the intricate ways that race is (always) socially constructed, Rankine at the same time finds a way to return us to the materiality of the body and visible identities, urging us to see that the public sphere consists of a series of embodied, racialized moments. The resulting wounds must be not just witnessed in art but in fact reembodied.

★

This embodiment is the most fundamental project of *Citizen*, which extends Rankine's work as a cultural critic (and as a text-image, mixed-media artist), at the same time lending focus to that work: here Rankine narrows her explorations of embodiment to the dynamics of racism in contemporary U.S. life. *Citizen* contains several of the scripts used in the "Situation" videos, here adapted to the page. Like the videos, and even more clearly than in the varied narratives of *Don't Let Me Be Lonely*, *Citizen* roots itself in the events of a historical moment terrifying for its racism, from Hurricane Katrina to the deaths of Trayvon Martin, James Craig Anderson, Jordan Russell Davis, and other black men, whose bodies pose a grave threat to the white imaginary and are therefore most vulnerable to brutalization. On the page, the Zidane piece and several other video scripts address themselves to such moments of violence. The dedication of the book to the several men known as the "cooler bandits" announces Rankine's intention to refute mainstream narratives and their representations of race; the lengthy sentences imposed on these teenage boys for nonviolent offenses became the subject of an award-winning documentary by John Lucas that examines the dysfunctions of the criminal justice system.[13] A lengthy section of the book reflects on Serena Williams's struggles with deeply embedded racism in tennis over a period of years. Another section deconstructs emotional reactions to stop-and-frisk incidents. In all the cases described in *Citizen*, Rankine explores the ways in which race and racism, however socially constructed, can be comprehended only by seeking to understand the experiences of bodies themselves. In this way, Rankine addresses herself to the American present and demolishes the myth of a "postracial" America.[14]

If Celan is the muse of *Don't Let Me Be Lonely*, James Baldwin is the muse of *Citizen*. Just as Baldwin wrote essays at once analytical and personal, political and poignant, Rankine attends here less to "media events" than to the ephemeral experiences of daily life. As important as a few nationally covered stories are in *Citizen*, even more significant are the book's short narratives, which Rankine collected from friends and colleagues over a period of years. In exploring not just the kinds of occurrences that make the news but also the kind that don't, Rankine moves the conversation about race away from media representations—their disembodied information—to the everyday life of bodies. As one highly lyrical section puts it, the question that haunts *Citizen* is "How to care for the injured body, // the kind of body that can't hold / the content it is living?" This body—injured psychically and physically—needs what Rankine calls simply a "place," both in itself and in the material world. Neither seems available: "And where is the safest place when that place / must be someplace other than in the body?" (143). Rankine's subject is not so much the ways that mass media encourage our denial of corporeal experience—the primary issue Rankine explored in *Don't Let Me Be Lonely*. By contrast, in *Citizen*, Rankine reveals how the violation of bodies leads to disembodiment—the disassociation following trauma that makes the "safest place" to be "someplace other than in the body."

The moments narrated and dissected in *Citizen* also portray violations of intimacy through conscious or unconscious acts of microaggression, experienced as bodily trauma. Whether life-altering (even life-threatening) or fleeting, these narratives, even more directly than those in *Don't Let Me Be Lonely*, trace the effects of our culture's denials about race on both individual and social bodies. Of particular importance are public places as settings and trust as a concept that binds us to one another in the spaces we share. One of Rankine and Lucas's videos, *Situation 8*, explores this implied contract as "an unconscious reliance on public trust." The video opens with Rankine's voice-over establishing our mutual vulnerability: "Daily we share the same elevators, streets, corridors, stairways, sidewalks, highways, arenas, restrooms, lobbies, subways—in short, all public spaces. . . . The understood question is always, Can I trust you?" Berlant raises similar questions, focusing on "the affective components of citizenship and the public sphere" (3). A further parallel emerges in the term "situation" itself, which Berlant uses to distinguish a moment of incipient change from Alain Badiou's concept of the "event" ("a drama that shocks being into radically open situations"). For Berlant, a "situation is a state of things in which *something* that will perhaps matter is unfolding amid the usual activity of life" (5). That *something* is distinctive for its potential, rather than for any undeniable "drama": a situation "produces a sense of the emergence of something in the present that may become an event" (5).

In Rankine and Lucas's "Situation" videos, the "usual activity of life" is similarly altered—but in indefinite ways—by the "emergence of something." Like the "Situation" videos, *Citizen* too exposes that incipience—its potential for injury and, at least at times, for healing.

A primary concern in *Citizen* is to embody the *language* of race. As Ralph Ellison attests (cited in the script to the Zidane video), "Perhaps the most insidious and least understood form of segregation is that of the word" (122). As a poet writing an "American lyric," Rankine returns dead metaphors about race to their corporeal realities. In *Citizen*, "micro" moments of racism appear not as the workings of a given ideology but rather as sensory shocks. A refrain brings home this bodily experience—a corporeal reaction to language. Repeatedly, the question arises—"What did you say?" or "What did you mean?" Capturing not only incredulity but also the distrust of one's senses—as in, *Did I just hear that?*—this recurring question portrays the racist moment as an exchange between two bodies, rather than the effect of a political platform or even a belief system. Everyday racism, Rankine implies, evades cognition. It is inflicted by one body on another, individually, and it is the more powerful for its sometimes unconscious emotional origins. When a friend claims that she is just joking when she calls the "you" in one narrative a "nappy-headed ho" (41) for being late to meet her, "the incoherence feels violent," and the "cut" is all the more painful because it comes—so shockingly—from an intimate. That intimacy, a compact between two embodied subjects, is ripped apart: "you watch [the cut] rupture along its suddenly exposed suture" (42).

Just as she reveals the effects of words on bodies, Rankine also unpacks the metaphor of being visible (or invisible). These narratives show concretely how seeing and being seen are deeply contested realities. The script for a "Situation" video about Hurricane Katrina asks repeatedly, "Have you seen their faces?" (83, 85). Rankine includes in *Citizen* another text she identifies as the script from a "Situation" video, this one called *Stop-and-Frisk*. The men pulled over or accosted in the *Stop-and-Frisk* scenario similarly are not *seen*. The refrain in that piece shows the ways in which day-to-day racism violates the most fundamental sensory inputs, because "you are not the guy and still you fit the description" (105). The same is true for the most "visible" media figures. Serena Williams cannot be "seen" for the racial fantasies projected onto her body. The workings of the white imaginary is most grotesquely represented in the photo of Caroline Wozniacki "impersonating" Serena "by stuffing towels in her top and shorts, all in good fun, at an exhibition match," thereby "embodying Serena's attributes while leaving Serena's 'angry nigger exterior' behind"—that is, erasing Serena herself (35, 36). In the same way, Rankine demonstrates the roles acted in a perverse American morality play. "In line at the drugstore it's finally your turn," one anecdote begins. When the female "you" is cut off by a man walking in front of her, and the cashier points this out, the man is "truly surprised": "Oh my God, I didn't see you," he says. The "you," placating, returns, "You must be in a hurry." The piece ends with his disconcerting reply, insistent with repetition: "No, no, no, I really didn't see you" (77). How can anyone miss another person, not notice that person's body, right there? The man caught in this situation is in fact more "surprised" than the person he stepped in front of, suggesting how common this experience is for the "you" in the story. Without any mention of race, this event relocates the floating concept of invisibility in specific bodies, showing the workings of privilege in our shared public spaces.

This episode parallels several others. In one, a little boy is knocked down by a stranger on a subway platform, a "person that did not see him, has never seen him, has perhaps never seen anyone who is not a reflection of himself" (17). The incident illustrates a friend's theory, described a few pages earlier, "that Americans battle between the 'historical self' and the 'self self,'" a battle in which race, especially its visible markers, continually impedes intimacy "with the full force of . . . American positioning," a force that will "wipe the affable smiles right from your mouths" (14). In its more despairing moments, Rankine's book depicts this "American positioning" as a given, unchangeable. In response to "another, What did he say?"—that is, another racist slur, this time launched at a couple in a car by "a mouth" in another vehicle—the only possible reaction is stoicism: "This is how you are a citizen: Come on. Let it go. Move on" (151). In Rankine's portrayal of the "self self" versus the "historical self," the latter seems always to trump the former.

In *Citizen*, what happens in the national eye is reflected, directly or indirectly, in daily interactions across the country. All affective relations are scarred. The verdict of the Trayvon Martin case—the finding of George Zimmerman as not guilty of second-degree murder—is evoked in the title of the piece from which the above passage about citizenry is drawn: "July 13, 2013" is the date of that verdict. There is only one mention of the case within the piece, though, in an indirect reference that "Trayvon Martin's name sounds from the car radio a dozen times each half hour" (151). The meditative pages that follow address not the trial, nor even the shooting itself, but rather the struggle to feel something in its wake. "What feels more than feeling?" (152), Rankine asks with pointed tautology. If feeling can "be a hazard, a warning sign, a disturbance," then too often the "warning" is disregarded: "Don't be ridiculous," the internal monologue runs. "None of the other black friends feel that way" (152). But the problem remains, a "displacement of feeling back into the body, which gave birth to the feelings that don't sit comfortably inside the communal." Here the body is like a holding area. Because of the conflict in "the communal," that body must, unhealthily, house the affect that seeks expression. In this circular economy, the "you" struggles to comprehend what is felt, to move that feeling toward language, but the struggle is overwhelming, and it yields neither utterance nor knowledge: "You are still feeling if only the feeling could be known" (153).

Such passages are deeply pessimistic. But *Citizen* also shows that we have the opportunity—at least on occasion—to transform our social reality through our bodies. The incident of the boy on the subway platform reveals how such change can work. The woman speaking to the "you" describes what happened *after* she attempted unsuccessfully to get the man who pushed the boy to apologize. The man in question will probably never "see" the boy. But for the woman telling this story, "The beautiful thing is that a group of men began to stand behind me like a fleet of bodyguards . . . , like newly found uncles and brothers" (17). It is no coincidence that this hopeful instance involves bodily presence. It describes an action that is at once an individual choice and a public act, one that is soon shared with others and that has an aesthetic dimension—it is a "beautiful thing." The men stand "behind" the woman, supporting her, synchronizing their bodies with hers, transforming themselves into "bodyguards." Importantly, they do this not in any political context (as in the activist injunction to "put your body on the line"). Rather, theirs is a private act, but crucially located in a public place. The men create intimacy by becoming "uncles and brothers." This is how change happens—on a small scale, in acts that forge community by redefining kinship as a matter of choice rather than blood. Rankine shows us that, acting under the most ordinary circumstances, individuals have the power to reclaim citizenry itself from the cynical mode of "go-along-to-get-along" (154) to a radical one of embodied change.

Another key section that evokes public space—and specifically mass transit—reveals the power of a quieter, but no less crucial, embodied act. In "Making Room" (the script for *Situation 7*), the rallying cry of identity politics—to put one's body on the line—is reconceived into an act of solidarity that emerges not from political speech but from simple physical contact. The scenario focuses on a common occurrence: a white woman in public is afraid of a black male body. She is reluctant even to sit beside a black man: because of the man's blackness, "Where he goes the space follows him" (132), and the white woman would "would rather stand all the way to Union Station" (131) than risk proximity, let alone contact. Here is where a small but radical act of one body in relation to another emerges: "You sit next to the man on the train, bus, in the plane, waiting room, anywhere he could be forsaken. You put your body there in proximity to, adjacent to, alongside, within" (131). The seeming excess, even redundancy, in the list of prepositions is precisely Rankine's point, because language can never exhaust all proximal relations; they must all be named, culminating with identity itself: "within." As the uneventful scene unfolds, reflection and determination *follow* the body's action, rather than the other way around, marking the action itself as deeper in its origin than any analytical function. We know this because it is only when the "you" overhears a conversation (about switching seats) that she *thinks* about what she has just done, what it means, and what may follow. The words that swim up in her consciousness have to do with her relation to the man, and in her mind these words are shared with the man himself: "as if from inside your own head you agree that if anyone asks you to move, you'll tell them we are traveling as a family" (133). Like the phalanx of newly created brothers and uncles emerging to support the woman and boy on the subway platform, this "you" has asserted familial relation. In this sense, kinship is at the core of *Citizen*. Experienced as one body choosing relation to another, such "traveling as a family" captures Rankine's own position as a writer bearing witness to the bodies of others.

★

Ever since the publication of *Don't Let Me Be Lonely*, Rankine's complex work in a range of media have signaled our shared uncertainty about the life of bodies. Although Rankine understands that no work of art can attain Celan's impossible ideal—to make flesh into text—she not only makes amply real the horrors of spectacle Césaire warns us of but also persistently does something even more important, culturally and politically. Revealing the lived realities of bodies, Rankine's work offers us the possibility of mutual recognition.

Notes

1. See Bell and Kimberley, both of whom address the themes of media and text/image hybridity in *Lonely*.

2. Rankine also notes that embedded within each static-filled TV screen is an image of George W. Bush (Flescher and Caspar)—a mark of Rankine's engagement, even in subliminal fashion, with the politics of the Bush administration in the book.

3. See Robbins, whose excellent chapter on *Lonely* explores the work as a hybrid form—a lyrical long poem. Robbins states that "Rankine uses the body to register the effects of a fundamentally asocial, antihumanist American culture" and argues that Rankine may "inherit from Walt Whitman's *Song of Myself* . . . the trope of the embodied speaker as a catalyst for a call to unity among the American body politic" (126). I see Rankine's speaker, by contrast, as a vehicle for parody and an example of the spectacle-riddled and disembodied; however, my own reading parallels Robbins's approach to raced bodies in *Lonely*.

4. Here Rankine's meditations on embodiment bring to mind inroads made in dis-

ability studies, including the appropriation of cyborg theory to consider new modes of understanding bodies and affect. For especially helpful and influential formulations, see Davis and Thomson.

5. Robbins explores as well Rankine's focus on the black body as always suspect (142–43).

6. For a discussion of this act, as well as the concept of "amendment" in relation to state violence and the liberal subject as both racialized and sexualized in U.S. law, see Chandan Reddy's introduction to *Freedom with Violence*.

7. See Robbins: "*Don't Let Me Be Lonely* issues an open call to all readers to *feel*" (147).

8. Elsewhere, we learn that the speaker is presumptively female-identified—if, that is, we assume that there is only one narrator in the book. In the episode cited earlier about the TV that is always on in the narrator's bedroom, the speaker mentions changing from skirt to slacks as a routine matter.

9. Rankine explains that she and her husband were on a plane sometime after 9/11 and saw a couple across the aisle, sleeping. Struck by how "trusting" these people looked while they were sleeping, she asked her husband to photograph them. She "started writing around that stillness and the trusting that goes along with sleeping in public, especially in an age of fear." They took over two years to accrue various photos of sleeping passengers (Buschner et al.).

10. Rankine has increasingly brought attention to the "pervasiveness of racism" in the United States (Keniston 245). Her "Open Letter" at the 2011 Associated Writing Programs Annual Meeting, in response to and dialogue with a poem by Tony Hoagland, spurred a national discussion among poets and writers about how they depict race in their work. The many responses gleaned—and posted online—now appear in the volume *The Racial Imaginary*, which Rankine coedited. Such projects make Rankine's most recent work and her role as a public intellectual urgently important.

11. Harmer points out that fewer than 30 percent of English-language words can be effectively read by sight alone. Further, many words and phrases look identical: "fifty" and "fifteen"; "go to Texas" and "no new taxes"; "suffering much" and "son of a bitch" (94).

12. This excerpt is taken from the script of *Zidane*, provided to the author (personal correspondence). The passage cited here is drawn (slightly emended) from "Many Thousands Gone," included in James Baldwin's *Notes of a Native Son*. For the original, see *The Collected Essays of James Baldwin* (Library of America, 1998), 29.

13. See http://coolerbandits.com.

14. A noteworthy aspect of Rankine's effort to document and bear witness to racism in America—especially in the justice system—is her updating of the book's memorials to black victims of white violence. The first print run of *Citizen* includes, alone on facing pages, the following brief texts: "November 23, 2012 / In Memory of Jordan Russell Davis" and "February 15, 2014 / The Justice System" (134–35). The first date marks the killing of the Davis by forty-five-year-old Michael Dunn, who shot the teenager after complaining about his music at a Florida gas station. The second date marks the declaration of a mistrial in the initial court case against Dunn. The next print run of *Citizen* added the name of Michael Brown. Finally, the most recent printing (as of this writing) includes on the left-hand page not only more names—Eric Garner and John Crawford—but also an open-ended list, with blanks beside the phrase "In

memory . . ." On the next page, Rankine has replaced the original text with three lines: "Because white men can't / police their imagination / black men are dying." See the coverage of these updates by Katy Waldman in *Slate*.

Works Cited

African American Literary Book Club. Contributors List: Step into a World: A Global Anthology of the New Black Literature. 2014. Web. 17 September 2014.

Alcoff, Linda Martín. *Visible Identities: Race, Gender, and the Self*. New York: Oxford UP, 2006. Print.

Bell, Kevin. "Unheard Writing in the Climate of Spectacular Noise: Claudia Rankine on TV." *The Global South* 3:1 (2009). 93–107. Print.

Berlant, Lauren. *Cruel Optimism*. Durham, NC: Duke UP, 2011. Print.

Buschner, Jenny, Braulio Fonseca, Kristen Paz, and Josalyn Knapic. "Interview: Claudia Rankine." *South Loop Review* 14 (2014). Web. 17 September 2014.

Butler, Judith. *Bodies That Matter: On the Discursive Limits of Sex*. New York: Routledge, 1993. Print.

Davis, Lennard. *Enforcing Normalcy: Disability, Deafness, and the Body*. New York: Verso, 1995. Print.

Flescher, Jennifer, and Robert N. Caspar. "Interview with Claudia Rankine." *Jubilat* 12 (2006). Reprinted in *Poetry Daily*. http://poems.com/special_features/prose/essay_rankine.php. Web. 17 September 2014.

Grosz, Elizabeth. "Notes towards a Corporeal Feminism." *Australian Feminist Studies* 5 (1987). 3–15. Print.

Hoover, Elizabeth. "Poet Claudia Rankine on Wounds We Should Not Forget." *Sampsonia Way: An Online Magazine for Literature, Free Speech and Social Justice*, November 12, 2012. Web. 17 September 2014.

Kimberley, Emma. "Politics and Poetics of Fear after 9/11: Claudia Rankine's Don't Let Me Be Lonely." *Journal of American Studies* 45 (2011). 777–91. Print.

Rankine, Claudia. *Citizen: An American Lyric*. Minneapolis, MN: Graywolf, 2014. Print.

Rankine, Claudia. *Don't Let Me Be Lonely: An American Lyric*. Minneapolis, MN: Graywolf, 2004. Print.

Rankine, Claudia. "Statement." *The New American Poetry of Engagement: A 21st Century Anthology*. Ed. Ann Keniston and Jeffrey Gray. Jefferson, NC: McFarland, 2012. 245–46. Print.

Rankine, Claudia, and John Lucas. Situations. http://claudiarankine.com. Web. 17 September 2014.

Rankine, Claudia, Beth Loffreda, and Cap Max King, eds. *The Racial Imaginary: Writers on Race in the Life of the Mind*. New York: Fence, 2015. Print.

Reddy, Chandan. *Freedom with Violence: Race, Sexuality, and the U.S. State*. Durham, NC: Duke UP, 2011. Print.

Robbins, Amy Moorman. *American Hybrid Poetics: Gender, Mass Culture, and Form*. New Brunswick, NJ: Rutgers UP, 2014. Print.

Thomson, Rosemarie Garland. *Extraordinary Bodies: Figuring Physical Disability in American Culture and Literature*. New York: Columbia UP, 1996. Print.

Waldman, Katy. "The New Printing of Citizen Adds a Haunting Message about Police Brutality." *Slate*, January 7, 2015. Web. 2 June 2015.

PART FOUR

REDEFINING POETICS

TEN

Echo Revisions

Repetition, Politics, and the Problem
of Value in Contemporary Engaged Poetry

Ann Keniston

A number of politically engaged American poems from the mid-2000s strongly belie Liam Rector's 2002 claim that "recent poems" reveal an "aversion for repetition" (43). The recurrence of repetition in these aesthetically diverse poems is significant partly because it supports a growing consensus that the so-called poetry wars of the past forty or so years—disputes between a range of polarized aesthetics—have finally ended.[1] Repetition, it seems, comes with little of the ideological baggage often associated with rhyme and meter, despite the fact that these techniques are themselves modes of repetition.[2] Repetition in recent poems also seems to respond to a twenty-first-century American culture characterized by events and stories that feel both familiar and redundant, to say nothing of means of reproduction that far exceed the merely mechanical ones described by Walter Benjamin in 1936.[3] At times, though, contemporary poetic repetition seems motivated by a quite different wish to avoid this sense of replay and the sensory overload that it implies; repetition is, after all, traditionally associated with the spell, incantation, chant, and lullaby, qualities that Jeffrey Gray has associated with several post–9/11 American poems.[4]

Recent poetic repetition, it might be hypothesized, thus signals both verisimilitude and unreality. In this way, it recalls Sigmund Freud's association of what he termed the repetition compulsion with both the reproduction of past events (especially traumatic ones) and their transformation, especially the change of the benign and familiar (Heimlich) into something "uncanny and frightening" (Unheimlich) ("Uncanny" 124).[5] Freud associates repetition with repression (Beyond 12) and concealment. In fact, Gilles Deleuze has argued that "the disguises and the variations, the masks and the costumes" evident in Freudian scenes of repetition constitute repetition's "internal genetic elements . . . , its integral and constituent parts" (16–17). Especially when associated with "lyrical language, in which every term is irreplaceable and can only be repeated" (2), repetition is for Deleuze a mode of "transgression or exception" that "is opposed to moral law" (5).

A related tension between similarity and difference is central to the concept of mimicry, which the OED defines as a mode of "copying or closely imitating" that is often intended "to entertain or ridicule."[6] Homi Bhabha, perhaps the best-known contemporary theorist of mimicry—others include Jacques Lacan, Luce Irigaray, and Judith Butler (Morton)—has, in one reader's terms, "applie[d]" this essentially psychoanalytic concept "to colonial discourse" (Morton 710). Mimicry for Bhabha involves a Freudian "*difference that is almost the same, but not quite*" (122); mimicry "*repeats rather than re-presents*" (125), a distinction also made by Deleuze.[7] More specifically, mimicry "mime[s] . . . [colonial] authority" in ways that "deauthorize" it (130). Through this indeterminacy, it "poses an immanent threat" to "disciplinary powers" (123).

For Bhabha, mimicry links a performative, often verbal strategy (repetition) with a social condition (colonial subjugation). Bhabha's focus on colonial and postcolonial texts is quite different from mine, but his reading method is similar: I too wish to argue that the *device* of repetition articulates *conditions* of twenty-first-century American culture. According to Bhabha, the colonizer as well as the colonized engage in mimicry; in the former case, mimicry both reinscribes and challenges colonial claims to authority (123). Repetition in twenty-first-century engaged poems reveals a related ambivalence toward the discourse of the (politically and economically) powerful. At times, these poems appropriate colonizing discourse in ways that indirectly challenge its authority; at others, they adopt non-Western verse forms. Mimicry is, I therefore wish to argue, central to not only the form but the political purpose of contemporary poems. In the terms of my title, which I have borrowed from the poem by Ann Lauterbach with which I close this chapter, the capacity to "echo" earlier language and ideas lets these poets "revise" them.

As the formally and thematically varied poems I discuss below (by Hugh Seidman, H. L. Hix, Maxine Kumin, and Ann Lauterbach) employ repetitive language and forms, they directly consider the topics of economics, measurement, and value. In fact, what is most striking about reading these poems together is that they all pose a version of the same punning question: what is the relation between (timeless, abstract, ethical) values and (material, economic) value? Although the exact relation between virtue and prosperity has been frequently debated throughout American history, these two modes of value are clearly linked: the same word describes both.[8] The poems I consider reveal the connection and also the tension between these ideas, often by considering practices of commodification and appropriation related to globalization.

They also explore, often less directly, a third sense of the term *value*—the concept of aesthetic worth. In quite different ways, each articulates deep anxiety about poetry's value in a culture that tends to ignore or deride it.[9]

I am by no means the first to point out the vexed relation between value and values in artworks, although many critics who have considered this issue have focused on the tension between economic and aesthetic value rather than ethical values. In 1988, Barbara Herrnstein Smith defined "a double discourse of value" that opposed "the discourse of economic theory" to that "of aesthetic axiology" (126–27).[10] Herrnstein Smith began to interrogate this dichotomy, but it is more definitively dismantled in John Guillory's 1993 *Cultural Capital*. Guillory's central claim is that aesthetic discourse is an effect of economic changes associated with modernity (316).[11] In his terms, "The very concept of aesthetic *value* betrays the continued pressure of economic discourse on the language of aesthetics," and aesthetic practices continually reinscribe principles that ensure the continued functioning of the marketplace (317).[12] Yet aesthetic discourse and acts of aesthetic valuation also deny "the fact . . . that the market is the historical *condition*" of aesthetics (324).

In this context, it is significant that much of the disagreement about the New Formalism of the 1980s and 1990s concerned the extent to which poetry could—and should—link ethical positions to poetic form. The advocates of New Formalism attempted to do just this, offering an appeal to what one advocate called "what is of most human value" through a formal traditionalism explicitly designed to appeal to "an audience of common readers" (McPhillips 207). Economics was not explicitly part of this equation, although it is often noted that, in one critic's terms, this poetry reflected "the socioeconomic fabric of America itself under the Reagan administration" (Holden, *Fate* 37). Certainly, many of New Formalism's detractors challenged this poetry by observing that nearly all self-identified New Formalists were affluent, white, and male. Critics also viewed New Formalism's apparently democratizing aesthetics—including the assumptions that a common reader and coherent sense of universal human values exist—as "nothing more than an ideological tool of right-wing politics" (Barron and Meyer xix). A similar alignment of political, economic, and aesthetic value, although with a decidedly different political orientation, is also central to—and disputed in relation to—other late twentieth-century poetic movements, including Language poetry.[13]

The poets I discuss below are, in terms of their demographics, vulnerable to charges similar to those leveled against the New Formalists: they too are white, privileged, and physically safe, although not all are male. The repetition on which their poems relies is also sometimes associated with an essentialized notion of (sometimes exotic) otherness. Repetition tends, as I began to suggest above, to be associated with the "primitive" (Shapiro) and non-Western, an association that seems especially problematic at a moment when the twenty-first-century U.S. global agenda is identified as imperialistic (Grandin). The recent poems I discuss do not express the remoteness, nostalgia, or condescension of which the New Formalists were often accused. But they also fail directly to refute such charges. Instead, they expose these dangers by mimicking them in contexts that destabilize—and reveal what Bhabha calls the difference of—their own repetitions. This mimicry is apparent on at least three levels: these poems use repetitive language and forms; they adopt and repurpose official discourse; and they consider, at times in apparently exaggerated ways, ethical dilemmas. All draw attention to appropriation and commodification (of others' language and suffering) as problems. In fact, tensions between safety and danger, complicity and complaint, and power and powerlessness recur.

In the remainder of this chapter, I will elaborate these claims by considering poems about recent public events by two pairs of poets. First, through readings of a poem by Hugh Seidman and several from H. L. Hix's sequence *God Bless*, I explore the use of repetitive renewable forms, which inherently foreground a tension between sameness (or what John Hollander calls in reference to poetic refrain a sense of "O, *that* again") and difference ("What is it to mean *this* time around?") (75).[14] Partly because these poems acknowledge their reuse of existing language, the effect is a sometimes vertiginous slippage between the original source text and the poet's implied (and often hard to pin down) commentary on it. The result is an unfixed mimicry that can be difficult to distinguish from reportage. In contrast, the second pair, including formally traditional poems by Maxine Kumin and poems in invented forms by Ann Lauterbach, does not reuse other people's language. Perhaps as a result, these poems refer more directly to their status as poems, partly by emphasizing commensurability and the incommensurable rather than valuation. (These concepts are directly associated by Guillory with the discourse of value [322–23] and by Deleuze with repetition [24].) Both poems also directly consider the topic of cultural appropriation, especially the extent to which physically and culturally remote events can be accurately described in poems. Something that might be termed linguistic mimicry (or what the OED calls "copying . . . the speech . . . of another") is thus especially evident in the first pair of poems I examine, whereas a kind of experiential mimicry, in which the poem attempts but fails to convey an extrinsic truth, is more apparently in the second.

*

As its title indicates, Hugh Seidman's 2005 "Found Poem: Microloans" is apparently made up entirely of "found" language. In generalizing and mostly monosyllabic terms and short, simple sentences, the poem praises microloans, small, low-interest loans generally granted by Western nonprofit organizations to women in developing countries in support of small-business development. These loans, the poem asserts, improve these women's lives. While

> Poverty lacks collateral[,]
> . . . .
> A woman fears risk.
> Mothers feed families.
> Microloans lift women.

Partly because of the choppiness of such assertions and partly because the poem's source text is not identified, it is difficult to ascertain whether the poet concurs with this advocacy of microloans: he may be celebrating microloans, neutrally documenting discussion of them, or criticizing them. The pantoum form, in which two lines from each quatrain are repeated in the subsequent one, complicates this confusion. Seidman has, we must assume, selected this repetitive form and ordered the original text's self-contained (even sound bite–like) phrases to conform to its rules. But the pantoum's repetitions defamiliarize the repeated phrases, and the poem as a whole refuses forward movements. (Pantoums always end by repeating two lines from the opening quatrain.) In "Found Poem," the form thus seems to challenge the poem's apparent narrative of upward mobility and progress. Seidman's use (and repetition) of found text intensifies the instability. The apparent redundancy of the text (which comes from elsewhere) combines with the form's repetitions to work, in Bhabha's terms, "both against the rules and within them" (128), impelling the poem onto an unstable ground in which critique (or what Deleuze calls "transgression") is simultaneously concealed and implied.

Concerns about value and valuation, especially the tensions implicit in Herrnstein Smith's "double discourse of value," are clearly central to the poem. It is often argued that microloans are especially valuable because they are so economically efficient; a loan of just a few dollars can make a big difference for an impoverished woman and her community. This difference is often depicted as not merely financial but ethical insofar as a financial contribution fosters a less quantifiable sense of self-worth and industry in the (usually racially other and geographically remote) recipient. "Found Poem" describes women engaged in productive activities ("A woman wove cloth. / A woman fired bricks. / A woman sold bread"), which seem to belie the "scorn" in which they are held by conventional "banks." Financial contributions to organizations that disburse microloans can also lead to feelings of satisfaction (even virtuousness) in donors, who believe that they have helped the deserving poor.[15] Yet this analogy between financial gain and self-worth is also problematic. Microcredit has been recently called not only ineffective but "a flood of hype" (Surowiecki), a phrase that implies an analogy between the rhetoric surrounding microcredit and conventional advertisements.

The poem successfully mimics economic-ethical arguments in favor of such loans. But repeating these arguments within a poem—and a pantoum in particular—exposes the clichés on which they rely. The poem reads as a typical marketing pitch, including both inspirational anecdotes (the snapshot-like descriptions of the various productive women) and implied threats about inaction (the final stanzas note that "One-fifth of Earth starves"). We are often told that it is good and right to donate money to charities, an ethical precept supported by the IRS deduction for such donations. But by conflating ethical values with moneymaking strategies, the poem implicitly asks whether financial contributions can effect social change.

The neocolonialist assumptions underlying this issue have been particularly evident in the years since September 11, 2001, when attempts to bring American-style democratic values to nations that did not ask for or necessarily want them have had deeply negative consequences. It has also been (perhaps especially) evident since 9/11 that ethical appeals often mask financial aims. For example, it is often noted that freeing Iraq from dictatorship was of particular interest to the United States because of Iraq's extensive oil reserves. Microloans may participate—if unwittingly—in such a dynamic, imposing capitalist values on remote others in ways consistent with the interventionism central to early twenty-first-century U.S. foreign policy.

In this context, the poem's pantoum form offers a different, and also highly ambivalent, mode of mimicry. This Malay form, though often and perhaps increasingly used by American poets, retains, as Vince Gotera has argued, a distinctly "postcolonial pedigree." By employing a pantoum to discuss Western interventions in foreign economies, Seidman exposes his poem's vulnerability to dangers (for example, of co-option, misrepresentation, and cultural insensitivity) that recall those associated with the overenthusiastic championing of microloans. It is thus both formally and thematically impossible to distinguish what Bhabha calls appropriation—in this case of (altruistic but also capitalist) ideology—from what "threat[ens]" this ideology (123). Seidman inhabits, and indeed profits from, this ambivalence, which is at least partly self-reflexive. "Found Poem," after all, would not exist without the system it seems to critique. Nor does the poem conform to traditional ideas of aesthetic value, partly because all its words are apparently plagiarized.

★

H. L. Hix's 2007 book-length sequence *God Bless: A Political/Poetic Discourse*, many of whose poems set language from public statements by President George W. Bush into traditional poetic forms, also considers the relation between repetitive forms and value(s). Like "Found Poem," the poems here function partly as documentary. The sequence includes two types of poems. Most, entitled sequentially with the name of a month and year, derive exclusively, as Hix indicates in a note, from "speeches, executive orders, and other public statements of George W. Bush" posted on the White House website during the titular months (n.p.). Interspersed with these are poems entitled "Interleaf," which combine writings by Osama bin Laden with original material that more generally "[imitates his] argument[s]" (n.p.). A subsequent prose section includes an interview in which Hix responds to questions about his poetic aims, followed by several interviews conducted by Hix, mostly with the authors of works related to Islam, recent wars, or American foreign policy. These interviews, Hix asserts in his own interview, let him move beyond the competing "*discourse(s)*" of the poems to actual (and more productive) "conversations" (67).

Hix is not only explicit about the sources of his poetic material but meticulous about his citational practices. In the Bush poems, on which I will focus, he claims to indicate omissions with ellipses; in the bin Laden poems, cited language is italicized. In contrast to Seidman, who seems to have revised an apparently nonrepetitive source text into something repetitive, Hix seems to be echoing preexisting repetitions. Yet, despite citations at the beginning and end of the sequence that express Bush's incredulity that he could actually be a poet (n.p., 65), it seems unlikely (although perhaps possible) that Bush actually spoke verbatim in the various forms employed by Hix, which include rhymed and unrhymed villanelles, sestinas, and ballads, along with a number of poems whose four- to eight-line stanzas end with the same refrain. Even assuming that Bush's language was unshaped by Hix, it is not clear whether the poems compile unwitting redundancies within individual statements by Bush or whether they were constructed by assembling either multiple copies (presented verbatim in different contexts) or sequential (and nonidentical) versions of a single speech.

Nor is it clear whether these poems should be read as dramatic monologues spoken by the invented characters "Bush" and "bin Laden," as original poems spoken by other speaker(s), as the actual utterances of these individuals, or as commentary by Hix on these utterances. Certainly the two kinds of poems differ. "Bin Laden" tends to prefer the sonnet form and anaphoric repetitions. Poems by "Bush" more often involve forms in which full lines or words at the ends of lines repeat. The volume further de-emphasizes Hix's role by identifying him as its "mediat[or]" rather than its author, echoing another recent volume of "poetry" based on quotations from a well-known political figure.[16] The term *mediate* is also ambiguous in that it refers both to the interpersonal (implying that the poems—or perhaps the poet—attempt to adjudicate between conflicting viewpoints) and to the textual (implying that the poems have altered the original text).

Hix's reliance on conventional verse forms clearly alludes to the tradition of (mostly) European poetry. But these poems contain none of the mellifluousness or beauty of conventional poems in these forms, partly because Hix often intensifies the repetition in already-repetitive forms, as when he imposes rhyme onto traditional nonrhyming forms such as the sestina (28–29). In fact, the poems in *God Bless* are defiantly antipoetic. Several rhyme on the final syllable of abstract polysyllables, including -y (57–8) and -tion (60), while others use flat or ungrammatical phrases as refrains, including, for example, "It seems to me like it makes sense" (51). Uneven line lengths and midword breaks intensify the awkwardness. The resulting poems look but don't sound or feel like poems. Certainly they fail to exemplify the appeal to universal values championed by earlier advocates of New Formalism, a movement with which Hix was loosely affiliated and several of whose adherents have praised his poems.[17] Rather, in ways consistent with Hix's prose writings on the topic, these poems seem to offer indirect but pointed critiques of—that is, they seem to mimic—New Formalist assumptions.[18]

Hix gives a hint of his poetic intentions when he expresses pleasure that an interviewer "get[s]" the "joke" ("Document" 20) of his use of the Persian ghazal form for two poems based on Bush's words (54–55). This choice is funny, it seems, because it offers an ironic commentary on the words within the poem. Bush (or "Bush") is here made to speak in a form about whose existence the actual George W. Bush was likely ignorant, one that implicitly pays homage to—or appropriates an element of—a Middle Eastern culture geographically adjacent to the one his words vilify.[19] The form thus, Hix's remark to the interviewer implies, lets him comment on the words the poem includes. The indirectness of this mimicry contrasts with Hix's assertion elsewhere that his sequence emerged from his "sense that our country is doing worse for itself right now than in the past" and from his "heightening sense of political obligation and civic responsibility" (Hix, "Philip" 69). This sense of "civic" or ethical responsibility is suppressed in the poems by Hix's refusal directly to critique the language he employs. Or perhaps the sequence reveals that such a critique is unnecessary, since Bush's words literally speak for themselves, and Hix's repetition and repackaging of them merely remind us of this fact.

Even more directly than Seidman, Hix links formal and syntactic repetition to a consideration of the multiple and conflicting definitions of *values*. Hix (via Bush) often uses the term in an ethical sense, as when one poem insists on the "universal[ity]" (36) of American values, which are elsewhere "fabulous" (21), antithetical to "evil" (18), and "God-given" (36). Yet these values are not in in fact universal, as other poems demonstrate. Other parts of the world "[don't] share" them (14), and "those responsible" for the 9/11 attacks "hate our values" (21), although the Iraqis "should cherish American values" (35). Several of the "Interleaf" sections expose a related contradiction between Bush's general insistence on "values" and his advocacy of "torture" and "murder" (54), although the fact that bin Laden—or Hix, speaking in conjunction with him—presents this critique also destabilizes it.

The poems also link American values to economic concerns. At times the two are simply juxtaposed, as when a reference to a U.S. "shortage of gas" follows an allusion to a "world / that sometimes does not share American values" (14). At others, they are linked, as in an extended discussion of the need to do something about "rising energy / prices": "To build freedom in the world . . . and enduring prosperity, / we need more refining capacity / in America, folks" (16; ellipsis in original). Other poems associate economic prosperity with charitable acts in ways that recall "Found Poem." "January 2002" exhorts Americans to "find somebody who is a shut-in, and say, / I'd just like to love you for a second" (24), while another poem follows the assertion that "we're an ownership society" with a reference to a recent "Senate / . . . bill to help ease the suffering on / the African continent" (44). Elsewhere, the expenditure of "taxpayers' money" on the war is justified through direct references to "the ideal of liberty," an ideal whose preservation has required both a past expenditure of "$87 billion" and an unspecified future one required "to protect this country" (57–58). Several of the "Interleaf" poems comment on such slippages, referring to the profits earned by "those who manufacture weapons / and . . . other large corporations" and claiming that "This is a war begun by the CEOs / of those [corporations] who receive the no-bid contracts" (63), an assertion Hix has made elsewhere.[20]

Hix mimics Bush's actual rhetoric by converting it into (bad) formal poetry, but *God Bless* also implies the limits of repetition as a strategy of resistance. Even when read alongside bin Laden's words, the Bush poems fail to interpret or transcend their own rhetoric. This situation is the result of the poet's compositional and formal choices, but it also reflects a political and temporal reality: the poems' redundancies exemplify their historical moment, as the dates affixed to each make clear. But these repetitive poems also seem motivated by a wish to ensure that none of these events will be repeated.

*

I have thus far been considering poems that are explicitly "found" or shaped from preexisting language and that engage directly with ideas about values. These poems, as I have been arguing, enact the ambivalent relation between neutrality and critique—or what the OED calls "ridicule"—central to mimicry. The poems by Maxine Kumin and Ann Lauterbach to which I now turn do not explicitly rely on found or appropriated language. Instead, they generally speak in the voice of a persona or in the poet's own voice, and their repetitions of words and phrases offer insight into the speaker's state of mind. But these poems also offer a more direct (and pointed) political commentary than those I have been discussing, often by insisting on the incommensurability of geographically remote events that recur despite the speaker's wish to contain or escape them.

Among the group of poems considering recent public events in Kumin's 2007 volume *Still to Mow*, two are in forms that involve repeated lines. Such "pattern[s]," Kumin has noted, "seem to free me to speak out" ("Statement"). Both poems—a villanelle and a pantoum—consider events associated with recent American-instigated wars elsewhere, although neither directly identifies its location or speaker. The villanelle "Entering Houses at Night" is narrated by one of a group of soldiers ("we")—likely Americans conducting house-to-house searches in Iraqi cities, but perhaps of another nationality in another time and place. Too late, these soldiers realize that, by following the order to use "force," they have caused the deaths of the "innocent" (*Still* 38). Seidman and Hix are primarily concerned with who is responsible for their text, but Kumin asks a far more difficult ethical question—whether civilian deaths are the responsibility of those who order these deaths or those who carry out those orders.

The 2006 pantoum "What You Do" (39–40), which appears just after "Entering Houses," formally and thematically intensifies this question of responsibility, partly through the use of address. In English, the pronoun *you* may be singular or plural; it may signal intimacy (the speaker understands what the other is feeling), distance (the speaker observes someone else's actions), participation (*you* can stand in for I), or judgment (the speaker criticizes the events she describes), among other qualities. "What You Do" exploits this ambiguity by refusing to reveal its addressee's identity. The poem seems stuck at a particular undefined moment ("when" begins over half its lines), a sense of paralysis intensified by Kumin's addition of extra repetition (as well as extra variation) to the already highly repetitive pantoum form, as the opening lines demonstrate:

> when nobody's looking
> in the black sites what you do
> when nobody knows you
> are in there what you do

when you're in the black sites
when you shackle them higher
in there what you do
when you kill by crucifixion

Here, the syntactic parallelism between acts perpetrated by "you" and the fact that "nobody" witnesses them confuse the poem's actors with its (non)witnesses. This confusion implies that the poem's readers must determine who is responsible, what transgressions have occurred, and what the implications of these violations are. (Here, then, Kumin extends Deleuze's claim that repetition resists moral law, since her poems expose the presence of preexisting and already-repetitive acts of ethical transgression.)

The poem is mostly descriptive, employing, like Seidman's, monosyllables and short, self-contained lines. Yet Kumin's use of the pantoum also impels her readers to witness each of the horrific acts it describes, according to the pantoum's logic, not once but twice. This repetition challenges the poem's repeated claim that torture occurs in private, both "when" and "where nobody's looking." In fact, the poem seems spoken (and written) partly to make public a series of hitherto clandestine physical acts (including the body "kill[ed] by crucifixion," "ice[d]," and "wrap[ped] . . . in plastic") that were subsequently concealed ("you swear it didn't happen / for over a year now"). A related but more explicit revelation of the truth occurs toward the end of "Entering Houses" when the soldier-speakers realize their "victory" is "Pyrrhic." Here, though, it is the poet, otherwise unidentified, who reveals what actually occurred.

Both of these poems seem, in ways quite different from those I discussed above, to assert that a singular truth exists and that it is ethically valuable to expose it. But this sense of revelation in "What You Do" is belied by the actual facts described by the poem. Although the poem's references are not identified, its images of the crucifixion, the iced body, and the body wrapped in plastic clearly refer to the notorious 2004 photos of the American-instigated torture at Baghdad's Abu Ghraib prison. As a result, its apparent revelations are actually descriptions of acts that were familiar to the poem's readers when the poem was published in 2006. These images are therefore redundant in a third sense.

In this context, the pantoum's repetitions seem to refer not only to the inescapability of actual acts of torture but to the failure of imagination that these acts engender. Like Hix's Bush poems, the speaker of "What You Do" can, it seems, only recycle preexisting images. As in "Entering Houses," it is unclear whether the poem condemns those who performed the horrific acts at

Abu Ghraib or the commanders and policymakers who impelled them to do so in ways that echo questions central to legal proceedings against the American soldiers represented in the photos. But Kumin also implies another, even more disturbing possibility. The speaker, by repeating already-known atrocities, may be manipulating (or even profiting from) them, partly by appropriating, as does Seidman, the non-Western pantoum for her own purposes. While profit and value are not explicitly discussed here, "What You do," like "Entering Houses," interrogates the ethics of depicting and manipulating suffering, an issue crucial to the distribution of these and other Abu Ghraib photographs.[21] Related ethical questions are crucial to poetry as an aesthetic and politically engaged medium.

The poem's circumspection further complicates these issues. Whereas the narrator of Hix's Bush poems insists on American innocence by vilifying those who "hate what America stands for" (21), Kumin focuses on situations that apparently involve American wrongdoing. Her use of *you* implies both intimacy with and a wish for distance from these transgressors. Nor does Kumin, in either poem, depict the actual suffering of Iraqis. Instead, by focusing on extant images, "What You Do" implies that such images, like the borrowed language used by Seidman and Hix and the familiar events in "Entering Houses," can be infinitely reproduced but not interpreted or revised. The poem's repetitions in this context signal not only redundancy but a melancholic inability to escape preexisting modes of representation. (This melancholy may inhere partly in the circularity of the pantoum form, which in Geoff Ward's terms, expresses the "basic failure of language as the bearer or sign of reality" [301].) The repetitions of "What You Do" thus both critique and perpetuate torture. They echo and revise, revealing a mimicry that is *"almost the same, but not quite."* Kumin's point seems to be that it is impossible to critically evaluate events accessible only in indirect and mediated ways.

★

The pantoum, I just suggested, may be linked to melancholy. Certainly both of the pantoums I have discussed, like Hix's Bush poems, seem confined by their form, ultimately unable to escape or evaluate their circular logic. But successful pantoums, Ward also asserts, transform this sense of failure into "consolation, even victory" (301). Repetition too is often associated with both comfort (as in lullabies) and anxiety (as in the Freudian uncanny). A number of recent repetitive poems by poets interested in "experimental" (or nontraditional) forms explore a related tension between the poles of "failure" and "consolation," often in relation to contemporary American political rhetoric and culture. Juliana Spahr's 2005 sequence *This Connection of Everyone with Lungs,* for example, uses long lines bound by anaphora to consider both the many "boundar[ies]" (19) separating us and "how connected we are with everyone" (9).

Two poems from Ann Lauterbach's 2005 volume *Hum* consider similar themes using invented repetitive forms that express psychological ambivalence. In the volume's relatively simple title poem, "Hum," repetition mostly functions as a spell or chant that only partly fends off the speaker's recollection of trauma. The more complex, impersonal, and extended "Echo Revision," as its title indicates, *explicitly* considers the efficacy of repetition as a strategy that not only reiterates (or echoes) but also interprets (or revises) traumatic events.

An attempt at self-comforting is evident in the first line of "Hum," "The days are beautiful." This line is repeated throughout the poem—Lauterbach has called it the poem's refrain ("Statement")—as are its central terms ("days" and "beautiful") and syntax ("The [noun] is/are [adjective]"). It is revealed early on that not only "someone" but "everyone" is "weeping." Late in the poem, a reference to "the towers," which "are yesterday" and "incidental," clarifies the reason: the poem is set in the aftermath of the September 11, 2001, World Trade Center attacks in New York, as Lauterbach has elsewhere confirmed ("Statement"). The poem's short, repetitive, syntactically simple statements express shock and paralysis but also offer a kind of counterstatement, which functions quite differently from the redundancy of the pantoums I discussed above. Here, insofar as "the days" can be understood, even in the abstract, as "beautiful," the possibility of what Ward calls (emotional) "consolation" remains possible.

Many of the poem's lines both echo and revise one another, as the opening reveals:

The days are beautiful.
The days are beautiful.

I know what days are.
The other is weather.

I know what weather is.
The days are beautiful.

That there remains a distinction between what "is" and what the speaker "know[s]" (as well as between what physically and metaphorically "is") recalls the tension, or perhaps false tension, between "you" and "nobody" in "What You Do."[22] Here, as there, it is unclear to what extent the speaker can intervene in, or even describe, what already exists, especially insofar as, as Lauterbach has noted, the reality of the attacks was immediately converted into a "discourse of vituperative violence" ("Statement"). Or perhaps the poem explores the relation between sensory immediacy and political rhetoric, as well as between what Lauterbach calls "fact" and "bare life" on the one hand and "massive tragedy and sorrow and spectacle" on the other ("Statement"). The poem's declarative present tense prevents the speaker from having to acknowledge that the often-noted "beautiful" Manhattan weather on September 11 was changed into a kind of ironic mimicry of beauty after the attacks. (The attacks also actually "*changed* the local weather" in Lower Manhattan, as Lauterbach has observed ["Statement"].) The refrain's affirmation of beauty thus implies a psychologically ambivalent response that elides physicality, hope, and emotional numbness.

Lauterbach's three-part "Echo Revision," published in the same volume, directly considers the topics that "Hum" enacts, including containment and measurement, grieving and temporality, and repetition itself. In this oblique and nonlinear poem, by far the least accessible (as well as the longest) of those I have discussed, Lauterbach repeatedly asks whether art can contain, or, as the poem indicates, "measur[e]" incomprehensible and/or remote events. The found poems I discussed above do not fully reveal the nature or extent of their authors' alterations to their source texts. It is possible, as I noted above, that Hix combined statements made by Bush over the course of a month into a single poem, converting the sequential into the simultaneous, possible actual revisions into textual echoes. Lauterbach does something similar, yet she reveals her own process of revision in ways that emphasize the gaps implicit in poetic composition: "Echo Revision," she explains, was composed by "enjambing early and late drafts of the same poem, placing single lines from each in couplets" ("Statement"). The poem thus renders simultaneous Lauterbach's sequential process of "revision," a strategy that creates a series of intertextual "echo[es]." In ways consistent with what she has called her wish in the poem to reveal "a rip or tear in the narrative continuum" ("Statement"), the poem's couplets also move from echo to revision. The verbatim or nearly verbatim repetition of the previous line predominates in the first section but is almost completely absent from the last. Both the title and the poem thus indicate the end result of the author's compositional strategy (the conversion of echo into revision) but also articulate the interplay between repetition and variation within the final text. This compositional strategy both evokes and transforms the critique implicit in the notion of mimicry: Lauterbach is, it seems, mimicking (or at least echoing) herself partly because she could not complete the poem until she devised this self-repeating form.

The form of "Echo Revision" thus, more directly than that of the other poems I have considered, emphasizes the quality of being "*almost the same, but not quite.*" The poem also more directly reveals the subversive potential of repetition. Hix's form, as I noted above, functions as commentary, indirectly revealing the aesthetic and ethical limitations of the poems' borrowed words. Lauterbach more directly asks what poetry, especially poetry in repetitive form, can accomplish. The poem begins by twice repeating a sentence, "Lest, forgetting, the branch-maiden lopped off," which, partly because it lacks an active verb, superimposes at least three time frames, the time in which the branch was lopped, the subsequent time of "forgetting," and an even more recent moment when this act of forgetting is disrupted ("lest"). But the line refuses to clarify or distinguish these (and perhaps other) time frames. The language itself, along with the syntactic and semantic difficulties it raises (who is forgetting? what is being forgotten? what is a branch-maiden?), emphasizes the act of speaking, a notion affirmed two couplets later, when a still-undefined entity is "Nagged by wind. Prose / Nagged by wind. Succulent prose." Here Lauterbach refers to an act of literary construction but does not disclose whose "prose" is being evoked or how it connects with the personified vocalization of wind. Prose seems to have been undermined, the poem implies later in the same section, because earlier modes of utterance persist. Rather than remaking earlier texts, as do Seidman and Hix, Lauterbach considers the relation between poems and preexisting forms:

Stumbling out from under the enunciated dirge
Stumbling out from under these forms

Of twilight's last screen
Sudden hatchings, partitions, reversals.

There were several hatchings, several namings,
The lesser and the leftover piled up

Several reversals of one into more than one.
Over the fecund industry

Had there ever been such magnitude, such spawning?
A counting of cast-off limbs.

Such counting of last limbs on the green?
To have unreason counted as reason

The poet here seems to be referring at least partly to her own position as a speaker who acknowledges and is physically overwhelmed by (she "stumbl[es] out from under") an already "enunciated dirge" and (perhaps earlier poetic) "forms."

As the minimalist, repetitive statements of "Hum" apparently attempt to control and align what is inexpressible, the speaker here attempts to master the uncontainable by measuring it. Terms of classification, counting, and organizing recur, especially in relation to what is intangible and abstract. The speaker first observes (already distinct) "hatchings, partitions, reversals," and then, in the next line, transforms them into the countable "several hatchings, several namings, / . . . / Several reversals." Soon after, she describes someone else's attempt to "count . . . limbs." Recalling the lopped-off branches of the first line, the (apparently human) limbs evoke both their origin (they are "cast-off") and their future loss (they are, like "twilight's . . . screen," "last"). Amid this attempt to impose what Deleuze calls an antirepetitive sense of "equality" (3), the irregularity of Lauterbach's repetitions antimathematically and subversively enable the "reversal . . . of one into more than one" and of "unreason" into "reason."

The poem's formal repetitiveness thus seems partly an effect of the psychological need to measure, accrue, and contain what resists these gestures. The unidentified protagonist seeks, it seems, to recast what already exists into an orderly form. Yet, as is evident in the interchangeable nouns and adjectives of "Hum," the attempt does not, and cannot, succeed. The poem keeps ungrammatically accruing new and irreconcilable "details" ("soldiers," "apples and pears, "the couple under the enormous tree"), which it fails to organize, even with the help of "a chart." As such, Lauterbach reveals the limitations of the poem's attempt to measure the incommensurable.

"Hum" early on describes repeated acts of "weeping" whose cause ("the towers") is only later revealed. In "Echo Revision," Lauterbach similarly depicts acts of counting and measuring before explaining their context. Like "Hum," "Echo Revision" never fully explains this context, instead alluding only to "details" (including "cast-off limbs" in Part 1 and "mourners," "crimes," "foxholes" in Part 2). The poem, Lauterbach has noted, "was written partly in response to the capture, trial for war crimes . . . , and death . . . of . . . Slobodan Milosevic" as well as to the "ongoing war in Iraq" ("Statement"). In this context, the act of "counting" is politically as well as poetically ambiguous. Lauterbach never specifies who is doing the counting or why, nor whether counting offers an antidote to or rationalization of violence:

> Some counting was included in the dossier of events
> The war was a separate entity, with its own turning dates.

Counting seemed to ease the ambiguity of the ocean.
The candles were lit.

There are the pluses and the minuses to add and subtract.
Nevertheless candles were lit.

The counting of crimes may enable their perpetrators to be brought to justice, or it may enable these perpetrators or those who support them to conceal what actually occurred. "Counting," after all, merely *"seemed* to ease the ambiguity" of something whose ambiguity—and unquantifiableness—cannot be alleviated. The problem, as in "What You Do" and the other poems I have discussed, is both ethical and aesthetic: insofar as language obfuscates meaning, it inflicts harm in ways that can't be measured. Kumin's "What You Do" implies that its speaker is complicit with the spectacularization and exoticization of the violence the poem apparently condemns, and "Echo Revision" does something similar. Or rather, there is no way out: counting, like repetition, both brings violence's perpetrators to justice and perpetuates the violence, as was perhaps evident in Milosevic's actual trial.[23]

But this instability also engenders a kind of beauty. The poem's third part echoes the turn at the end of the second toward an acknowledgment of "the innumerable and the inseparable," apparently personifying "the incommensurate" who are visible "in their separate, unique garb of silver / . . . / Riding up and over the long radiant angle." Here, the failure of quantification (the speaker's acknowledgment of "the incommensurate," "the innumerable and the inseparable") offers an alternative to mere counting, enabling the "separate" to become both "inseparable" and "plural." In this alternate space, "silver" and "radian[ce]" render the "angle" nearly angelic. But another, quite different reading of these lines is also possible: the riders may be old-fashioned armor-clad infantrymen bent on further destruction. This ambiguity implies, as does "What You Do," that atrocity is accessible to nonwitnesses, including Lauterbach as poet, only via images. Any poem that attempts to convey atrocity risks being overwhelmed not only by the need to "measur[e]" but by the force of its own images, which, as here, overwhelm logic.

This sense of what Bhabha calls "excess" (122)—in this context, what exceeds evaluating, valuing, and measuring—has recurred both formally and thematically in all the poems I have discussed. All in different ways imply that actual events can't be "echo[ed]" or directly conveyed; to depict them is inevitably to "revis[e]" them. A sense of distance that recalls Kumin's reliance on already-familiar snapshots of the atrocities committed at Abu Ghraib seems more benign in the final lines of "Echo Revision." Here, a man who "smiled to the camera" is depicted both as an "old man, now dead" and a "young man."

By conflating the two, Lauterbach implies that photos can at least partly resuscitate the dead. Because we do not know who this man is, we cannot evaluate the ethical implications of this antichronological slippage.

But Lauterbach also seems to be referring to poetry. In "Echo Revision," and by extension all poems, different moments coexist. Like photos, poems depict both past events and their remoteness and thus offer a replica of what can't be fully understood or counted. Their mode of repetition is, as Deleuze claims, partial and unscientific; poems are always both echoes and revisions. They mimic but also alter their subject matter. At the same time, echo and revision shield poetic speakers (and poets) from having to describe what actually occurred, and as a result they protect readers from having to experience these events. Repetition in all the poems I have discussed involves shielding and avoidance as well as critique. By preserving existing power structures, repetition reveals the poet's complicity with them. Repetition therefore also implicates the reader, who must navigate, using only the partial representations in and of the poem, its competing claims.

To echo is therefore always to revise. Inserting familiar language into a poem, including language familiar because it has already appeared in that poem, comments on that language. By insisting on the materiality as well as what Ward calls the "failure" of language, all the poems I have discussed reveal the discrepancy between experience and poetry. Questions about valuation and measurement are central to these poems insofar as they, like all poems, are formal, measured constructs. But by making such issues explicit, these recent poems reveal the centrality of value, valuation, and evaluation to contemporary experience, perhaps especially that of American civilians observing American-led military actions from afar or what Lauterbach has called the problem of the "near-far" ("Statement"). The recurrence of repetition in recent engaged poems seems to signal, among other things, a contemporary moment in which a sense of incommensurability coexists with both a rhetoric of quantification and a sense of powerlessness, in which the possibility of individual action or intervention, especially in relation to events occurring elsewhere, seems radically curtailed. In this context, repetition seems to be useful to a range of contemporary poets because its value and meaning can't be fixed. Among other things, twenty-first-century engaged poems suggest that their own curtailed language offers a source of resistance that is perhaps inevitably indirect and unoriginal.

Notes

1. These disputes have been variously characterized, but they often center on form, subjectivity, and accessibility. Jonathan Holden identifies Language poetry and New

Formalism as "the two . . . main developments" in 1980s American poetry (*Fate* 37), and he has characterized the years since then in terms of tensions between personal free verse and formally traditional public poems (*Old* 52). Other readers have contrasted the postconfessional valorization of a stable speaking subject or "I" with Language poetry's challenges to this idea. Cole Swensen has used the term "hybrid" to characterize a recent poetic mode that reveals "selectively inherited traits" from different earlier schools of poetry; in the hybrid, she adds, "the political is always" evident, even if indirectly (xxi).

2. During the 1980s in particular, poets adhering to traditional forms were often in conflict with those eschewing them. In contrast, repetition is evident in both formally traditional and innovative contemporary poems. Gilles Deleuze notes that "rhyme . . . is indeed verbal repetition, but repetition which includes the difference between two words and inscribes that difference" (21).

3. Examples of this experiential repetitiveness include the common phrases *endless war*—war, that is, keeps repeating itself—and *the Great Recession*, a term that alludes to an earlier similar event. The Internet's capacity to reproduce information ad infinitum has inarguably changed Americans' relation to this information.

4. Ward calls the pantoum the form, "more than other[s]," that "retains the audible resonance of incantation, and a sense of the spell" (293). Gray notes the prevalence of the "ancient . . . , incantatory, prophetic, [and] ceremonial" (266) in several poems, including Amiri Baraka's "Somebody Blew Up America."

5. The notion of the repetition compulsion is elaborated in *Beyond the Pleasure Principle*, in which Freud also notes the transformation of an originary "*passive* situation" into its "*active* unpleasant" subsequent repetition (10). In a discussion of the uncanny, Freud refers to the notion of "the principle of a *repetition-compulsion* in the unconscious mind. . . . Whatever reminds us of this inner *repetition-compulsion* is perceived as uncanny" (145).

6. Mimicry, the OED goes on, can also refer to the protective mechanism by which one species comes to resemble another.

7. "Because repetition differs in kind from representation," Deleuze claims, "the repeated cannot be represented: rather, it must always be signified, measured by what signifies it, itself making what it signifies" (18).

8. American culture is arguably based both on shared "values," including those of life, liberty, and the pursuit of happiness, and on the "American dream," which is often defined in economic terms. While some versions of the American national narrative associate ethical behavior (good values) with an increase in wealth (greater value) and the reverse, challenges to this equivalence have been frequent. In contemporary culture, it is often noted, capitalist values seem to have triumphed over the public good, or, to put it more bluntly, the economic has come to define, discipline, and control the cultural category of the good, partly through acts of cultural and linguistic repetition. See, for example, Naomi Klein.

9. Related tensions have recently been evident in discussions of (and hand-wringing about) the status of contemporary American poetry, which is often described as both separate from and imbricated in the marketplace. On the one hand, poetry seems to offer an antidote to the commercialization (as well as the sense of economic vulnerability) of contemporary American culture: poets, it is often remarked, seldom get rich from writing poems. Even as poetry has become increasingly marginalized in contemporary culture, however, it has become increasingly professionalized, due

largely to the rise of MFA programs and the need for creative writing professors to keep them going. For a discussion of these issues, see Silliman.

10. The former is associated with "money, commerce, technology, industry, production and consumption, workers and consumers," the latter with "culture, art, genius, creation and appreciation, artists and connoisseurs" (127).

11. Guillory notes that "the premise of our social life is the absolute commensurability of everything. The language of judgment has been transformed into the discourse of 'value-judgments'" (323).

12. These principles include the necessity (and cultural marginalization) of wage labor (318), the perpetuation of imbalances between production and consumption, and the existence of a market for artworks (321).

13. Language poetry is often associated with the political Left and with "a critique of bourgeois society" (Lazar 232) that, in George Hartley's terms, "bar[es] . . . the frames of bourgeois ideology itself" (qtd. in Lazar 232). However, others have interrogated the act of "equat[ing] aesthetic choices with political stances" (Keller 261).

14. Geoff Ward has defined the pantoum, a form in which each line is repeated in a different context, in analogous terms: "What looks like sameness turns out to spell difference" (294).

15. Because men tend to spend rather than invest the loaned funds, microcredit is generally offered only to women.

16. A volume of "poems" by Donald Rumsfeld that compiles often cryptic excerpts from briefings and interviews identifies its author, journalist Hart Seely, as its "compile[r]."

17. In a positive review of Hix's *Perfect Hell*, New Formalist poet and advocate Dana Gioia identifies its mixture of elements of "Language Poetry, . . . New Formalism . . . and early Surrealism."

18. Hix is the author of several essays, including "New Formalism among the Postmoderns" (*As Easy* 28–35) and "New Formalism at a Crossroads" (*As Easy* 26–49), that discuss the limitations of pure New Formalism.

19. "November 2001," for example, asserts, "We face an enemy . . . the likes of which we've never seen before" and "Our enemies . . . have no conscience. They have no mercy" (22; ellipses in original).

20. Hix criticizes the Bush administration for "things . . . such as non-compete bids awarded to companies with which he and others in his administration are closely affiliated, non-compete bids for billions of dollars of taxpayers' money and the decision to go to war to create the need for those non-compete bids," which he calls "lies" that "cause the deaths of thousands of people, and have a major impact on millions more" ("Philip Brady" 71–72).

21. In 2009, President Obama determined that additional photos of torture from the prison be suppressed because of what he called their potential "to further inflame anti-American opinion and to put our troops in greater danger" (qtd. in Zeleny and Shanker).

22. Lauterbach uses versions of "to be" as a descriptor ("The days are beautiful"), a signal of metaphor ("The sky is a cloud"), and something that joins them, as in the late "Here are the stones / loosed from their settings." She has described the poem's refrain as "both a [physical] fact" and "an assertion of bare life against . . . massive tragedy and sorrow and spectacle" ("Statement").

23. Milosevic died before his four-year-long war-crimes trial was concluded.

Works Cited

Barron, Jonathan N., and Bruce Meyer. "Introduction." *New Formalist Poets. Dictionary of Literary Biography*. Vol. 282. Ed. Jonathan N. Barron and Bruce Meyer. New York: Gale, 2003. xv–xxii. Print.

Beach, Christopher, ed. *Artifice and Indeterminacy: An Anthology of New Poetics*. Tuscaloosa: U Alabama P, 1998. Print.

Benjamin, Walter. "The Work of Art in the Age of Mechanical Reproduction." *Illuminations*. Ed. Hannah Arendt. Trans. Harry Zohn. New York: Schocken, 1969. 217–52. Print.

Bhabha, Homi. *The Location of Culture*. New York: Routledge, 1994. *EBL Reader*. Web. 10 June 2014.

Butler, Judith. *Gender Trouble*. New York: Routledge, 2008. Print.

Deleuze, Gilles. *Difference and Repetition*. Trans. Paul Patton. New York: Columbia UP, 1994. Print.

Freud, Sigmund. *Beyond the Pleasure Principle*. Ed. and trans. James Strachey. New York: Norton, 1961. Print.

Freud, Sigmund. "The Uncanny." *On Creativity and the Unconscious*. Ed. Benjamin Nelson. New York: HarperCollins, 2009. 122–61. Print.

Gioia, Dana. "Consummately Infernal." Rev. of *Perfect Hell*, by H. L. Hix. Orig. pub. *Ploughshares* Winter 1996–97. Web. 10 June 2014.

Gotera, Vince. "The Pantoum's Postcolonial Pedigree." *An Exaltation of Forms: Contemporary Poets Celebrate the Diversity of Their Art*. Ed. Annie Finch and Kathrine Varnes. Ann Arbor: U Michigan P, 2002. 254–58. Print.

Grandin, Greg. *Empire's Workshop: Latin America, The United States, and the Rise of the New Imperialism*. New York: Metropolitan, 2006. Web. 10 June 2014.

Guillory, John. *Cultural Capital: The Problem of Literary Canon Formation*. Chicago: U Chicago P, 2013. Print.

Herrnstein Smith, Barbara. *Contingencies of Value: Alternative Perspectives for Critical Theory*. Cambridge, MA: Harvard UP, 1988. Print.

Hix, H. L. *As Easy as Lying: Essays on Poetry*. Wilkes-Barre, PA: Etruscan, 2002. Print.

Hix, H. L. "A Document of Listening." Interview with Philip Metres, November 2007–May 2008. *Jacket* 36 (2008). Web. 10 June 2014.

Hix, H. L. *God Bless: A Political/Poetic Discourse*. Wilkes-Barre, PA: Etruscan, 2007. Print.

Hix, H. L. "Philip Brady Interviews H. L. Hix, 18 February 2007." *God Bless*. 69–78.

Holden, Jonathan. *The Fate of American Poetry*. Athens: U Georgia P, 1991. Print

Holden, Jonathan. *The Old Formalism: Character in Contemporary American Poetry*. Fayetteville: U Arkansas P, 1999. Print.

Irigaray, Luce. *This Sex Which Is Not One*. Trans. Catherine Porter and Carolyn Burke. Ithaca, NY: Cornell UP, 1985. Print.

Keller, Lynn. "Measured Feet 'in Gender-Bender Shoes': The Politics of Poetic Form in Marilyn Hacker's *Love, Death, and the Changing of the Seasons*." *Feminist Measures: Soundings in Poetry and Theory*. Ed. Lynn Keller and Cristanne Miller. Ann Arbor: U Michigan P, 1994. 260–86. Print.

Keniston, Ann, and Jeffrey Gray, eds. *The New American Poetry of Engagement: A 21st Century Anthology*. Jefferson: McFarland, 2012. Print.

Kumin, Maxine. "Statement." Keniston and Gray. 229.

Kumin, Maxine. *Still to Mow*. New York: Norton, 2007. Print.

Lacan, Jacques. *The Four Fundamental Concepts of Psychoanalysis.* Trans. Alan Sheridan. New York: Norton, 1998. Print.

Lauterbach, Ann. "Echo Revision." *Or to Begin Again.* New York: Penguin, 2009. 79–83. Print.

Lauterbach, Ann. "Hum." *Hum.* New York: Penguin, 2005. 76–78. Print.

Lauterbach, Ann. "Statement: Writing in the Near/Far." Keniston and Gray. 230–31.

Lazer, Hank. "The Politics of Form and Poetry's Other Subjects: Reading Contemporary American Poetry." Beach. 222–45.

McPhillips, Robert. "What's New about the New Formalism?" *Expansive Poetry: Essays on the New Narrative and the New Formalism.* Ed. Frederick Feirstein. Santa Cruz, CA: Story Line, 1989. 195–208. Print.

"Mimicry." *Oxford English Dictionary Online.* Oxford UP, 2012. Web. 3 May 2015.

Morton, Stephen. "Mimicry." *The Encyclopedia of Literary and Cultural Theory.* Ed. Michael Ryan. Vol. 2. Malden, MA: Wiley-Blackwell, 2011. 709–13. Print.

Rector, Liam. "Repetition: A Column." *American Poetry Review* 31.3 (2002): 43–46. Web. 5 May 2014.

Seely, Hart, ed. *Pieces of Intelligence: The Existential Poetry of Donald H. Rumsfeld.* New York: Free P, 2010. Print.

Seidman, Hugh. "Found Poem: Microloans." *Somebody Stand Up and Sing.* Kalamazoo, MI: New Issues, 2005. 68–69. Print.

Silliman, Ron. "The Political Economy of Poetry." Beach. 190–200.

Spahr, Juliana. *This Connection of Everyone with Lungs: Poems.* Berkeley: U of California P, 2005. Print.

Surowiecki, James. "What Microloans Miss." *New Yorker,* 17 March 2008. Web. 10 June 2014.

Swensen, Cole. "Introduction." *American Hybrid: A Norton Anthology of New Poetry.* Ed. Cole Swensen and David St. John. New York: Norton, 2009. xvii–xxvi. Print.

Ward, Geoff. "On the Pantoum, and the Pantunite Element in Poetry." *A Companion to Poetic Genre.* Ed. Erik Martiny. New York: Wiley, 2012. 293–305. Print.

Zeleny, Jeff, and Thom Shanker. "Obama Moves to Bar Release of Detainee Abuse Photos." *New York Times,* 13 May 2009. Web. 7 July 2014.

ELEVEN

Ambivalence and Despair

Kevin Prufer

I was living in a very small town in west central Missouri during the run-up to our disastrous wars in Iraq and Afghanistan. Just a few miles down the road was Whiteman Air Force Base. I won't forget the sound of the Stealth Bomber (never all that stealthy) rumbling over our house in the mornings. Many of my students were in the military and quite a few felt ambivalent about the wars. They understood their immediacy and complexity in ways the rest of us probably couldn't, knowing that they might soon be called up to fight. My position was safer, though in its way also uncomfortable. I'd lie in bed reading the newspaper, growing increasingly furious with the likes of Paul Wolfowitz and Dick Cheney, filled with a rage that was nearly blinding. I couldn't sleep. I'd pour myself another drink.

This was not an especially productive time for me as a writer. I wanted to speak out about the ways enormous national power was being misdirected and used for evil purposes. I wanted to create a poem that would open Americans' eyes to the dangers of the nearly unlimited reach of our empire, the porosity of our borders, the strange sense of national exceptionalism that washed over us at the beginning of the twenty-first century. I wanted to write a big poem, but was plagued by false starts and feelings of despair as my work turned away from what I imagined poetry to be into something more closely resembling dogma.

Those days, I spent much of each day at work editing *Pleiades: A Journal of New Writing* and directing Pleiades Press. Most of this involved reading thousands of poetry manuscripts by aspiring, generally youngish American authors, the vast majority of whom had studied in university workshops. I remember how around the turn of the century, I began to see an uptick in apocalyptic poetry, which grew enormously after September 11, 2001. The tone was ambivalent and despairing, much of it meditating on the simultaneous beauty and terror of destruction, the poetic mind searching through the chaos of conflagration for some political sense of how we went wrong, how we came to destruction—never finding any. These new poets, above all, abhorred sentimentality and what I came to think of as sentimentality's cousin, dogmatism.

Inspired, perhaps, by my present moment, I was also reading about the war fever that spread across Europe during the run-up to the Great War. There were parallels—vast numbers of people eager to rush recklessly into a war they (or I) didn't really understand, convinced that it would all be over in a few months . . . followed by a poetry of horror, ambivalence, emptiness, and apocalyptic vision. I reread *The Waste Land* in the context of Arielle Greenberg's "City of Paper" or Noelle Kocot's *Poem for the End of Time* and found new resonances. And, one way or another, these observations led me to rethink Wilfred Owen's great war poem "Dulce et Decorum Est," his horrifying descriptions of soldiers "bent double like old beggars under sacks, / knock-kneed, coughing like hags," or the image of one of them suffocating in a gas attack, "flound'ring like a man in fire or lime." What, I wondered, might Wilfred Owen's canonical poem say about our contemporary moment of politics, war, and poetry?

"Dulce et Decorum Est" is addressed to a "you," whom I knew to be Jessie Pope, a war propagandist who lured young men into the trenches with sentimental, patriotic poetry. I imagine Owen's dislike of Pope resembled my own loathing of the talking heads on the news, each of them trying to sell me (with slogans and flags) a war that I believed would ensnare thousands of people in decades of misery.

These visceral feelings—a then-hazy sense for the importance of Owen's poem in understanding twenty-first-century political poetry, that feeling of despair and rage and impotence—grew stronger when another poet, Joy Katz, asked me if I'd write a piece on sentimentality for a print symposium. What, she asked, does it mean to call a work of art sentimental? Is the word particularly political or gendered? Do we wield it as a way of ushering young people into wars? Or keeping women poets in their place by making subjects that might especially concern them—including female sexuality—off limits? Or is sentimental language a way that we comfort ourselves in the face of an oppressive status quo? (Think of the images of happy slaves asleep after a day's work, or descriptions of pure, white, innocent womanhood—all constructed, I think, not just to make us smile, but to assure us that the status quo is sweet and right.)

The more I thought and read about it, the more I became convinced of two even more primary ideas. First, I grew certain that our accepted definition of the word—an overabundance of inappropriate or contrived emotion—was totally inadequate. And I decided that our cultural suspicion of sentimentality had deep, political roots, roots that stretched back (at least) to Wilfred Owen's anger and despair about Jessie Pope and the Great War—and forward into our current sensibilities about "political" poetry.

Back in 1967 in the pages of *College English*, Brian Wilkie considered a deeply sentimental, Victorian song about the father of a poor family who, instead of caring for his dying son, goes out drinking every night. The lyrics, from Henry Clay Work's "Come Home, Father," conclude

Father, dear, come home with me now!
The clock in the steeple strikes three.
The house is so lonely, the hours are so long
For poor weeping Mother and me.
Yes we are alone, poor Benny is dead
And gone with the angels of light;
And these were the very last words that he said:
"I want to kiss Papa good night."

Is this, Wilkie asked, sentimental because it is overly emotional? Of course not. There is nothing exaggerated about the level of emotion here. The death of a neglected child is, after all, very emotional territory. Nor, he observed, is the situation contrived. In Victorian London, as now, this kind of situation—alcoholism, sickness, untimely death—is unfortunately common. Is the poem, he asks, sentimental because it asks for our participation in an affair that doesn't concern us? But of course it concerns us as much as any human situation . . . so being emotionally moved by it is probably natural and right. By any standard definition, Wilkie observes, this very sentimental song is not sentimental at all.

Perhaps, I thought, reading Wilkie's essay, the root of the sentimentality in "Come Home, Father"—and in many works we call sentimental—isn't an overabundance of emotion but a simplification of emotion to a single channel. Poverty is complex, as are sickness, alcoholism, and death. Work's piece doesn't fail because it's inappropriately emotional, I decided, but because it's inappropriately simple. It doesn't really *think* about the situation—what has caused it, why a father would do this, what larger social forces are at work; rather, the writer offers up a reductive moral message: It is wrong of that man to be out drinking while his son is dying.

By this time, I'd tracked down some of Jessie Pope's writing, and it reminded me of Work's song. Here's an example:

Who's for the trench—
Are you, my laddie?

Who'll follow French—
Will you, my laddie?
. . . .
Who'll earn the Empire's thanks—
Will you, my laddie?
Who'll swell the victor's ranks—
Will you, my laddie?
When that procession comes,
Banners and rolling drums—

Like Henry Clay Work, Jessie Pope approaches complex topics—including, for her, the Great War, our responsibilities to our nation and to ourselves, the meaning of victory and power, and the morality of combat—with an inappropriate simplicity. She, too, is sentimental. And this kind of political sentimentality—a way of thinking that requires no thinking from the reader but excites powerful, simplified political emotions—is dangerous. "My friend," Owen writes to Ms. Pope

You would not tell with such high zest
To children ardent for some desperate glory
The old Lie; Dulce et decorum est
Pro patria mori.

One thing we may have learned from the disastrous twentieth century is to be mistrustful of totalizing, sentimental art because sentimental language is politically dangerous. It whips us into frenzy and shuts down thinking. Stupid, fervent nationalism is not only dangerous, but it almost always comes wrapped the gauze of sentimentality.

The World War I poets saw the rhetoric of late Romantic and Victorian writers—their longing for transcendence, moral clarity, and ethical purity, their belief that great truths might exist outside of the mind of the observer—twisted into the radical nationalisms that led to tragedy. And, while many modernist authors and artists fell for the banality and sentimentality of fascism, much of the new modernist (and, in different ways, postmodernist) sensibility retreated from Victorian rhetoric (and its many attendant dangers) into often radical interiority, uncertainty, suspicion of totalizing truths, and fragmentation. Where the Victorian "man of letters" wrote poetry to instruct and to offer a system of moral or ethical values, the twentieth-century poets I grew up reading were suspicious of this position, preferring the notion that we create the world in the act of observing it, the subjectivity of stream of consciousness, and the belief that the experience of truth (moral, religious, ethical, political) depends on the mind that does the experiencing.

These days, still near the start of the twenty-first century, we seem generally to have accepted the centrality of radical subjectivity without necessarily remembering its historical and political roots. Moreover, we tend to conflate political poetry with dogmatic poetry, which knows the answers and advocates for them (and, therefore, with sentimental, simplifying poetry). Our current distrust of political advocacy in poetry (what my students might call "heavy-handed" or "perhaps ironic?") has deep historical roots—roots we sometimes forget exist. One of those many, many roots might just be visible in Wilfred Owen's pain and rage at the sentimental political poetry of Jessie Pope.

Although one might not find a poet more at odds with Owen's formal sensibilities, political activist-poet Denise Levertov addresses many of the same ideas in her famous essay on the function of the line. The ascendant sensibility of her age, she wrote in 1979, is uninterested in bearing witness to what she calls dogmatic certitudes. We live in an age of open forms of poetry because open forms are more suitable for expressions of the uncertain mind, of the mind in motion—a kind of poetry she finds more suitable to the late twentieth century than, for instance, Wilfred Owen's rhymed and metrical lines. A Shakespearian sonnet, she suggests, contains within it its own inevitable conclusion at roughly the 140th syllable. Rhetorically speaking, received forms have built into their underlying structures the implicit idea of arrival at a conclusion. Open forms, however, are exploratory, and exploration—a resistance to the idea of totalizing truth and an affirmation of the psychologically interior nature of poetry—is one of the hallmarks of an age that has too often seen in the sentimental, the dogmatic, the nationalist, and the religiously zealous an inclination toward oppression, cruelty, war, injustice, and genocide. People who come to us bearing large truths are not to be trusted, and poems wrapped in the formal cloth of certitude are unlikely to be welcome.

Although her suspicion of totalizing political thought (and sentimental propaganda) mirrors Wilfred Owen's, her arguments are more formally based. With open forms, she implies, poems engage in open-ended thought, creating the sense of a mind at work on a problem, a position that undercuts the nonsense Wilfred Owen abhors in Jessie Pope. Where the line breaks, she says, we sense the mind reaching outward, hurtling forward. A series of quick interrupted syllables suggests a false path the mind started to take, then doubled back on. In the white space between lines or series of words, the mind hovers in unarticulated anticipation, in a momentary wordlessness from which the ideas that follow are sprung.

These two strands, Owen's and Levertov's, seem to me to say a great deal about the political sensibility of my generation of poets, who came of age at the beginning of the new millennium and are probably nearing the height of their power as I write. Like both poets, we are deeply suspicious of sentimentality (and its cousins, uncomplicated dogmatic certitude and dangerous totalizing thought). Though we may have forgotten why this is—my own students tell me sentimentality is icky and unpleasant, but often can't define the term or explain why—we have nevertheless inherited previous generations' sense of the dangers of reducing complex situations, political or otherwise, into emotional simplicity. Somewhere inside us, we know that this kind of thinking is dangerous. We know enough not to participate in it, and so, many of us have found in intense poetic interiority a solution. Resistant to rigid poetic forms and seduced by the polyvalent possibilities of a poetry adept at enacting the nuances of a mind in motion, we write politically in ways that are thoughtfully engaged but do not, often, advocate directly.

I have often wondered, thinking about these issues, if ours isn't an age partly defined by a kind of muscular political ambivalence in poetry—our best political poets expressing a polyvalence of political thought, enacting in their poetry the turnings of minds at work on political problems that can't be reduced to single channels. The point isn't necessarily to advocate for a political position (though that certainly might be one end result), but rather to express the complexities of living in a political world, our many emotional and critical responses going in conflicting directions. We circle questions of race or gender, our thoughts and feelings never lining up in the same direction, but we understand that the act of creating muscular, ambivalent poetry is itself conducive to a deepening of political and social understanding. We look at the war in Iraq and are outraged, sad, hopeless, frustrated, inspired.

Back in Missouri, as the Stealth Bomber flew over my house, I found a solution by retreating into the distant past, writing a series of intensely interior poems taking place in a number of historical periods simultaneously, always meditating on the many possible ways of understanding empire—the fluidity of our borders, the failures of ancient emperors, the complexity of cultural hegemony. The poems thought hard in multiple directions, but didn't exactly draw conclusions.

I'm not sure how good they are, but I think they're probably typical of many in my generation of political poets, mostly trained in MFA programs and employed at universities. (It seems to me that other poetries—spoken word, performance poetry, or, for instance, poetry strongly rooted in the experience of ethnic, cultural, gender or sexual minorities, etc.—have often responded quite differently to these and other historical forces, more vigorously and directly.) Still, I see similar approaches to political subjects by many of the younger poets who I think are among the most vital and interesting at work in America today.

This is perhaps best represented by Arielle Greenberg's "City of Paper," which I believe is one of the truly extraordinary (and largely unrecognized) political poems of our time. Greenberg begins with a scrap of charred paper that has floated to the speaker from what we can only imagine is the destruction of the Twin Towers. On it, she finds a person's name and, throughout the poem, the speaker addresses her thoughts to that person, considering the role of paper—at times a site of self-expression, at times suggestive of political bureaucracy ("The city runs on paper. / We run through the paper city"), monetary power ("Our money is paper / and it can and does burn"), or, as the ash falls around her, powerlessness and political despair:

> They spread the paper across the neighborhoods
> so everyone could have some.
> This is what it can mean to live in a democracy.
> The disaster was flesh-bits and twisted steel, as they say,
> but even as far away as here we got paper
> floating down over us.

It's an extraordinarily thoughtful poem, one that probes for answers but never finds any. From the chaos of disaster, Greenberg emerges in deep ambivalent thought, counting the forces that have come together to create this destruction, asserting, finally, the existence of the thinking individual who would make sense of a situation that confounds political sense. "Some sheets," she tells us in the final lines, "seemed perfectly new, fresh from the ream. / Some had only a word left." (Noelle Kocot's *Poem for the End of Time*, Cathy Park Hong's "The Word Cloud," and much of the environmentally inflected new work of Timothy Donnelly exist in similar landscapes.)

Vastly different in voice, though similarly ambivalent, is Brian Barker's "A Brief Oral Account of Torture Pulled Down Out of the Wind," which, inspired by the images of torture victims at Abu Ghraib prison, is another of the great, though little mentioned, political poems of the beginning of this century. Here, the political mind—a mind that seems to exist on the wind—comes to us fractured into multiple harrowing (and sometimes mordantly witty) individually titled perspectives: "What the Torturer Whispers to Himself in the Mirror," "What the Hood Whispers to the Head," "What the Boot Whispers to the Heart Beneath its Heel," "What the Dog Whispers to the Shape Cowering in the Corner," and so on. Again, if there's a dominating tone, it's horror and despair, laced through with an obsessive attention to particularities of detail and polyvalent human experience. The scene of torture is ultimately phantas-magorical and surreal, resisting clear sense and articulable meaning. The final voice belongs to a fly, who tells us,

> once when you could not lift your arms
> I partook of your bodies
> now you're no more than puddles trapped in stone
> forgive me my old opprobriums
> as even tonight I'm about my father's business
> the world churns on
> through endless joy and oblivion
> so speak to me now as you disappear
> and I will carry your message
> to the cold lips of the sleepers
> yes I will tell them I saw you standing amazed
> smiling in another life
> I will look them in the eye
> I will tell them you longed to be loved

Although the poem ends with a yearning for human connection, the work otherwise doesn't allow for much possibility of that, not in a world of forces so much bigger than ourselves, forces enacted in many competing, harrowing perspectives on the scene of torture before us.

While memorable and extraordinary, the tone of despair and of energetic thinking without conclusion will seem familiar to anyone who reads through the work of the younger poets in the two leading anthologies of political poetry in print today, State of the Union (edited by Joshua Beckman and Matthew Zapruder) and The New American Poetry of Engagement: A 21st Century Anthology (edited by Ann Keniston and Jeffrey Gray). Again and again I encounter its muscular ambivalence, its representations of the motions of thought, its conflation of intricate detail, beauty, horror, and sadness—in the work of Matthew Zapruder, Rachel Zucker, Forrest Hamer, Matthea Harvey, Lisa Sewell, Claudia Rankine. When I encounter Matthew Rohrer's "Elementary Science for Dick Cheney," in which the speaker asserts "It is you, the vice / president of our country, / who is despicable . . . you set the people up to die . . . / and walked away," the moment of arrival at a conclusion, of pure assertion is astonishing.

In one of the most frightening moments of my life, I had to interview W. S. Merwin on a stage in front of about five hundred people. The lights blinded me. I had a few questions written down on notecards, but the conversation had run away from them and now he was talking about politics. I didn't know what to do. "Do you think," I asked him (because it was foremost in my mind), "ambivalence is a viable political position for a poet?"

"No," he said. "Not at all." And then he continued with his other thought, his real point.

I kept returning to his answer in my head. It bothered me. At the time, I was still articulating for myself how, for poets of my generation, disturbed ambivalence might be one of the engines driving our political poetry. But, of course, ambivalence contains its own dangers—in its refusal to take a stand, in its insistence on thought alone and on the value of circling a problem and allowing it to exist in its complexities. A political movement, for instance, cannot afford too much rhetorical complexity if it is going to make its position known. No one will shout Peter Gizzi's political poetry at a rally the way they might have declaimed Jessie Pope's (though they would certainly find some deepening of their political worldview from it). And a truly ambivalent political sensibility might, having lost its urgency, verge into mere noodling with political ideas (something I also encountered in my position as a literary editor). Mere vagueness or, worse, irresponsible political disengagement, can often pass, at first glance, for serious, thoughtful ambivalence (or, just as frequently, for a winking, ironic wordliness—a reduction of complex political feeling into simplifying irony, a kind of masked sentimentality in itself, I'd argue). Maybe this is what bothered Merwin about my question.

But, like others, I have come to believe that the complex thinking and feeling that arise from deep political conflictedness are, in other ways, a good antidote for the dangers of our century's political dogmatism, sentimentality, and shouting. I turn on the television, the radio, the computer, and am accosted by slogans, tweets, political talking points, and complex issues reduced to tiny nuggets of opposing processed thought. We all are. These are the enemies of real political thought and dangerous to political feeling (as well as to the well-being of our country). We live in a world in which too many vehicles of communication are too good at delivering this kind of simulated thought to vast numbers of ready minds.

In its many ascendant sensibilities, poetry will never be as good as television, Internet, and radio at telling us whom to vote for or convincing us to enlist in the army. At its best (in our age of lyric interiority), it is too complex and intricate for that, and its reach is smaller. The days when Jessie Pope's poetry convinced men to die in the trenches seem, for now, far away. And that's all for the best, because it seems to me that the twenty-first-century political poem engages in a kind of thinking that no other art form I know of is quite as adept at. Poetry as I conceive it creates the possibility of a simultaneity of conflicting meanings, the experience of productive ambivalence, the chance to begin to understand enormously complex questions with a large-mindedness that can contain multiple, conflicting beliefs or feelings. The work of Greenberg or Barker, for instance, accepts that this containment is part of the process of thinking about not wholly answerable questions.

Provoking deep, ambivalent thought about political questions is not just a prelude to a political act but, also, I think, a kind of political act in itself—in that it makes us more humane, serious, and insightful thinkers about politics. Near that air force base in Missouri, where this essay began, I observed that my military students had an understanding of the human and political implications of our wars that the rest of us did not. It's this sort of nuanced understanding that I expect the new political poetry will communicate to those of us who have not yet been born.

Works Cited

Barker, Brian. "A Brief Oral Account of Torture Pulled Down Out of the Wind." *The Black Ocean*. Carbondale: Southern Illinois UP, 2011. 54–63. Print.

Beckman, Joshua and Matthew Zapruder, eds. *State of the Union: Fifty Political Poems*. Seattle: Wave, 2008.

Greenberg, Arielle. "City of Paper." *Pleiades: A Journal of New Writing* 23.1 (2003): 14–16. Print.

Keniston, Ann, and Jeffrey Gray, eds. *The New American Poetry of Engagement*. Jefferson, NC and London: McFarland Publishers, 2012. Print.

Levertov, Denise. "On the Function of the Line." *Light Up the Cave*. New York: New Directions Press, 1982. 67–77. Print.

Owen, Wilfred. "Dulce et Decorum Est." *The Poems of Wilfred Owen*. Norwalk, CT: New Directions, 1949. 66. Print.

Rohrer, Matthew. "Elementary Science for Dick Cheney." *State of the Union*. Ed. Joshua Beckman and Matthew Zapruder. Seattle: Wave Books, 2008. 10–11. Print.

Wilkie, Brian. "What Is Sentimentality?" *College English*. 28.8 (1968): 564–75. Print.

TWELVE

Getting the World into the Poem

Information, Layering, and the Composite Poem

Tony Hoagland

For to exist on earth is beyond any power to name.
— Czeslaw Milosz, *Facing the River* (30)

At one time, even before writing existed, poetry was a repository for knowledge—not just stories of battle, love, and national identity, but of practical things, like how to break a horse or how to raise honeybees. Virgil, in his Georgics, will still tell you where to place your beehives (under a shady tree, near freshwater); he will describe to you the distinct social roles in bee society and tell you how to heal your bees when they are sick and listless:

> Since life has brought the same misfortunes to bees as ourselves,
> if their bodies are weakened with wretched disease,
> you can recognize it straight away by clear signs:
> as they sicken their color immediately changes: a rough
> leanness mars their appearance: then they carry outdoors
> the bodies of those without life, . . .
> or else they hang from the threshold linked by their feet, or linger
> indoors, all listless with hunger and dull with depressing cold.
> . . . .
> Then I'd urge you to burn fragrant resin, right away,
> and give them honey through reed pipes, freely calling them
> and exhorting the weary insects to eat their familiar food.
> It's good too to blend a taste of pounded oak-apples
> with dry rose petals, . . . or dried grapes from Psithian vines,

with Attic thyme and strong-smelling centaury. (IV, 251–80, "Disease
in Bees")

Information and poetry have had a long, sometimes ambivalent relationship.
It was the Romantic movement in particular, in the nineteenth century, that
pushed information toward the margin of poetry, and replaced it, or dis-
placed it, with sensibility and inspiration. Blame Coleridge, who allocated
fact-checking and memory to the inferior poetic faculty of Fancy. Poetry, said
Coleridge, does not record or describe the material realm, but transforms it
(325). Though some poets of the twentieth century have worked counter to
that trend, we still can feel, in contemporary poetry, a strong prejudice in fa-
vor of subjectivity, not information. Poetry, as it is generally understood by the
American public, records and rewards the quivering inner life of hypersensi-
tive individuals—not analysis of Israeli politics nor facts about male-pattern
baldness.

When inner life is privileged over facticity, the representation of outer life
recedes to the periphery, or disappears from art; fact and its physics, and even
its vocabulary, become the property of scientists, economists, and carpenters.
For the Romantics, and their many aesthetic progeny—the Confessionals,
the Beats, the New York School poets, the Deep Imagists, and others—it was
emotion and imagination, not facts, that counted. In contemporary poetry,
despite our postmodern skepticisms about the self, the poetic emphasis on
personal subjectivity remains strong. It could be said that much American po-
etry remains closeted from the wide, unruly realms of knowledge, history, and
current events.

In the midst of this argument about the nature and duty of poetry, one ca-
pacious formal strategy for handling reality—a form worth exploration and
consideration—is the composite poem. The composite structure offers some
formal tools with which to address and depict the era in which we live be-
cause it offers a strategy capable of joining the field of personal subjectivity to
worldly knowledge.

Through its techniques of layering and metaphor, the composite poem
provides a way of mixing scale, type, and tone into an arrangement which is
parallel, not integrative. Such techniques can capture the mosaic nature of
experiences that can't necessarily be accommodated in the typical dramatic
poem. The layered poem might include a weather report, a two-dollar hot dog
for lunch, a reference to history, existentialist musing, and an incidental con-
versation; between these elements a resonant comprehension is elicited. Such
suggestive dialectics of fact, ignorance, and imagination are aspects of the
composite poem explored in this chapter.

★

Reece: Diverse Data

The composite poetic method is usefully visible in the "Florida Ghazals" of Spencer Reece. Reece combines samples of worldly information interleaved with fragmentary yet passionate testimonies related to subjective life. Using the free-floating, capsule-like couplets of the ghazal form, Reece arranges his errant materials to evoke an impressionistic sense of experience, not a narrative. The resulting counterpoint is satisfyingly crisp and convincing:

> Down here, the sun clings to the earth and there is no darkness.
> Down here, the silence of the sea and the silence of the swamp seep
> into our
> muscles.
> . . . .
> All night Dolores labors between the sea grapes and the empty park.
> Our town prostitute, she listens for a long time. Her listening makes
> her strong.
>
> The teenage boy locks his door and combs the obscene magazine.
> His calloused left hand chops the gloss in waves. The silence of the
> naked ladies
> builds.
>
> The Cape Sable seaside sparrows population dropped 25 percent.
> Females are silent.
> Male calls are counter and multiplied by sixteen: this is how we track
> what cannot
> be seen. . . .
>
> Egas Moniz wins the Nobel Prize in 1949 for pioneering lobotomies.
> I am a pioneer of silence but the silencing of madness haunts me
> because it is
> unresolved. ("Florida Ghazals" 1–12, 17–19)

By layering and juxtaposing data from different arenas, and by shifting between private and public narratives, Reece sets up complex strata and resonances of representation. Here the factual data validate the speaker's credibility, as well as providing subtle analogues to the speaker's inner life. The result is a poetry more expansive and polyvalent than either a sheerly personal "subjective poem" or a purely "reportorial" poem. Here is a poetic in which information and private life haunt each other.

Take, for example, Reece's oddly factual couplet regarding sparrow populations in Cape Sable. We are told how the data about males and females are counted; one gender, we learn, the female, is silent. The existing population of that gender is extrapolated from the number of male sparrow calls. This information, layered alongside the other, peopled vignettes of the poem—the teenage boy who masturbates, the town prostitute who works the park—infiltrates the poem with a nuanced atmosphere of loneliness. We recognize the loneliness of sexuality itself—especially in this place, where one is noticeable only by being invisible and absent. Similarly, the first-person narrator of the poem, who only appears in the poem's final line, is, he says, "a pioneer of silence" (18). This intimate testimony is layered alongside another piece of "data" from the public world, including the invention of the lobotomy, "split-brain" surgery. Collating these episodic sentences and couplets, we recognize a gathering host of complex, nuanced patterns in this troubled world.

Through layering and triangulation, Reece's ghazal achieves a deeper, more capacious relationship to the real. The composite poem alloys chunks, bits and bytes of the objective and the subjective into a loose kind of composition—one whose hybrid roughness does not smooth out the heterogeneity of the real, but nonetheless seeks to harmonically organize it, to arrange it into a credible, believably disorganized form.

Reece's poem is representative of the composite strategy in other ways as well. His ghazal appears to take a place, Florida, as its central focus, rather than a personal story—this choice allows the poem to assemble diverse voices and sources that exist in counterpoint, and collectively create a "field" of sensibilities, and a field of realities. By declining to place a singular, introspective self at the poem's center, Reece's field of vision becomes wider and perhaps even more complexly moving.

By such strategies, perhaps it is poetically possible to have it both ways: to infuse the poem with the credibility, textural wealth, and fascination of worldly data, and also to delve deep into the precincts of the soul.

Labeling such poetics is difficult. "Florida Ghazal" might be called a "collage," and yet it's not, quite—the juxtapositions are not violent or abrupt. Reece's poetic method could also be tagged with the label of "associative imagination," and yet that doesn't seem quite accurate either, for Reece's technique involves overlay and simultaneity, as well as stratification, rather than depicting a mind leaping forward from point to point.

Poetry and Information

The challenge of inclusiveness is complicated by plenty of factors. Our age is characterized by a constancy, diversity, and immensity of data that has never before been encountered. Even to contemplate it is overwhelming. When the world is too big to see or understand, how does one approach it, let alone construct an inclusive poem? When so many things are happening simultaneously, how can a poem or a work of fiction possibly convey the way that it feels to be an individual human consciousness? Wholesale withdrawal from the world almost seems to be a precursor for the making of art. Given such an environment, one can see why many poets would prefer the segregated terrain of the subjective—it is a matter of self-preservation.

Moreover, our sense of our own cognitive limitations has never been so acute. Increasingly, we recognize randomness rather than causality as a governing principle in life, fortune, and experience. We are more aware than ever how our cognition, perception, and emotional lives are prejudiced and swayed by systems in whose design we have had no say—economic systems, ideological systems, linguistic systems. In our time, information is no longer simply information—it is understood to be always inflected by the manners of its presentation. Even to claim that the world is "knowable" can seem like a grandiosity. And how can poetry acknowledge its own fallibility?

And yet our poetic responsibility to reality—to what Czeslaw Milosz has named "the passionate pursuit of the real"—persists (*Witness* 75). As a poet and a person, I want to include both Lyme disease and moonlight in my poems. I want economics and racial reality, and bootleg pharmaceutical companies in India. I want reggae music coming out of the perforated speakers on the gas pump, while a block away, a twenty-nine-year-old paralegal reads the result of her pregnancy test and rolls her eyes in disbelief. I value art that looks outward as well as inward, that sees the world cross-eyed as well as through a cold eye. I want to include a world larger than that of my personal experience.

But how can a poem manage and orchestrate it all?

How can I get this giant ship into that small bottle?

The Test Tube Paradigm

One helpful thought-experiment is to visualize the poem as a kind of test tube, or terrarium, into which the poet allows a limited but generously diverse sample of the world. This data sample should have something unedited and wild about it in terms of selection—but not so much quantity that its plenitude overwhelms the poem. Once that datum is inside the glass container of the poem, says the poet, let us see if we can organize and then orchestrate it, arrange it into the poignant suite of harmonics and disharmonies that we call a poem.

The hazards are clear. If the poet allows in too much information, or too big an information sample, then she may be showcasing an abundance that verges on shapelessness. If the poet allows too little data, or too little disorder into the test tube, she is running a rigged game, an arrangement with a fixed outcome. Such a poet is in danger of writing the same poem again and again, like a laboratory that makes the same discovery year after year.

The novelist Milan Kundera addresses exactly these issues of ambition, scale, and structure in his critical book *The Art of the Novel.* "Encompassing the complexity of existence in the modern world," says Kundera, "demands a technique of ellipsis and compression," yet the modern novel, he says, must also maintain an architectonic clarity; "when you reach the end of a book you should still find it possible to remember the beginning" (71–72). In other words, Kundera implies, the goal is not vertigo or overwhelmedness.

Modernism, of course, was an artistic revolution conceived in part to handle the surfeit and swirl of the twentieth century. Eliot's *The Waste Land,* Pound's *Cantos,* Gertrude Stein's circularity, Berryman's *Dream Songs:* new forms arise when existing modes no longer seem to be adequately keeping up with reality, experience, and our age.

If one considers the sorts of technique that have appealed most to literary writers and readers in the last century—fracture, collage, abcedarium poems, poems that flirt with sampling and randomness or Oulipo techniques—we can recognize how craft has been attempting to keep up with the Information Problem—to poetically accommodate a reality in which more data, more speed, and less fixity have been evident. If these are the parameters of contemporary experience, it is no wonder that modern aesthetics has gravitated toward collagist, typed-over, fragmentary, skewed artistic forms.

Of course, the true subject here is not merely information, but our ongoing, as-yet-unsuccessful attempt to find a postmodern humanism.

Ironically, as contemporary poetry has sought formal ways to accommodate our era, with its instabilities, multiplicities, and interpenetrations, it has inadvertently lost much of its soulfulness. The sophistication elicited by the challenge of representing modernity has frequently sabotaged the result, producing at times a hopelessly over-cerebrated and obscure art—the so-called L-A-N-G-U-A-G-E poetry movement is one example. At other times, poetic art slips into an intoxicated engagement with disorientation and disjunction, and produces what seems a parody funhouse mirror of the zeitgeist. Postmodern poetry, with its default setting of irony, often has fashioned itself into an entertaining or dismaying barrage of fragmentation, surfeit, and colorful flotsam. Such a poem may skillfully imitate the milieu of the world, without mediating or shaping that chaos. Here, for example, is a passage from the opening of "Rotation," by the poet Ben Lerner:

> I was going to praise the transpersonality of print over the
> individuality of
> handwriting
> I was going to praise the viewer constructed by monochromy
> I was going to describe the remarkable comeback intention is making
> in new music
> and praise that
> Desire for accessibility flaring up inside me as I praise the fantasy of
> corporate
> personhood
> In the brief window between takeoff and the use of approved
> electronic devices I
>
> believe great change is possible
> I believe it while banking hard to the east to find smoother air
> When I can't tell if a person is joking I believe in the power of poetic
> modality, to
>
> hear this as music,
> to see this as an experiment in the collectivization of feeling.
> (1–13)

Lerner's poem is rife with knowing references to the world, but within the framework of these postmodern manners, every assertion is equally weighted; no relative value is assigned to this or that, no hierarchy imposed, and the affect of the speaker toward his subject matter is indecipherable. "Corporate personhood" is praised in the same breath as the "desire for accessibility" as is the "transpersonality of print" over handwriting. Such floods of speech-data convincingly mime the informational deluge of contemporary experience, but the velocity and surfeit of this catalog both begins and ends in a sort of numb, ironic vertigo. After a few reams of such manic, oscillating texts, one starts to wonder, So what? The end product disorients more than it connects.

The Self Also Can Be Portrayed as a Composite

Anne Carson's short poem "Strange Hour" demonstrates that composite techniques can also be used to present *selfhood* in a manner more encompassing than do conventional techniques. Like Reece, Carson is deft at collaging and blending, fusing and juxtaposing data and selfhoods. Her poems collate outer and inner realms, contradictory sensations and thoughts, feeling and perception; the result is an evocative array of dimensions, which are at once fragmentary and inclusive. An especially economical, but layered example is her lyric poem "Strange Hour."

Because "Strange Hour" is narrated by one speaker, and is largely scenic, it might initially appear to be staged in a rather conventional poetic mode. But closer inspection reveals some oddities in its composition that add unexpected registers and angles to its lyric psychological portrait.

> 3 a.m. cool palace roar of Oakland night.
> Not even a siren then a siren far off.
> Train passed a while ago now nothing.
>
> Bare lightbulb in garage across the street who left it on.
>
> Every sentence should contain a fact at least.
> No one but myself ever seems to set foot on this balcony
> Strange to say.
> Undertone of hatred I cannot eliminate
> From my feelings of friendship for most people.
> Clear at this hour. (1–10)

"Strange Hour" is, on first encounter, a quiet urban lyric—a compact, largely descriptive poem that might be likened to a longish haiku. But though the poem offers a unified scene, its special compressed radiance arises from its unusual composite of (at least) three distinct "layers" of consciousness and data: precise perceptual information; linguistic self-consciousness; and a terse, almost dislocated report from the interior emotive self.

Carson's first stanza is austere, intimate, and observant. These three quiet lines record external data unobtrusively filtered by a solitary receiving consciousness, in a voice so unself-conscious in register that it forgoes personal pronouns. This intimate moment is interrupted at the exact middle of the poem, in line 5, by a sudden, solitary admonition about the act of writing: a declaration of aesthetic principle very consistent with the theme of this chapter: "Every sentence should contain a fact at least."

How abrupt! Although this single end-stopped line is attached to stanza 3, it arrives seemingly out of nowhere, and its subject matter ("What Are the Rules for Making a Poem?") is not developed in any subsequent lines. This inserted idea belongs to a different, one could say, neural category than what precedes and what follows. Yet we accept it, because (a) it is interesting, (b) it complicates our notion of what a poem is, what this poem is, and who the speaker is, and (c) its appearance is so brief. In short, as readers, we are willing to tolerate considerable inconsistency; in fact, we are enlivened by it, especially if the result is a rewarding complexity.

After the speaker's aesthetic endorsement of the factual world, the first self-reference to the physical presence of the observer appears; "no one but myself ever seems to set foot on this balcony," she says (6). And then—again, abruptly—a revelation spikes through, in fragment form, as if torn off the flank of the inner life. "Undertone of hatred I cannot eliminate / From my feelings of friendship for most people" (8–9). This sentence fragment delivers an incongruously intense piece of private confession. Hatred is a strong emotion, and "most people" is a lot of people. It is a very interesting exclamation—one that has had no preparation or real context in the poem, and one that receives no development after its appearance. These "extraneous" moments provocatively strain the seams of the lyric container. Yet consequently, they distort and enlarge the poem into something more mysterious, alert, and beautiful than it would otherwise be. In another, more "romantic" kind of poem, the revelation of hatred would beg exploration, development, and transformation. In the composite poem, even a charged subjective "declaration" possesses the status of only one objective fact among others "clear at this hour."

In its use of disparate angularities, Carson's soliloquy presents an unconventional, stratified vision of the self, one that implies that a world in which the material and spiritual, the inner and outer, the perceptual and the linguistic coexist but do not entirely match up. Human nature inhabits multiple worlds nonexclusively, simultaneously, and discontinuously. Such a version of the self may be less unified in its presentation, but poetically more trustworthy than the average confessional poem, which tends to operate entirely within the psychological realm. As a result the poem slips free of its pastoral identity, and it becomes that much more intriguingly, complexly contemporary.

The composite poem is not driven by cause and effect; it does not arise from antecedent, nor spawn consequence; it does not insist on conflict. Instead, it creates spaciousness through variety, and through an implicit assertion of coexistence.

Characteristics of the Composite Poem

The composite poem approaches the real through an aesthetic process of sampling, counterpoint, and dialectic. It has a desire for inclusiveness—yet, knowing that actual inclusiveness is impossible, it gathers a harmonics of unlike things into its landscape. Here is a list of some of its features.

1. The composite poem likes information. It incorporates data from a range of realms—history, science, economics, politics, personal life,

and news. These data serve as counterweight to the powerful convention of the personal and subjective in the recent history of poetry. By counter-pointing facts, styles, and information systems, the realms of the exter-nal and internal reality haunt each other in the composite poem.

2. The composite poem aims to capture the irregular character of experi-ence, its lopsidedness and illogic. It is disproportionate and disheveled by design, deliberately making it difficult to determine a single, reductive meaning. Likewise, the composite poem also often nods to the impreci-sions, limitations, and difficulties of mimesis, and to the influence of language and ideological systems for how they affect our vision. Toward that end, it mixes notes of tragedy, whimsy, indifference, and cheerful-ness.

3. The composite poem sometimes involves a relative tonal impersonality, offering an appearance of detachment. Or perhaps it is truer to say that it contains simultaneous levels of detachment and attachment.

4. The composite poem thus avoids one prominent liability of the Roman-tic temperament: it refuses the paradigm of a singular heroic speaker, who occupies the center of the poetic monologue. Instead, it brings to-gether diverse voices and sources, which exist in counterpoint and, only collectively, create a "field" of knowing. The poetic center might be built around a place or a motif rather than a single self.

5. When the composite poem fails, it is often from a surfeit of randomness. Similarly, it may be susceptible to a lack of progression or to passivity. Because its parts are free-floating and more or less discrete, they may seem self-sufficient, or merely fragmentary. Ideally, however, the parts must complicate and activate each other. They must resonate dynami-cally.

The Composite Poem as a Reprieve from Narcissism

Robert Hass is one of the best contemporary practitioners of the composite mode. Hass also understands the tonic, contrapuntal value of data in a poem that might be otherwise entirely psychological or narrative. "August Note-book: A Death," a multisectioned poem about the death of a brother, displays the tempering effect of information on subjectivity. Aside from the sheer plea-sures of facticity, the speaker's brief sociological lecture provides a place in which to stand free of sentiment and from the habit of psychologizing that sometimes seems to dog the American poem:

Because I woke again thinking of my brother's body
And why anyone would care in some future

That poetry addresses how a body is transferred
From the medical examiner's office,
Which is organized by local government
And issues a certificate certifying that the person
In question is in fact dead and names the cause
Or causes, to the mortuary or cremation society,
Most of which are privately owned businesses
And run for profit and until recently tended
To be family businesses with skills and decorums
Passed from father to son, and often quite ethnically
Specific, in a country like ours made from crossers
Of borders, as if, in the intimacy of death,
Some tribal shame or squeamishness or sense
Of decorum asserted itself so that the Irish
Buried the Irish and the Italians the Italians.
In the South in the early years of the last century
It was the one business in which a black person
Could grow wealthy and pass on a trade
And a modicum of independence to his children.
I know this because Earlene wrote a paper about it . . . (2.1–22)

In a poem necessarily addressed to personal loss, this sociological digres-
sion acts to freshen the air before the return to grief. A poem is "the cry of
an occasion," but each occasion, we are reminded, is infiltrated by manifold
contexts—economic, civic, historical, racial. If invoked skillfully, such data
can save a poetic occasion from easy sentimentality, or, alternatively, can
deepen our recognition of how every story extends in many human directions.
The hyperfactual register of voice in the passage makes us aware that even the
most personal moment is touched, backstage, by commerce, history, tribal-
ism, and all the circuitous paths toward worldly dignity. Hardship and strug-
gle, it turns out, are plentiful in all quarters of the world. Such a "digression"
sheds light backward on the poem's "main" occasion.

Moreover, through this curious digression, the speaker is relieved of a
different, potentially costly freight—self-absorption, and the grandiose pre-
sumption of the self's uniqueness.

Tranströmer: The Power of Disarray

It is no coincidence that Hass, one of our most sophisticated American poets,
is also a diligent translator of international poetry—in particular that of To-
mas Tranströmer, of Sweden, and Milosz, the Polish émigré poet. From these

two poetic masters, Hass's own poetry has absorbed many strategies of form and attitude relevant to our topic. It is therefore worth examining one of them in more detail. Tranströmer is one of the most interesting poetic dialecticians of the twentieth century, and has certainly influenced other contemporary American poets. Tranströmer's sensibility refuses to segregate the personal-subjective from historical and objective realities. His poems accommodate many octaves and key changes in their range. They layer and conglomerate the spiritual and the informational, the existential and the scientific, the narrative and lyrical. They smuggle and camouflage direct meaning through a broad variety of methods. They are almost subliminal "fields" of understanding, fields in which insight, experience, and ignorance coexist comfortably with factual precision. In Tranströmer's poems, the speaker's subjective mind-set provides only one source of information; other sources include historical records, weather reports, and scientific data. Here's an example of a composite poem by Tranströmer, entitled "Oklahoma":

I.
The train stalled far to the south. Snow in New York,
but here we could go in shirtsleeves all night.
Yet no one was out. Only the cars
sped by in flashes of light like flying saucers.

II.
"We battlegrounds are proud
of our many dead . . ."
said a voice as I awakened.

The man behind the counter said:
"I'm not trying to sell anything.
I'm not trying to sell anything.
I just want to show you something."
And he displayed the Indian axes.

The boy said:
"I know I have a prejudice.
I don't want to have it, sir.
What do you think of us?"

III.
This motel is a foreign shell. With a rented car
(like a big white servant outside the door).

Nearly devoid of memory, and without profession,
I let myself sink to my midpoint. (1–20)

What a strange poem "Oklahoma" is. Tranströmer presents its mysterious parts without assembly instructions, and without any overarching statement that would divulge a secret order. Imagine how convenient it would be, for example, to have a title like "History" placed over this poem—a single idea that would lock the poem into a thematic framework, that would be more directive and determinate, thus saving us a lot of uncertainty about the shape and disposition of this diverse data.

Instead, the segments of "Oklahoma" conjure up an ambiguous atmosphere in which various narratives are suspended, like particles. The relation between these particles is neither linear nor hierarchical. The poem's overall tone is studiedly neutral, and the lack of connective language, transitions, or mediation between the poem's parts is notable.

Consider the rather amorphous middle section of the poem. What are its various floating "voices"? These fragmentary speeches seem to issue, respectively, from a battleground graveyard, a boy, and a merchant of Native American relics. In the context of the poem's title, "Oklahoma," they might be heard as the various voices of the place itself. We might go farther, and say they are the spectral voices of commerce, history, and anxiety, expressing themselves equally, a series of past injuries that persist into the present. The poem itself is a constellation, a "field" of impressions about a place—Oklahoma. But Tranströmer devises an odd, nonlogical and nondiscursive form in which to present these inflected impressions.

I don't think Yeats would have granted much credibility to this poem. "Oklahoma" doesn't exert power in the Romantic sense of great verbal music, nor the gathering persuasive push of rhetoric. It doesn't possess a heroic mounting cadence, nor plant a flag of beauty or truth on top of Mt. Experience. It doesn't conquer anything. The poem's claim to unity is sketchy. Even its principal speaker is indistinct, nearly anonymous.

And yet, this poem feels quite convincingly engaged with reality to me. "Oklahoma" emanates a quality of mystery, without the taint of intentional mystification or coy elusiveness. Its poetic form feels adequate to the flavor of the modern condition. Undeniably, the risk the poet assumes with such a nondirective form is an appearance of passivity or noncommittedness. Yet the poem's reserve comes through as a register of modesty, even of soulful maturity. We sense an integrity, that is, an underlying structure beneath the poem's fragmentary surface.

Tranströmer's poem also unobtrusively conveys, in its ambient way, many different kinds of information—kinds of information that would not ordinarily occupy the same plane of poetic consciousness, including the ghost-voice of battlegrounds, the soulless commercialism of merchants, the guilt of self-consciousness. The speaker himself is not just a witness or innocent bystander; he is complicit in this world, his car like "a big white servant" outside his door; one can hear the jingling chains of association attached to that description—inferences about race, privilege, and historical capitalism.

"Oklahoma" offers no final opinions. Rather, the poem is a delicate field of inferences and relationships. The speaker is neither arbiter, victim, nor soliloquizing hero, but only, as the poem says, trying to arrive at his "midpoint." That is, he is trying to arrive at a center, one that bears a resemblance to negative capability—what Keats described as "when a person is capable of being in uncertainties, mysteries, doubts, without any irritable reaching after fact and reason" (48). Poised amid, and surrounded by, such ghostly forces as those represented in the poem, isn't his insomnia understandable?

Rigorous Intuition

The composite structure offers some formal tools with which the era in which we live can be addressed and depicted. It is a strategy capable of joining the field of personal subjectivity to worldly knowledge. Perhaps in this way the factual and the personal can use each other as insurance policies—or as outriggers, each preventing the other from capsizing into its respective monopolizing preoccupations. But, the question arises, what are the principles of composite organization? Can the apprentice poet simply drink a bottle of vodka, and throw a lot of unlike yet interesting things together, and voilà, produce a poem? Without conventions of prosody to guide it, or a conventional dramatic device (like narrative) to organize the shape of the poem, what is the difference between the peculiar orchestration of a good composite poem and the haphazard assemblage of a magpie's nest?

The novelist Milan Kundera, cited above, emphasizes that even a postmodern work of art, one that strives to be polyphonic, must retain what he calls an "architectonic clarity" (72). In other words, even a poem of many different voices and parts must nonetheless have a perceivable unity, an involute intention and design. The point of contemporary work is not to defeat the mind but to expand the parameters of the represented world—allowing for its diversity and irrationality but not conceding its shapelessness.

The well-orchestrated composite poem (as embodied in earlier examples of this chapter) might include a weather report, a two-dollar hot dog for lunch, a reference to history, existentialist musing, and an incidental conversation; and yet between these elements a resonance exists. A few of the practicing poets to whom I would assign this label of composite poem-makers are, in addition to those I have discussed, Campbell McGrath, Khaled Mattawa, and Fanny Howe. Other, somewhat experimental writers like Lyn Hejinian, C. D. Wright, and Michael Ondaatje sometimes use the composite poetic structure. So-called lyrical essayists like John D'Agata and Eula Biss also structure their work along these modular lines. Poems written in the Persian form called the ghazal often seem intrinsically composite in their design—their spiritual intention is to inspire associative thinking about the world and the spirit without consenting to too much closure or to the arrogance of certainty.

Caveat about New Forms

This chapter does not intend to glorify asymmetry and disassociation for their own sake. Nor does it mean to claim, as some postmodern aesthetics do, that artistic techniques of "randomness and shuffling" construct a better or truer portrait of the world. There is something wrong, perhaps even adolescent, about the celebration of disorder as an artistic principle or virtue. Such sport is a kind of aesthetic drunkenness. I once watched a speaker shuffle the index cards on which his lecture was written, then read them in the resulting random sequence. He had a point to make about the intrinsic arbitrariness of order, but there is often a self-conscious "shock the bourgeoisie" agenda to such claims and performances, which recall modernist preening. The avantgarde correlation between a given structure and an oppressive rationality is false, anyway. And the celebration of randomness in our era, from a certain perspective, seems like playing video games while Rome burns.

The Quixotic Quest

No literary form has a monopoly on success or excellence. But contemporary poetry is also obligated to be worldly. The full, passionate, and discriminating engagement of poetry with the outer world is urgently important. In some cultures outside the United States, poets and poetry have traditionally served as a mediating, evaluating intelligence between ordinary citizens and the larger forces of history. Our need for that function of literature is alive and well. Poetry, with its compression and agility, possesses cognitive as well as affective powers, ones very well suited to the tasks of reportage, analysis, and judgment. At its best, it functions as a kind of passionate civic watchdog, neither complicit with nor subservient to dominant values. It is an arbiter of realism as well as a protective redoubt for the inner life that keeps us human. It can also serve as a reservoir for cultural values, a reliable source of proportion and perspective in a blurred, fractious world. In this sense, memory is no nostalgic prison, but a guardian of proportion.

What the composite poem models in the work of its best practitioners is a skillfully contrapuntal amalgam of experience, the greater world, and human nature. In such a representation, psychology and personal stories are present, but are not granted a higher status than economic statistics, historical fact, biology, nationalism, or climate-related details. In such an environment, the acknowledgment of cynicism can cohabitate with declarations of love and aspiration. The synthetic breadth and dynamic of such a poem can exceed analysis in its depiction of the world. For poetry to continue to serve its deepest functions, we must seek inclusive structures and inclusive visions that do not simplify, but can integrate disintegration into their narrative without conceding to absurdity and consciencelessness.

If these values sound idealistic, so what? They are nonetheless perennial. That they have been somewhat misplaced is itself a symptom of the authority surrendered by poetics and poets to the narcotic powers of the global Frankenstein, capitalism. Poetry's range of attention, the sense we have of its value and authority, and even our sense of its power, have been compromised. However, they are recoverable. The issuing institution for that recovery of authority will be the next generation of poets who rediscover their own means, mission, and courage.

Works Cited

Carson, Anne. "Strange Hour." *Threepenny Review* 72 (Winter 1998). Web. 1 May 2015.

Coleridge, Samuel Taylor. *Biographia Literaria*. Ed. David H. Richter. Boston: Bedford / St. Martin's, 2007. 325–29. Print.

Hass, Robert. "August Notebook: A Death." *Paris Review* 191 (2009): 151. Print.

Keats, John. "To George and Thomas Keats Dec. 22, 1817." *Letters of John Keats to His Family and Friends*. Ed. Colvin Sidney. London: Macmillan, 1925. 47–48. Print.

Kundera, Milan. *The Art of the Novel*. New York: Grove, 1988. Print.

Lerner, Ben. "Rotation." *American Poetry Review* 41.1 (2012): 14–15. Web. 1 May 2015.

Milosz, Czeslaw. *Facing the River: New Poems*. Trans. Robert Hass. New York: Ecco, 1996. Print.

Milosz, Czeslaw. *The Witness of Poetry: The Charles Eliot Norton Lectures*. Cambridge: Harvard UP, 1984. Print.

Reece, Spencer. "Florida Ghazals." *Blackbird: An Online Journal of Literature and the Arts* 4.2 (2005). Web. 1 May 2015.

Transtsömer, Tomas. "Oklahoma." *Windows and Stones: Selected Poems*. Trans. May Swenson. Pittsburgh, PA: U Pittsburgh P, 1972. Print.

Virgil. *Georgics: Book IV*. Trans. A. S. Kline. Poetry in Translation, 2001. Web. 2 May 2015.

Contributors

Steven Gould Axelrod is Distinguished Professor of English at the University of California, Riverside. He is the author of *Robert Lowell: Life and Art* (Princeton, 1978), *Robert Lowell: A Reference Guide* (G. K. Hall, 1982), and *Sylvia Plath: The Wound and the Cure of Words* (Johns Hopkins, 1990). He is coeditor of the *New Anthology of American Poetry*, volumes 1–3 (Rutgers, 2003, 2005, 2012). He has also edited *Robert Lowell: Essays on the Poetry* (Cambridge, 1986); *Critical Essays on Wallace Stevens* (G. K. Hall, 1988); *Critical Essays on William Carlos Williams* (G. K. Hall and Macmillan, 1995); and *The Critical Response to Robert Lowell* (Greenwood, 1999). He is presently completing a new book titled *Cold War Poetics* and a coedited volume, *Robert Lowell's Memoirs* (forthcoming from Farrar, Straus & Giroux).

Elisabeth Frost's books include *All of Us: Poems* (White Pine Press, 2011); *The Feminist Avant-Garde in American Poetry* (Iowa, 2003); and *Bindle* (with artist Dianne Kornberg; Ricochet Editions, 2015). With Cynthia Hogue, she also edited *Innovative Women Poets: An Anthology of Contemporary Poetry and Interviews* (Iowa, 2006). She has received grants from the Fulbright Foundation, Yaddo, MacDowell, the Rockefeller Foundation's Bellagio Center, the University of Connecticut Humanities Institute, and elsewhere. Frost is Professor of English and Women's & Gender Studies at Fordham University, where she also edits the Poets Out Loud Prizes book series from Fordham Press.

Jeffrey Gray is Professor of English at Seton Hall University, New Jersey. He is author of *Mastery's End: Travel and Postwar American Poetry* (University of Georgia Press, 2005) and of many articles on poetry and American culture. He is editor of the five-volume *Greenwood Encyclopedia of American Poets and Poetry* (Greenwood, 2005); coeditor (with Ann Keniston) of the recent *The New American Poetry of Engagement: A 21st Century Anthology* (McFarland, 2012); and translator of Guatemalan novelist Rodrigo Rey Rosa's *The African Shore* (Yale University Press, 2013). He was born and raised in Seattle, Washington, and has lived in Asia, the South Pacific, Europe, and Latin America.

Joseph Harrington is the author of *Poetry and the Public: The Social Form of Modern U.S. Poetics* (Wesleyan, 2002), portions of which appear in *Poetry and Cultural Studies: A Reader* (Illinois, 2009). He is also the author of *Things Come On (an amneoir)* (Wesleyan, 2011), part of a mixed-genre series about his mother's life and times. He has published articles in journals such as *Jacket2*, *American Literary History*, and *American Literature*. His creative work has appeared in *Bombay Gin*, *Hotel Amerika*, and *Colorado Review*, among others. Harrington is the recipient of a Millay Colony residency and a Fulbright Distinguished Chair. He is Professor of English at the University of Kansas (Lawrence).

Tony Hoagland's books include *What Narcissism Means to Me*, *Unincorporated Persons of the Late Honda Dynasty*, and *Donkey Gospel*. He has received the Mark Twain Award, the James Laughlin Award, the Jackson Poetry Prize, and the O.B. Hardisson Prize for teaching. His second book of prose essays, *Twenty Poems That Could Save America*, was published in 2014. The title essay appeared in *Harper's* online magazine. He teaches at the University of Houston, and elsewhere.

Lynn Keller is the author of *Re-making It New: Contemporary American Poetry and the Modernist Tradition* (Cambridge, 1987), *Forms of Expansion: Recent Long Poems by Women* (Chicago, 1997), and *Thinking Poetry: Readings in Contemporary Women's Exploratory Poetics* (Iowa, 2010). She coedited *Feminist Measures: Soundings in Poetry and Theory* with Cristanne Miller and is one of the editors of the University of Iowa Press Contemporary North American Poetry Series. She is the Martha Meier Renk Bascom Professor of Poetry at the University of Wisconsin–Madison, where she is a member of the Department of English and the Center for Culture, History, and Environment. With the support of a Guggenheim fellowship, she is writing a book on twenty-first-century ecopoetics.

Ann Keniston is Professor of English at the University of Nevada, Reno, with a specialty in postwar American poetry. She is the author of two monographs, *Ghostly Figures: Memory and Belatedness in Postwar American Poetry* (Iowa, 2015) and *Overheard Voices: Address and Subjectivity in Postmodern American Poetry* (Routledge, 2006) and two volumes of poetry. She is also coeditor (with Jeanne Follansbee Quinn) of *Literature after 9/11* (Routledge, 2008) and (with Jeffrey Gray) of *The New American Poetry of Engagement: A 21st-Century Anthology* (McFarland, 2012). She is at work on a new book on twenty-first-century American engaged poetry.

James McCorkle is the author of *The Still Performance* (a study of postmodern American poetry) and the editor of *Conversant Essays: Contemporary Poets on Poetry* and most recently, with Jeff Gray and Mary McAleer Balkun, of the *Greenwood Encyclopedia of American Poets and Poetry*. He is also the author of two collections of poetry: *Evidences*, the recipient of the 2003 American Poetry Review / Honickman Award for poetry, and *The Subtle Bodies*. He is an Assistant Professor of Africana studies at Hobart and William Smith Colleges. He also currently serves as the Director of the Africa Literature Association's Headquarters.

Bob Perelman is a poet and scholar who is Professor Emeritus at the University of Pennsylvania. He has published numerous books of poetry, including *Iflife*, *Playing Bodies* (with painter Francie Shaw), and *Ten to One*; his critical books are *The Marginalization of Poetry*, *The Trouble with Genius*, and *Modernism the Morning After* (forthcoming).

Kevin Prufer is the author of six books of poems, most recently *Churches* (Four Way Books, 2014), *In a Beautiful Country* (Four Way Books, 2011), and *National Anthem* (Four Way Books, 2008). He has also coedited numerous volumes, including *New European Poets* (Graywolf, 2008) and the forthcoming *Into English: Essays on Multiple Translations* (Graywolf, 2015). With Wayne Miller, he codirects the Unsung Masters Series. He is Professor of English in the Creative Writing Program at the University of Houston.

Vernon Shetley is the author of *After the Death of Poetry: Poet and Audience in Contemporary America* (Duke, 1993). His essays on poetry, film, and dance have appeared in *Raritan*, *MLN*, *Science Fiction Studies*, *Genre*, and other venues. He is currently at work on a study of neonoir filmmaking.

Eleanor Wilner has published seven books of poems, most recently *Tourist in Hell* (Chicago); *The Girl with Bees in Her Hair*; and *Reversing the Spell: New & Selected Poems* (both Copper Canyon). Her awards include a MacArthur Fellowship, the Juniper Prize, three Pushcart Prizes, and a National Endowment for the Arts and PA Council on the Arts Fellowships. She teaches in the MFA Program for Writers at Warren Wilson College. She has been politically engaged since she was eight years old and saw the captured Nazi films of women in the death camps and the photos in *Life* of the burned "Hiroshima Maidens."

Index

Note: Page numbers in *italics* refer to illustrations.